HENRY VENN—
MISSIONARY STATESMAN

Henry Venn, B.D.

Prebendary of this Cathedral:
for thirty years Honorary Clerical Secretary
of the Church Missionary Society.
Born February 10, 1796,
Died January 13, 1873.

"Stedfast, Unmoveable,
Always Abounding
in the work of the Lord."

(Bust located in crypt of St. Paul's, London.
Photo by Alan F. Kreider.)

American Society of Missiology Series, No. 6

HENRY VENN—
MISSIONARY STATESMAN

Wilbert R. Shenk

ORBIS BOOKS
Maryknoll, New York 10545

Ibadan, Nigeria

Manuscript editor: Lisa McGaw

Published in the United States by Orbis Books, Maryknoll, NY 10545, in collaboration with the
American Society of Missiology

Library of Congress Cataloging in Publication Data

Shenk, Wilbert R.
    Henry Venn—missionary statesman.

    Bibliography: p.
    Includes index.
    1. Venn, Henry, 1796–1873. 2. Church Mis-
sionary Society—History—19th century.
3. Missions—Theory—History of doctrines—19th
century. 4. Church of England—England—Clergy—
Biography. I. Title.
BX5199.V443S53   1983   266'.3'0924 [B]   82-18779
ISBN 0-88344-181-0 (pbk.)

Published in Nigeria by Daystar Press, Daystar House, P.O. Box 1261, Ibadan

Daystar ISBN 978-122-166-6

The American Society of Missiology Series, in collaboration with Orbis Books, seeks to publish scholarly works of high merit and wide interest on numerous aspects of missiology—the study of mission. Able presentations on new and creative approaches to the practice and understanding of mission will receive close attention.

Previously published in the American Society of Missiology Series

No. 1   *Protestant Pioneers in Korea,*
         by Everett Nichols Hunt, Jr.

No. 2   *Catholic Politics in China and Korea,*
         by Eric O. Hanson

No. 3   *From the Rising of the Sun—Christians
         and Society in Contemporary Japan,*
         by James M. Phillips

No. 4   *Meaning across Cultures,*
         by Eugene A. Nida and William D. Reyburn

No. 5   *The Island Churches of the South Pacific:
         Emergence in the Twentieth Century*
         by Charles W. Forman

Contents

Preface to the Series

The purpose of the ASM Series is to publish, without regard for disciplinary, national, or denominational boundaries, scholarly works of high quality and wide interest on missiological themes from the entire spectrum of scholarly pursuits, e.g., theology, history, anthropology, sociology, linguistics, health, education, art, political science, economics, and development, to articulate but a partial list. Always the focus will be on Christian mission.

By "mission" in this context is meant a cross-cultural passage over the boundary between faith in Jesus Christ and its absence. In this understanding of mission, the basic functions of Christian proclamation, dialogue, witness, service, fellowship, worship, and nurture are of special concern. How does the transition from one cultural context to another influence the shape and interaction of these dynamic functions?

Missiologists know that they need the other disciplines. And other disciplines, we dare to suggest, need missiology, perhaps more than they sometimes realize. Neither the insider's nor the outsider's view is complete in itself. The world Christian mission has through two millennia amassed a rich and well-documented body of experience to share with other disciplines.

Interaction will be the hallmark of this Series. It desires to be a channel for talking to one another instead of about one another. Secular scholars and church-related missiologists have too long engaged in a sterile venting of feelings about one another, often lacking in full evidence. Ignorance of and indifference to one another's work has been no less harmful to good scholarship.

We express our warm thanks to various mission agencies whose financial contributions enabled leaders of vision in the ASM to launch this new venture. The future of the ASM series will, we feel sure, fully justify their confidence and support.

William J. Danker, Chairperson,
ASM Series Editorial Committee

Foreword

A biographical study of Henry Venn, concerned especially with his theoretical principles and administrative practice, has long been desired. Venn was the most influential theoretician of mission in the United Kingdom in the nineteenth century and the most powerful and authoritative administrator of the largest missionary society within the established Church of England during that century. He, through personal relations, consultations, lectures, writings, and participation in the London Secretaries' Association, exerted great influence on the officers and missionaries of the other British mission societies. As the chief executive officer of the Church Missionary Society of the Church of England, Venn also exercised great influence in British colonial affairs.

Although he towered high above contemporary mission administrators and strategists, at his death British missionaries and mission executives made a sharp turn away from his fostering of indigenization and autonomy towards the furtherance of ecclesiastical colonialism. The repudiation of missionary imperialism and paternalism and the advocacy of indigenization and devolution of authority by the Jerusalem Conference of 1928 induced missionaries again to seek the guidance of Henry Venn.

Since Henry Venn never systematized his theory and practice in a book and never had a posthumous disciple to continue his teaching and advocate his principles, the reappropriation of Venn's views was more difficult to achieve than was a renewed acceptance of the principles and practice of Rufus Anderson in America, because Robert E. Speer kept alive Andersonian missiology west of the Atlantic Ocean. Venn did write an enormous quantity of documents and articles, mostly preserved in the Archives and Library of the Church Missionary Society and in the British Museum, but they had disappeared from general circulation soon after Venn's death, when an outlook absolutely contrary to his captured the British missionary mind. Because of the documentary nature of Venn's writings, full recovery of his missiological principles and guidelines was slow, although after the Jerusalem Conference of 1928 there was a growing awareness of them. Canon Max Warren, Venn's successor in a later era, made available a very helpful introduction to Venn's thought in the book, *To Apply the Gospel, Selections from the Writings of Henry Venn* (Grand Rapids: Eerdmans, 1971). Wilbert R. Shenk published a *Bibliography of Henry Venn's Printed Writings with Index* (Scottdale, Pa.: Herald Press, 1975). There have been a few studies of Venn published, including Peter Beyerhaus and Henry Lefever, *The Responsible Church and the Foreign Mission*, pp. 25–30, 65–73 (Grand Rapids: Eerdmans, 1964); F. D. Coggan, *These Were His Gifts*, pp. 21–31 (Exeter: University of Exeter, 1974); and T. E. Yates, *Venn and Victorian Bishops Abroad* (London: SPCK, 1978).

A biography of Henry Venn focusing on his mission theory and administrative policy has long been desired. Now it has been provided by Dr. Wilbert R. Shenk, Vice President for Overseas Ministries of the Mennonite Board of Missions. Dr. Shenk is well qualified for this task since he, like Venn, is a creative thinker in the realm of world mission theory and strategy and an experienced administrator.

Venn never had overseas field experience, and he refused appointment as Bishop of Madras, preferring participation in mission as the general of a worldwide enterprise at its home base. His intimate association with missionaries kept him from becoming merely an armchair strategist. He grew up from childhood in the bosom of the Clapham Sect into a full-orbed evangelicalism concerned both with evangelization and the furtherance of the Kingdom of God on earth through the abolition of slavery and other evils. The fortune which came to him as his wife's dowry enabled him to serve CMS without salary, and that may have given him greater influence.

Americans are especially interested in the similarity of administrative policy and mission theory between Henry Venn and Rufus Anderson of the American Board. Their views and policies corresponded in most important details. The great difference was that one was an Anglican who saw the maturity and autonomy of the new church achieved in the consecration and enthronement of its own native bishop, while the other was a Congregationalist who recognized the local congregation as responsible and autonomous just as soon as it had a native pastor, was self-supporting, and engaged in mission. The two men are independently the authors of the "Three-self Formula." Together they established the charter of the indigenous church, although that goal would not be attained for many decades, because Protestant missionaries became infected with imperialism and racial superiority and turned to ecclesiastical colonialism in the last quarter of the nineteenth century. Dr. Shenk treats well the relationship of the two men.

Henry Venn intervened frequently with the Colonial Office and the Foreign Office, going far beyond the guidelines which he set for missionaries in political matters. He had an especially powerful impact on African affairs and much influence in India. As the Senior Clerical Secretary of the great CMS he had what is today called "clout," far beyond the influence of a secretary of any American mission board.

One of the greatest puzzles and mysteries in Protestant mission history has been the almost complete reversal of Venn's policies and practices in the CMS immediately following his death, marked at once by the troubles of Bishop Crowther. Ecclesiastical colonialism characterized by disdain of indigenous abilities became the new order. A sense of intellectual and spiritual superiority along with rigorous paternalism infected all British missions. This writer once asked Max Warren why that happened. He attributed it to negative aspects of the Keswick Movement. Add to that the fact that the British people were swept up into imperialism. Dr. Shenk throws some light on this problem, but it is to be hoped that he will eventually deal further with this question.

Wilbert Shenk has in this study made a noteworthy contribution to mission history.

R. Pierce Beaver

Acknowledgments

This study is one of the fruits of a study leave that the Mennonite Board of Missions granted me during the years 1973–75. I especially wish to thank H. Ernest Bennett, at that time executive secretary of the Board, who arranged for me to have time off from regular duties for research and writing. Associates on staff who shouldered additional burdens during my absence deserve special commendation.

A. F. Walls, head of the Department of Religious Studies, Aberdeen University, first suggested that I undertake a study of Henry Venn and then guided my research. He shared generously of his encyclopedic knowledge of missionary history.

Without the help of the following libraries and their staffs, this study would never have been possible: Aberdeen University, the British Museum, and the Church Missionary Society. Rosemary Keen and Jean Woods, archivist and librarian, respectively, of the CMS Library, proved to be especially valuable allies in this undertaking because of their knowledge of the primary sources and the personal interest they take in those who do research at CMS House, London.

This project provided occasion to consult with other scholars. Special mention must be made of the late Dr. Max Warren who succeeded to the general secretaryship of the Church Missionary Society exactly a century after Henry Venn. Warren took a deep interest in Venn and personally started the demanding task of indexing Venn correspondence after he retired from the secretaryship in 1963.

Nancy Kinsinger Halder completed the indexing of Venn correspondence, a service for which all future researchers in CMS history will join me in expressing hearty thanks.

Two secretaries, Esther Graber and Barbara Nelson Gingerich, have provided excellent and efficient service, thus lightening the load in a variety of ways.

Special editorial assistance in getting the manuscript ready for publication was rendered by Mary Ann Halteman Conrad. Dr. and Mrs. J. W. Longacher and Mr. and Mrs. Kenneth M. Shenk generously provided financial assistance for this phase of the work.

My family and I enjoyed our sojourn in Aberdeen. They often had to sacrifice their interests in exploring the delightful sights and sounds of Scotland to enable this project to be completed. I am grateful to them for their encouragement and support.

Abbreviations

AIC	African Improvement Committee
CMI	*Church Missionary Intelligencer*
CMR	*Church Missionary Reporter*
CMS	Church Missionary Society
CO	*Christian Observer*
Knight, 1880	William Knight, *Memoir of the Rev. H. Venn*
Knight, 1882	William Knight, *Memoir of the Rev. H. Venn* [2nd edn.]
LMS	London Missionary Society
LSA	London Secretaries' Association
MR	*Missionary Register*
Proceedings	*Proceedings of the Church Missionary Society*
SCM	Student Christian Movement
SPCK	Society for Promoting Christian Knowledge
SPG	Society for the Propagation of the Gospel
VB	*Bibliography of Henry Venn's Printed Writings with Index* (see Bibliography, p. 138, for explanation of citations)
Venn MSS	Venn manuscripts deposited in Church Missionary Society Archives, London (see Bibliography, p. 138, for explanation of citations)
Warren	Max Warren, *To Apply the Gospel—selections from the writings of Henry Venn*

1

Evangelical Son

Grandpa's Boy

Born at Clapham, on the outskirts of London, February 10, 1796, Henry was the fifth child and first surviving son of John and Catherine (King) Venn. He was named for his grandfather, a prominent personality in the eighteenth-century revival.[1]

Until Grandfather Venn's Evangelical conversion around 1750 the Venn family had been devoted traditional Anglicans. From this time on they were identified as Evangelicals. In a movement that was torn between Whitefield and the Wesleys, Anglicans like Henry Venn took a mediating position. They affirmed the need for conversion, genuine piety, warm fellowship, and evangelism, but challenged Whitefield's and Wesley's readiness to flout traditional church polity. Although it was often questioned by his critics, Grandfather Venn remained committed to the Church of England.

Henry Venn was too young when his grandfather died in 1797 to remember him. Nevertheless, the two Henrys felt a special filial bond. The old man lived out his last days with his son John in Clapham. The family insisted that young Henry showed a marked preference for his grandfather's lap, and Grandfather Venn took particular delight in his namesake.

Many years later Henry related to his own children how as a child he was moved to tears as he read the account of Jacob giving his blessing to the two sons of Joseph (cf. Gen. 48:15). Clearly, this conjured up for him the scene when his own grandfather had given him his patriarchal blessing, "the influence and benefit of which cannot be known till the last day. But thus early did it please God to bestow upon me tokens of his free and special grace."[2] The meaning of this benediction deepened for him as he grew to adulthood.

Both father and grandfather decisively influenced the formation of Henry Venn. Venn spent more than ten years intermittently editing his grandfather's *Life and Letters*. Published in 1834, the bulky volume consisted largely of his grandfather's letters. In the preface Venn tried to come to terms with and disentangle the origins of Evangelicalism. Grandfather Venn became a commanding presence in Henry's life.

Son of Clapham

Another commanding presence in Henry Venn's life was the Clapham Sect.[3] These pious and powerful Evangelicals, many of whom were members

1

of Parliament, were the spiritual children of old Henry Venn. Though not a formally organized group, they made the village of Clapham on London's outskirts the center of Evangelicalism in the 1790s. Not all were Anglicans and not all were regular residents of Clapham. Approximately a dozen men comprised the group of which William Wilberforce, prominent antislave campaigner, was the best-known member. To accomplish their purpose the Clapham Sect enlisted the cooperation of others who shared their Christian principles and vision.

These Evangelical activists worked essentially on two fronts: the public and the church. They assumed that Great Britain was a Christian nation. Government and church together maintained the social order and preserved public morals. The Clapham Sect shared the prevailing view of the social order as a static class system. They saw themselves as trustees under God to use their favored social position and wealth in ameliorating the ills of society.

Henry's father, John (1759–1813), was rector of Clapham parish and a member of the inner circle of the Clapham Sect. He shared their concerns and supported them in their causes. As spiritual leader he taught them week after week. They discovered in him a discerning critic and astute counselor. At crucial points he helped turn some of their designs into reality through his leadership.

The early 1790s saw the formation of William Carey's Baptist Missionary Society and the interdenominational London Missionary Society. Even though most of them gave support to both of these new societies, the Clapham Sect remained dissatisfied. They wanted a fully Anglican missionary society. Struggling for several years against apathy, opposition, and their own inexperience, they finally organized the Church Missionary Society (CMS) on April 12, 1799. It was John Venn who presided over the meetings that confirmed the need for a society attached to the established church and culminated in the formation of the CMS. To John Venn belongs credit for the basic principles that have since undergirded the CMS. The CMS, said Venn, should be "founded upon the Church principle, not the High Church principle." With one phrase he staked out a position different from either the Society for the Propagation of Christian Knowledge/Society for the Propagation of the Gospel (SPCK/SPG) or the London Missionary Society (LMS).[4] John Venn also played an important role in the Clapham Sect's founding of the *Christian Observer.* Launched in 1802, the *Christian Observer* won a respected role as an authoritative Evangelical voice.

This then was the Clapham where Henry Venn was born and spent his first seventeen years. His father was the respected rector of a parish whose leading citizens were men of affairs—members of Parliament, bankers, lawyers. Devout Christians, they believed their faith should be lived. They spent their wealth solving human problems and spreading the gospel of Jesus Christ. They pioneered Christian philanthropy and created institutions for Christian missions and humanitarian services. It was no ordinary village and it was no ordinary movement.

Strong Family Life

Family records tell little of what it was like to be one of John Venn's children. Evangelicalism found its center in the home. The Clapham Sect made wholesome family life an article of faith. The Thorntons, Grants, Stephens, Wilberforces, Macaulays, Venns, and Shores all had large families and cultivated strong family life. What set them apart was the sense of a larger community, which allowed them to share their homes freely with each other. They lived not as nuclear families, but as a family of families. Their children played together in the spacious gardens; they shared in picnics and constantly visited with each other.

The Venns lived comfortably on their modest means. They disciplined their children wisely and provided for their cultural enrichment. John Venn bought the novels of Sir Walter Scott for his family to read. He did not allow his children to attend parties where there was dancing or card playing. Evangelicals did not condemn these activities outright, but they argued that people who spent their time in this way were often not really serious about their spiritual welfare. Family life must be based on spiritual values. The Venns taught their children to rise early, engage in private devotions, and keep diaries as acts of personal discipline. The whole household participated in daily prayers.

John Venn had begun conducting family prayers for his household even before he was married. Henry Thornton, still a bachelor when the Venns moved to Clapham, appreciated this feature of Venn family life. He wrote in his diary: "Breakfasted yesterday with Venn . . . attended his family prayer . . . if there be happiness in this world this is it."[5]

Rector's Boy

The warmth and joy of wholesome family life frequently mingled with illness, even death. Soon after John, the youngest of the Venn children, was born in 1802 their father took ill and was unable to work for the next fifteen months. The following spring Kitty Venn fell from a stool and sustained serious injuries. More concerned for her husband's welfare than her own, she continued nursing him when she should have been hospitalized. As a result, she died April 15, 1803, leaving her ailing husband with seven young children. All that Henry remembered about his mother's death was that his father announced the sad news to the family after morning prayers.

A week later John Venn's sister Jane came to be mother to seven-year-old Henry and his brother and sisters. According to Marianne Thornton, the Venn children did not really welcome Aunt Jane.[6] Nevertheless, Jane Venn ran the Venn home competently and the children developed respect and affection for her. Jane made her home with John's children the rest of her life, dying at age ninety-two in 1852.

John Venn's long illness marked the end of his most creative years. After

1803 he continued to write for the *Christian Observer,* but gave up almost all active participation in the Church Missionary Society. The sect still carried on some of its activities from Clapham. They had organized the Society for the Education of Africans in 1799 when Zachary Macaulay brought twenty-five children from Sierra Leone for training. The society set up a special school at Clapham and appointed William Greaves as headmaster.

One Sunday afternoon Zachary Macaulay invited eight-year-old Henry Venn to go along to the African Seminary to hear the students examined in Bible knowledge. As Venn recalled the scene nearly seventy years later:

> They stood in a semicircle round Mr. Macaulay while he questioned them in Scripture history; and Mr. Henry Thornton stood by Mr. Macaulay's side, evidently much interested in the group before him; while Mr. Wilberforce, on the outside of the group, went from boy to boy, patting them on the shoulder as they gave good answers. . . . [7]

The following year John Venn baptized these youths in Clapham church. The experiment ended pathetically as the Africans, unable to adapt to the climate, died one by one. The presence of these African children for five years in Clapham stimulated in Henry Venn a lifelong affinity with Africa and .Africans.

Much to Henry's regret, John Venn was schoolmaster to his own children. He also accepted Samuel Thornton, Jr., as a student in 1805. This provided Henry companionship, and teaching two was as easy as teaching one. Venn listened to the boys recite for him each morning between eight and nine o'clock while he shaved and dressed—provided he had no other interruptions. He left the boys largely on their own the rest of the time.

John Venn set high standards, emphasized the importance of good writing, and encouraged Henry to pursue a broad range of interests, including astronomy, mechanics, electricity, heraldry, and gardening. He had strong and clear views on education and was a gifted teacher.

When Wilberforce and company won the great twenty-year campaign to abolish the slave trade, John Venn used the occasion to teach his young pupils a lesson in current affairs and Christian responsibility. He knew how to make his students eyewitnesses to history.

John Venn discerned Henry's character early and found much for which to praise him. Henry felt deeply attached to his father, but could never be completely familiar with him. His father's failing health, financial concerns, and other preoccupations prevented him from taking time for real companionship.

John Venn was not the only one to notice that Henry developed early into a serious and sensible person. Dutiful, reliable, and completely lacking in selfish ambition, Henry possessed a feeling for what was right and wrong and encouraged his peers to act accordingly. More than once he took a hand in settling quarrels among the children or set an example for which, to his surprise, he later received commendation. These qualities quickly commanded the confidence of other people and he was treated by his father's friends with a respect and trust beyond his years.[8]

It is not suprising that Henry's earliest memories were all associated with religious activities. He even took the lead in some of them. When he was five or six years old, he wrote his first sermon. His sisters were assembled and he proceeded to deliver his homily from a chair-turned-pulpit to his loyal congregation. Throughout his childhood he had many "strong religious feelings." His nine-year-old sister Maria's death when he was in his early teens measurably deepened his interest in things of the spirit. He began to pay close attention to his father's sermons and hymns and copied extracts into a notebook. These he used in his devotional meditations. In May 1811, at the age of fifteen, he was confirmed in Holy Trinity Church, Clapham.

In a large parish like Clapham, where Evangelical influence had become dominant, the children seldom met anti-Evangelical prejudice. But as the rector's son, Henry Venn did not escape entirely. On one occasion the bishop of London was entertaining a relative at Fulham Palace. This guest also wanted to call on John Venn at Clapham. The bishop, unwilling to have his carriage seen calling at Clapham rectory, arranged a place of rendezvous. Henry's father dispatched him to meet the distinguished lady who was set down at the Bull's Head, three hundred yards from the rectory—the bishop being more willing to have his carriage call at a public house than an Evangelical rectory.[9]

Family Head

When Henry was seventeen he was sent with his friend Francis Baring to Cambridge to study under Henry's father's mathematician friend, William Farish. But already in 1813 John Venn's health began failing. By May he knew he was dying of dropsy and jaundice. Henry was recalled from Cambridge to be with the family during their father's last days. John Venn died on July 1, 1813, leaving Henry responsible for the rest of the family.

"Your dear brother will be your protector," he said. "Henry, look after your sisters, they must be your charge." He reassured his daughters, saying: "It relieves me much to think you have such a prudent and cautious and kind and affectionate brother—I do not doubt that he will do well at the university, and that he will be everything to you, my dear children, that you could wish."[10]

During this time at his father's bedside Henry committed himself to the Christian ministry. This gave his father much satisfaction. He charged Henry: "Give yourself wholly to it. . . . You have a holy work before you, Christ to help you, the Holy Spirit to enlighten you, heaven for your home, the Bible for your guide. Travel with these companions through this world as a pilgrim and a stranger seeking one above, and may you bring many sons to glory."[11]

To seventeen-year-old Henry fell responsibility for his father's financial affairs and helping William Dealtry, who succeeded Venn as rector of Clapham, get settled into the living. Though Henry Thornton and Zachary Macaulay provided counsel, Henry did most of the work of preparing for publication two volumes of his father's sermons. These were published in 1814. Four years later Henry published a third volume. The income from the sale of John Venn's sermons helped finance Henry's college education.

In October, Henry returned to Cambridge to continue his study under Professor Farish in preparation for entering college the following year. Aunt Jane took the rest of the family to live with her at Brighton.

Off to College

Henry entered at Queens' College, Cambridge, in 1814. He began college with his religious convictions settled. Both Charles Simeon and William Farish, as longtime friends of his father, took special interest in him. Henry had already formed his loyalties. He identified fully with the Evangelicals in the university; but religious seriousness was no more popular in 1814 than it had been in his father's and grandfather's time.

Henry did not lack friends, of course. His boyhood friends from Clapham—George Stainforth, Charles Shore, Francis Clement, and Henry Venn Elliott—were all at Cambridge. A year later he met Joshua King, who became Henry's closest associate for the next ten years. Henry soon settled into a disciplined routine. Elected a scholar in his second year, he won the college prize for a Latin declamation and two prizes in mathematics.

Venn deplored the feeble missionary spirit at the university. All his life he urged the universities to greater missionary responsibility and support. He argued that the scale of values was wrong, for it placed the greatest worth on service in the university itself. A few years after leaving college, as a member of the CMS Committee, Venn listened in disappointment as members discussed a Cambridge graduate's candidacy for missionary service: "A man of so many accomplishments," according to the predominant view, "should go out as a Chaplain and not as a Missionary: he will have greater influence on the cause of Christianity."[12] Venn would have none of that. At an early age he became convinced that missionary service required not only dedication but the very best in intellectual gifts available. He would not accept second-class standards.

The focal point for missionary interest during these years was the Cambridge men who had gone to India as chaplains. From India, Claudius Buchanan offered prizes in the universities in Great Britain for compositions on missions. When the first awards were made in 1805, Charles Grant (1778–1866), son of Charles Grant of the Clapham Sect and East India Company director, won one of them. In his winning entry he wrote:

> Britain, thy voice can bid the dawn ascend,
> On thee alone the eyes of Asia bend.

High Arbitress! to these her hopes are given,
Sole pledge of bliss, and delegate of heaven,
In thy dread mantle all her hopes repose,
Or bright with blessings, or o'er cast with woes,
And future ages shall thy mandate keep,
Smile at thy touch or at thy bidding weep.
Oh! to thy godlike destiny arise!
Awake and meet the purpose of the skies!
Wide as thy scepter waves let India learn
What virtues round the shrine of empire burn.

In his poetry Grant successfully captured the main themes that were to influence both missionary and colonial policy for the next two generations.

In January 1818 Henry took his B.A. degree. He emerged from the Mathematical Tripos nineteenth Wrangler. That summer Henry traveled north with Robert and Samuel Wilberforce to join their family for a long vacation at Rydal, Westmoreland. During this time he met the poets William Wordsworth and Robert Southey and spent one day walking with the latter. The summer at the Wilberforce home cemented the friendship between Venn and William Wilberforce.

St. Dunstan's

Following his election to a fellowship at Queens' in January 1819, Henry returned from Cambridge to London. During the next months he attended the Bible Society meetings, saw Wilberforce frequently, and often went to Clapham to visit the Thorntons and other old friends.

In October the bishop of Ely ordained him a deacon on his fellowship title. On November 28 at the age of twenty-three Henry performed clerical duties for the first time, reading prayers and preaching at Clapham, the church where he had been baptized and confirmed. A few weeks later he wrote to his uncle George King:

I have never been troubled with what are called nervous feelings. I felt while standing in that pulpit a lively though melancholy satisfaction in the idea of representing my father in a far more worthy way than I shall ever be able to do in any other situation, standing before the same congregation, invested with the same office, endeavouring to set forth, however imperfectly, the *same truth*.[13] [Emphasis in original.]

Though his father and mother were not there to celebrate young Venn's accomplishments, old friends of the Clapham Sect took note and maintained a parental interest. "I heard Henry Venn (our dear friend Venn's oldest son) preach yesterday for the first time," wrote Zachary Macaulay to Hannah More on May 24, 1820. "It was a sermon of great power and still greater promise. It is delightful to see a fourth generation of Venns thus taking their stand on the Lord's side."[14]

At the end of 1819 Henry Venn first entered the committee room in Salisbury Square as a CMS member.[15] He became a regular visitor to meetings of the religious societies. For several months he served as curate at Beckenham and later preached Sunday evenings at Spring Garden Chapel while searching for a regular curacy. For his family's sake he wished to remain in London. Equally compelling was his desire to stay in close touch with the CMS and the Bible Society. He felt drawn to that work.

The year 1821 saw some milestones for Henry. In January he assumed responsibility as curate at St. Dunstan's. In June he was ordained priest by the bishop of Norwich in the cathedral. In July he completed his M.A. degree at Cambridge.

St. Dunstan's was a church of historical importance, having been served by William Tyndale, John Donne, and well-known eighteenth-century Evangelical William Romaine. Venn was virtually in sole charge at St. Dunstan's. The task was not easy for an inexperienced curate. The parish consisted of six thousand people, many of them tradesmen living over their shops. The district was in general not high class. During pastoral visits to some houses Henry found it prudent to post his beadle (church officer appointed by the vestry) at the door to protect his own reputation.

At this time Venn's qualities still did not suggest particular leadership gifts. Like his father, he seemed quite lacking in personal ambition. Rather, he demonstrated solid dependability and conscientious application. R. B. Seeley, Fleet Street publisher who later did work for Venn, was one of the St. Dunstan's parishioners. He recalled:

Few people, certainly at the period of my first acquaintance with him, would have been able to anticipate the position which he occupied half a century later. The quietness of his demeanor, the absence of everything pretentious or aspiring, and his freedom from that sort of perhaps allowable ambition, which is so common now-a-days [1873], all tended to prevent the thought from arising that in the curate of St. Dunstan's, Fleet Street, in 1821-2, men beheld one who half a century after would possess a degree and extent of influence in the Church, which no other man, apart from rank and official dignity, could pretend to wield. . . .[16]

Already at this stage, however, Venn's interests were growing in the direction of the societies rather than the parish. His sister Emelia must have felt intuitively the direction Henry would develop when she observed him in a missionary meeting in Clapham schoolhouse in March 1821. "After a long speech from Mr. Bickersteth, Henry got up, and with an air of perfect composure and self-command stood and for twenty minutes spoke in a manner that astonished one and filled me with gratitude and thankfulness," she wrote to her brother John in India. "Not only did he speak in support of missions, but he wanted to publicly avow his willingness to assist in so great a work as that of mission."[17]

Henry continued his parish work because nothing else was open to a young clergyman. Yet it was mission that caught his imagination from the first.

Despite the heavy work load, Venn found time for CMS meetings and occasional Bible Society functions as well. He was appointed to a special CMS committee charged with setting up a missionary training college at Islington. The Islington Institution opened in late 1824 and Venn was offered the post of vice principal. He declined, saying that teaching was not one of his gifts.[18]

Though the St. Dunstan's curacy confined him to the London area, Henry continued to see his old friends. At least once each month he went to Clapham. During this time he began working on his grandfather's biography. His research of family origins took him to Devonshire and Yorkshire. While traveling to Yorkshire he visited the Nicholas Sykes family, who were relatives of the Clapham Thorntons. He found Mrs. Sykes and her daughters at home, "presenting a most cheerful and pleasing family picture." On his return from Yorkshire he took the occasion to call again at the Sykes's where he spent several hours with the young women. "Miss Sykes walked with me to the Hamleen and talked well," he observed in his journal.[19]

Cambridge Again

After five years at St. Dunstan's, Venn was convinced that he needed to deepen his preparation in theology and biblical studies. He resigned the curacy and returned to Cambridge to study for his bachelor of divinity degree. During his second year at Cambridge he was appointed proctor. This involved not only student discipline but community relations as well. Town–gown tensions rose and fell. On one occasion Venn and Joshua King quelled a riot.

The proctor position allowed him to exert moral influence. His grandfather had enforced Sunday observance at Huddersfield and his father did the same thing at Clapham. Henry Venn worked to rid Cambridge of its houses of ill-fame during his tenure as proctor. At year's end only two remained in operation and he instituted legal proceedings against them.

In the midst of tutorial and other official duties, Venn pursued his theological studies. He also followed lectures on the French Revolution and medicine. His excuse for the latter was that as a parish priest he felt he ought to have some rudimentary understanding of medical science. In truth he shared his father's penchant for applied science. He was not interested in it as a theoretical exercise, but in its manifold practical implications. In this Venn's lifelong emphasis on utility shows through; when he preached in the college chapel he spoke to student needs rather than discoursing to impress the Fellows.

In spite of his long association with the university, Venn never felt entirely at home there. He did not develop into a serious scholar. Perhaps his Evangelical predilection led him to value results over theory; he was by nature a preeminently practical man of great common sense. He criticized as insular and self-validating the values by which academe lived. In a sermon preached at Queens' College Chapel in his final term he showed his bias. The title: "Academical studies subservient to the edification of the church."[20] In this sermon he argued that the student should seek to excel, but that the grand motive was to edify the church. The "mock pageantry" of academic struggles should not be mistaken for reality. The true value of the academic would be realized when it served the Christian cause.

No one ever accused Venn of lacking intelligence or wisdom. Many nineteenth-century Evangelicals were anti-intellectual; Venn was not. He valued knowledge and encouraged others to get training. Yet Venn dissented from the prevailing views of university education. He disliked the pompous airs a university could affect while disregarding its moral responsibility.

In the spring of 1828 Venn left academe to again work in the church. He assumed the curacy at Drypool located on the outskirts of Hull.[21] The place was dull and uninviting, but not without its redeeming features. There his casual acquaintance with the Nicholas Sykes family rapidly became intimate. He courted and won the hand of Martha Sykes, the woman who had "talked well" on his previous visit. Martha's father, who had died in 1827, was a Hull businessman with a large fortune and a family to match.

On January 21, 1829 Henry and Martha were married at Swanland. He was thirty-three, she twenty-eight. It was a cold, inhospitable day and, according to Emelia Venn, "Henry was very composed, but looked rather like a person in a boat who is not ill but knows he is going to be."[22]

Whatever the wedding lacked in style was more than made up for in the success of the marriage. Henry and Martha were completely devoted to each other. Martha's marriage settlement also assured their financial security and allowed Venn to work for CMS for more than thirty years on an honorary basis.

Venn threw himself into his parish work at Drypool with great energy. He performed the usual clerical duties conscientiously but introduced innovations. Distressed at the general biblical illiteracy among parish homes, he was convinced that ministers should revive the old practice of catechizing the young people (not children). "I believe multitudes are as ignorant of the first and simple principles of Christianity as the children of the heathen,"[23] he said.

In 1829 he had 160 young people enrolled in confirmation classes. They received three lectures on the church each week and were interviewed personally at the end of the course. For adults Venn introduced Sunday evening catechetical lectures. To his surprise more than one hundred people were soon coming. "The room is crowded, and they are very attentive," wrote Martha to Emelia Venn. "There seems to be a remarkable degree of . . . enquiry amongst the people, more particularly amongst the soldiers and their wives (from the nearby garrison). I cannot tell you how many of this class have come to this house desiring to see Henry, not a week passes without two or three, sometimes more."[24]

In order to strengthen pastoral care, Venn introduced the visitation scheme his father had pioneered at Clapham. The District Visiting Society met both spiritual and physical needs. Visitors covered the entire parish periodically. Because Drypool was a poor parish with considerable physical need, Venn also founded the Clothing Society. Hundreds of people enrolled in the Society.

Word of Venn's good work at Drypool spread. People sent inquiries about his various schemes and asked advice in starting similar societies. Zachary Macaulay held up Drypool as an example of what the church must do to be revived.[25] On short notice Dr. Thomas Chalmers of Edinburgh visited Drypool the summer of 1833. "Hull is particularly well off both for its Christian clergymen and its Christian citizens," he wrote. "Mr. Venn, in whose house I am, is still among his thirties, and a most active, intelligent, and zealous minister."[26]

It was of course impossible for Venn to participate regularly in CMS affairs from Hull. But from the CMS viewpoint he was a model parish clergyman; he organized regular meetings at Drypool in support of the CMS.

St. John's

The years at Hull were fruitful, but Venn longed to return to London. When offered the curacy at St. John's in 1834, Henry moved his young family (Henrietta, two years, and John, two months) from Drypool to Holloway. At St. John's Venn once again set about improving the pastoral care of his people. To help improve the general education of the community, he founded the Institution for Promoting Useful and Religious Knowledge in 1838. "In subservience to the interests of morality and the glory of God," the institution featured a lending library, reading room, and lectures on literary and scientific subjects. Venn wanted it to benefit especially the working classes of the district.

Martha also took an active interest in the parish. She founded Grove Lane Infants' School in 1836. The Venns built and maintained this institution entirely at personal expense.

Immediately after returning to London, Venn began attending CMS meetings. He was soon serving on important subcommittees, which involved him in the most vital questions facing the society.

In 1837 when Daniel Corrie, bishop of Madras, died in India, Evangelicals were eager to see him replaced by another of their persuasion. They turned to Henry Venn. Venn found the offer attractive but declined after careful thought for two reasons. First, he pleaded lack of qualification. The second reason was more weighty: family health.

Martha Venn's health was waning. Her favorite sister, Anne, who lived with the family, died of tuberculosis in 1835. In 1837 their third child died when he was just a few months old. These were heavy emotional burdens for Martha. When she was expecting their fourth child in 1838, her health was poor. Venn recalled:

I had great anxiety about her health. Between the pressure of my parish duties and my attentions to her, I was often in a state of extreme mental torture. I frequently went from her to my church with so heavy a heart, that I could have sunk into the earth with every step I took. . . . I can scarcely recollect any moments of my life when I suffered such intense distress as during those sad hours.[27]

Each day he carried her up and down stairs to conserve her strength. He dared not tell her—or even admit to himself at first—that he was beginning to have strange symptoms. His pulse was becoming rapid. He had pain in his arm, and he sat up many sleepless nights.

The baby, Henry, was born July 27 and on August 2 Venn went to see a doctor. The doctor said he had "all the symptoms of an enlargement of the heart." The next day he went to another physician who confirmed the diagnosis and prescribed total rest for an indefinite period of time. At this point he was forced to tell Martha of his serious ailment. From August 1838 until the following August he performed no clerical duty.

In the spring of 1839 he took his family on a trip through Wales, and when Dr. Jephson saw him in summer he assured Venn that he was much improved and that Martha's health was good. Venn intended to return to his parish duties in August, when his wife became ill once more, with tuberculosis. The doctor frankly explained the situation to both of them. He held out little hope of recovery. A year before Venn was living "under the sentence of death." Now Martha was under the same sentence. Martha immediately wrote letters to all her family members informing them of her illness and began making preparations for the end.

Naturally she was much concerned for the welfare of the children. Henrietta was high-strung and Martha felt she required gentle but firm discipline. She encouraged Henry to remarry, provided the children's welfare was also taken into account. But Venn's own health was far from good, and they had to consider the possibility that their children might be left without either parent before long. They went over the list of relatives who might be suitable guardians. Their first preferences were Henry's unmarried brother and sister, John and Emelia Venn of Hereford. Throughout these months Martha amazed Henry repeatedly with her composure and self-control. They both firmly believed that the Christian faith was based on hope. They did not accept death easily or treat it sentimentally, but they knew that for the Christian death does not have the last word.

Venn stayed by his wife's side throughout her final illness. Day by day they faced the inevitable outcome together. They ran back over the events of the past several years, asking what they might have done differently. They were tempted even to question whether they had failed to follow God's leading. On one occasion Henry "had been speaking about the remarkable providence connected with the Bishopric of Madras three years ago." Spencer's wife had also been in consumption and he went to India assuming she would not live.

She not only recovered, but she was able to go to India to join her husband. Had Henry played Jonah?[28] Martha rejected this line of reasoning.

She especially wanted to ensure that the children not retain "unpleasant recollections connected with her illness—and that they might have no terrific impressions respecting death. . . ."[29] When the children came to her room, even after she had grown weak, she always tried to be as natural and interested in them as usual.

By March 10 the disease had advanced so far that Martha was seldom conscious. The night of March 20 she roused in agitation. Henry prayed with her and concluded with "Lord Jesus receive her spirit." Calmly she responded: "I had thought long ago to have been at rest and slept in Jesus. How long I have waited." These were her last words. The morning of March 21, 1840, Martha died.[30] Together with his brother John, Venn took his wife's body back to Highgate for burial at St. John's. After their mother died Venn continued to speak of her to the children to keep her memory fresh and "to familiarize to them death and heaven and reunion with those who have slept in Jesus—as events supremely desirable."[31]

Henry and Martha Venn had enjoyed an unusually happy marriage. Leslie Stephen, a nephew, said that "Venn's closest relations used to speak with a kind of awe of the extraordinary strength of his conjugal devotion."[32] Even though she had encouraged him to think of marrying again, he never did. At least part of the explanation lies in Venn's strong conviction about the communion of saints. Many years later when his old friend Lord Chichester, CMS president, lost his wife, Venn confided to him that this sense of continuing communion had been a source of comfort and strength to him in the years since his own wife had died. "You know I am not sentimental," said Venn, "I never was. I have a horror of what is called spiritualism. But through the grace of God I have enjoyed a constant communion with the spirit of my dear wife since she was taken."[33] This was not a doctrine Venn expounded, but a deep personal experience. His sympathy for others who suffered was profoundly affected and enriched by his own sufferings.

In the spring of 1840 Venn returned to London with his children. His doctor told him that he was still in no condition to work and would have to give up all responsibilities for a period of several years if he wished to recover even a measure of health. Instead, he ignored the advice and returned to his parish duties and participation in CMS affairs.

During the two years of enforced absence, a curate had carried on the work. By 1840 two curates were assisting Venn at St. John's. Though he had returned to St. John's expecting to throw himself into the pastorate, he never quite settled down to being a parish priest. Each new step now led him in another direction. The magnetic pull of the CMS proved more powerful than the parish. Gradually—inexorably—another calling was unfolding. By the end of 1843 he confided to his diary what would not be official for another two years: that he would give himself fully to the CMS and the missionary cause.

Meanwhile Venn had to provide for his family. He was a devoted father and tried to compensate for Martha's absence. Where the children's education was concerned he sought to provide the best. During their first years he employed a governess. After 1846 his sons attended Cholmondeley School, Highgate, and later Islington Proprietary School, founded by Daniel Wilson. Son John later said, "Our general life at home as children was not, I think, a joyous one, though it was far from being actually unhappy."[34] Running the household was left to a succession of governesses and the family nurse. Since Venn was often absent, household staff set the tone for family life more than he knew or wished.

Aunt Emelia and Uncle John filled an important role for the Venn children. For several years Venn took summer vacation trips to Europe to recuperate, while his children spent delightful days at Hereford. Emelia also helped Henry decide on new household staff. Unfortunately, she could not be present all the time to manage the household. Aunt Emelia's visits brought lightness and cheer. She had an unusual gift for understanding young people and the Venn children considered her their second mother.

The children felt near-awe for their father. For them he was goodness itself. He could condemn falsehood overwhelmingly, but quietly. He was thoughtful and affectionate and they were ever surprised by his generosity. Venn tried to take time with his sons. He bought tools for them and took them on occasional hikes or rides. But he was an increasingly busy man and could not give them the attention he intended—much less substitute for a mother.

When Venn consulted his doctors in May 1844, they were surprised at his good recovery. He had learned to pace himself and his heart had gradually accommodated itself so the doctors assured him he could expect to live a normal lifespan. He was advised to guard against sudden overexertion, improper diet, mental anxiety, and agitation. In fact this was the regimen he had already set for himself. In future years the doctors might well accuse Venn of constantly violating the rule about overexertion; his health was never perfect again, but he had found a *modus vivendi*.

NOTES

1. Cf. Wilbert R. Shenk, "T'owd Trumpet: Venn of Huddersfield and Yelling."
2. Venn MSS F17.
3. At the time, of course, many opposed them and their efforts. Posterity has generally taken a more positive view. Among the many accounts of this remarkable group, see Sir James Stephen, "The Clapham Sect," *Essays in Ecclesiastical Biography*, II:289–385; E. M. Howse, *Saints in Politics*; and the following biographies: R. Coupland, *Wilberforce*; M. M. Hennell, *John Venn and the Clapham Sect*; M. G. Jones, *Hannah More*; V. Knutsford, *Life and Letters of Zachary Macaulay*; S. Meacham, *Henry Thornton*; and H. E. Hopkins, *Charles Simeon of Cambridge*.
4. For a full account of the founding of the CMS and Venn's part in it, see Hennell,

John Venn, chap. 5; C. Hole, *Early History of the Church Missionary Society*, pp. 25–51; E. Stock, *History of the CMS*, I:63–78.

5. Hennell, *John Venn*, p. 160.

6. E. M. Forster, *Marianne Thornton*, p. 39.

7. VB 206.

8. Venn MSS F17.

9. VB 183.

10. Venn MSS, June 12, 1813.

11. Venn MSS, June 22, 1813.

12. VB 171:350.

13. Venn MSS, C62, Oct. 16, 1819.

14. V. Knutsford, *Zachary Macaulay*, p. 355.

15. Venn's CMS membership usually is dated from 1821, when he became curate at St. Dunstan's-in-the-West. E.g., William Knight, *Memoir of the Rev. H. Venn*, 1880, p. 27. Stock, *History of the CMS*, I:241, gives the year as 1822. Venn himself consistently dates his membership from 1819. Cf. VB 130:172 and 147:129. He joined in late 1819 and began attending regularly from January 1820. The Minute record shows he was present for ten committee meetings in 1820 alone.

16. Knight, 1880, p. 26.

17. Venn MSS C26, March 26, 1821.

18. Venn MSS C36, Dec. 14, 1824, and G/AC3, Dec. 20, 1824.

19. Venn MSS F13.

20. VB 2.

21. The Drypool living was in the gift of William Wilberforce, who was diffident about offering it to Venn (Venn MSS C35, Oct. 26, 1826).

22. Venn MSS C75, Jan. 22, 1829.

23. Knight, 1880, p. 49.

24. Ibid., p. 55.

25. Venn MSS C35, Feb. 18, 1832.

26. Thomas Chalmers, *Memoirs*, II:416.

27. Venn MSS F61.

28. Ibid.

29. Ibid.

30. Venn MSS F11.

31. Venn MSS F22.

32. *Life of Sir J. F. Stephen*, p. 36.

33. Venn MSS C36. Also cf. Venn MSS F61, where he summarizes his theology of suffering.

34. Venn MSS F27.

2

Honorary Clerical Secretary

Master of the Committee Room

Venn resigned his pastorate at St. John's, Upper Holloway, in 1846 and was appointed honorary clerical secretary of the CMS on April 13, 1846. The decision to leave the pastorate was not without struggle. For years he had divided time between the parish and the CMS. Since 1841 he had served as interim honorary clerical secretary. The two responsibilities were too heavy. "I believe I have been called of God to undertake the secretaryship," he wrote. "I dare not give up my parish."[1]

Venn was dissatisfied with his performance as pastor while at the same time he found CMS work satisfying and challenging. He finally turned to brother John and old friend Charles Baring for counsel. Both agreed that Venn's vocation was CMS service. Baring pointed out that Venn's real value was seen in the committee. His straightforward manner, calmness of judgment, and an ability to take a long-range view had given him authority with the committee that in Baring's words "no other secretary has before possessed."[2]

When Venn joined the secretariat in 1841 Dandeson Coates was the dominant figure in office and committee affairs. Venn was assigned to help answer special inquiries in home correspondence and was responsible for communications with ecclesiastical authorities, letters to individual missionaries and colonial bishops overseas, instructions to missionaries, and the annual report. With Coates, he oversaw publication of occasional papers.

Even before Coates's death in 1846 Venn had become the leading secretary. Major Hector Straith, appointed to succeed Coates, became office supervisor. Venn took charge of the work of the committee. The committee did not attempt, however, to name him general or senior secretary. Venn argued against a pattern that formally set one man over the rest of the secretariat. He was, nevertheless, the undisputed leader.

Venn always carried the title honorary clerical secretary, despite the committee's urging that he receive the normal salary. He served as secretary for thirty-one years, declining to receive so much as reimbursement for travel costs for official deputation.

Leadership of the CMS in Victorian Britain required the gifts of a churchman combined with those of a statesman. Anglican missionary societies, as a part of one of the established churches of the major colonial power, were

16

intimately linked to the state both at home and abroad. The church-state relationship was fraught with danger and difficulties. Venn understood the need to balance disparate interests. He knew that missions dare not become tools of the state.

The Anglican Church presented similar complexities. The CMS was one among several church societies. The CMS finally won the blessing of the hierarchy in 1841, but tensions and problems did not disappear. Churchmanship was needed both to resolve new problems and to improve the system as it faced new situations.

Venn brought to the secretaryship the experience of a pastor and churchman. His familiarity with church societies gave him valuable background. Clapham had exposed him to men and affairs of state. Some of his boyhood friends from Clapham were now influential members of government. These advantages of experience and relationships united in a person who possessed gifts of administration, strength of statesmanship, and keen awareness of spiritual principles. Venn possessed considerable self-confidence, which less secure people saw as imperiousness. His dogged defense of Society principles and reputation was matched with flexibility in questions of method. To critics he appeared unduly stubborn. He made decisions rapidly and had an outstanding capacity for work.

One of Venn's great strengths was his shrewd insight into human nature. His nephew, Leslie Stephen, suspected that Venn's irrepressible story-telling and good humor must have been an embarrassment in what were generally serious-minded circles, even though they made him a delightful companion.[3] He enjoyed people and entertained a steady stream of missionaries and other friends in his home.

One of the keys to Venn's success as a secretary was his relationship to the committee. The CMS General Committee consisted of twenty-four laymen and all clergymen who subscribed half a guinea annually. The lay members were typically men with experience in the commercial or political world. Although he was not a public speaker and increasingly avoided the platform after he became secretary, Venn was master of the committee room. He respected the committee and, in turn, commanded their respect. He knew the reason. He told his son, "All the influence I gain in committees, etc., arises from the habit I early formed of 'getting up' a question thoroughly. . . . As old Boston [the gardener] used to say of pumping the cistern full at Highgate, 'It requires one to stick to it.' It is a habit which once formed applies to everything—religion as well as science—personal and ministerial religion."[4]

He also knew when to drop a proposal that failed to win support. Once he brought a recommendation to the committee, only to have it rejected. Some months later the same idea was proposed by a committee member and it was enthusiastically adopted. Venn quietly called for his paper and read it to the committee. "When I brought this to you, you would not have it," he reminded them.[5]

Venn had a clear concept of a committee's function and working processes.

He feared the formation of parties or factions in a committee. Following one difficult committee meeting, he confided to his son: "By dint of putting the matter in various phases, I was enabled at last to shape it so well that all consented; which is a far greater triumph than carrying one's own proposition by a majority of votes."[6] Venn knew how to expedite the work of a committee. He also respected the personalities of committee members.

As chief secretary Venn took the lead in recruiting new members. He observed the difficulty new committee members sometimes faced in being accepted and feeling useful. Some would join, but then become discouraged and drop out. Venn once counseled a prospective member that the committee dealt with both great issues and routine business. Matters of substance might arise quite spontaneously. One could not get a fair impression of the work of the committee on the basis of one or two meetings. It was partly up to the novice to win his way with the committee through patience and perseverance.

What kinds of issues did the committee face? Venn listed for the prospective member questions before the Society in 1866: "What are the proper relations between the foreign missionary and the native pastor? What is the normal organization of a nascent native Christian Church? How to dispose of a very limited amount of European agency over a very wide and expanding field of labour to the best advantage?"[7] The committee dealt with difficult personnel problems such as the case of a man who got on badly with fellow missionaries but was nonetheless bringing people to faith. The principles of the Society needed to be defended but in a constructive way. Relations to government posed delicate problems. Missionary methods had to be evaluated. The committee needed variety in experience and competence in order to make deliberations productive.

Lord Chichester, CMS president 1834–86, characterized Venn's ability in conducting interviews with missionaries before the committee. He did not waste time on preliminaries. In fact, he could be blunt. He would begin: "Now, Mr. ———, what have you to tell us?" If the witness hesitated, Venn prodded him. "You have seen so and so," he would say, "now tell us about it."[8] This got the results he wanted.

Chichester also noted Venn's skill in relating to government officials. Usually special delegations comprising Society members and secretaries made representation to government. The person of highest rank led the delegation and served as spokesman. Venn was the acknowledged CMS authority on such occasions. When Parliament was debating the question of the British Squadron Patrol of the West African coast in 1849, Venn drafted a sixteen-page memorandum outlining the issues and specific recommendations to be placed before Lord Palmerston, foreign minister. "Whatever impression was made upon the Queen's Minister, was mainly owing to the clear, intelligent, and business-like statements of our honoured Secretary," said Chichester. "I know that this was the opinion of several of the Ministers with whom I conversed upon the subject afterwards."[9]

Venn found the challenges of the CMS invigorating. On his fiftieth birthday he wrote: "How differently should I have once regarded this day—as the entrance upon old age. Now I seem to myself still essentially a boy." He was thankful that God had made his way clear for the resignation of St. John's, permitting him "to devote a freer mind wholly to the delightful work of the Church Missionary Society."[10] He confided to his diary: "Wonderful beyond my present conception also is the mercy of God towards me in placing one in so honourable and influential a position in his church who have deserved rather to be cut down as a cumberer of the ground—to be cast aside as one unfit for the Master's use."[11]

Bishop Blomfield honored Venn on his fiftieth birthday by making him an honorary prebendary of St. Paul's. Blomfield's action showed the respect in which he held Venn. This esteem was mutual.

Venn's Interpretation of the Church Missionary Society

There was never a time in Venn's memory when the CMS was not a part of his life. A son of one of the founders, Venn knew the leaders of the Society and the missionaries they sent out. As a young man he had supported the Society, becoming a member in 1819. Despite family illness he rendered important service to the CMS as a committee man. In short, his commitment to the Society was an act of filial piety as well as personal conviction. He felt duty-bound to pass this trust on to the succeeding generation whole and untarnished.

Venn's ambition to write what he termed the "constitutional" history of the CMS was never fulfilled. His interpretation of the Society is found instead in four sources: *Sermon on the occasion of the death of Josiah Pratt,* "The origination of the CMS," *The founders of the Church Missionary Society and the first five years,* and "Retrospective Address." In addition, Venn's writings and correspondence include many references to CMS origins and Evangelical principles.[12]

While the Church of England formally acknowledged the importance of mission long before 1799, it had not really taken mission to heart. The Society for the Propagation of the Gospel (SPG) and the Society for Promoting Christian Knowledge (SPCK), founded a century earlier, did not get the support they deserved. The eighteenth century saw a gradual awakening to mission beginning with the Moravians in 1733. By 1786 and 1792 the Methodists and Baptists had organized missionary societies. The interdenominational London Missionary Society (LMS) followed in 1795.

During this same era a series of discussions among Evangelicals, most of which occurred in the Eclectic Society in London, paved the way for the formation of the CMS. The world was opening up to Christian consciousness in a new way. A budding antislave movement exposed the moral squalor of white traders and explorers from the "Christian" nations. Evangelicals felt the obvious response was to bring the gospel to peoples who had never heard it. Not least among the reasons, they wanted to atone for the wrongs whites had committed against other races.

It was Charles Simeon, influential rector of Holy Trinity Church, Cambridge, who proposed in 1796 that the Eclectic Society discuss the possibility of mission linked directly to the established church. The circle of interest was growing, with Evangelicals like William Wilberforce and Henry Thornton lending support. When the Eclectic returned to the question three years later, influential laymen gave their encouragement. Their goal was to establish a missionary society sponsored by Evangelicals of the church.

At the last minute some Eclectic members wondered if it might still be possible to collaborate with the LMS; but John Venn and Charles Simeon were convinced this was impossible for members of the church. John Venn proposed four principles that must undergird a missionary society. First, a successful mission depends on the Holy Spirit to open doors and guide in steps taken. Second, the strength of mission is in the quality of persons sent out. In the third place, mission must begin small and grow from the ground up. And fourth, the Society should be founded upon the church principle, not the high-church principle.[13] With this statement Venn rejected both the LMS nondenominational approach and the SPG/SPCK "high-church" tradition.

Henry Venn believed that the CMS was a direct product of the Evangelical Revival, despite absence of reference to its Evangelical character in the founding document. Evangelical ideals were incorporated into early decisions and policies. CMS founders felt personally responsible for the conversion of the world. While some argued that it was the bishops' responsibility to preach the gospel, CMS founders claimed that nobody was excused from this responsibility. They accepted the priesthood of all believers. At the same time these men worked on the basis of both ecclesiastical and spiritual principles. They were committed to the Church of England as well as to Evangelical convictions. Their work was conducted as an act of faith and in a spirit of prayer. CMS founders were men of hope even in difficult days.

The CMS was established as a society within the church and in subordination to church authority. It did not have a Crown charter, but was to function on the basis of voluntary association. Voluntary association was a time-honored institution in British society. Although the roots reach back into history much further, the forms known to CMS founders were the fruit of the flowering of religious societies in the latter half of the seventeenth century. The basic idea was similar to that underlying a religious order: a group can best accomplish its agreed-on objects by a discipline that sustains and directs it in the pursuit of that purpose.

Venn considered the voluntary character of the Society second in importance only to its Evangelical foundation. He defended the voluntary principle against all critics, whether they urged formation of a union of societies or placing the missionary societies under direct control of the hierarchy. Venn argued that the mission of the church within the Anglican communion could best be prosecuted by voluntary societies of like-minded, fully committed supporters. But he also believed that such societies should operate within the church.

This design, however, contained a constitutional contradiction. How could a voluntary society composed primarily of laymen be subordinated to the church hierarchy? The traditional solution was to win the patronage of the hierarchy without ceding control to the bishops. The point was not lost on the bishops, of course. Although the archbishop of Canterbury unofficially admitted to William Wilberforce that he personally favored the CMS, he claimed it was impossible to declare this support publicly.[14]

Venn defined the Church Missionary Society as a governing body that maintained the broadest possible perspective on all questions. It guarded basic principles, which met their real test once missionaries were sent out. It served as the buffer between the church and the missions when criticisms arose. It was responsible for selecting fields of labor, appointing workers, and developing the principles by which work was conducted.

Venn liked to claim that patterns and policies evolved by the CMS were unique and that the CMS contributed to the development of the missionary society as an institution.[15] He exaggerated the point. The CMS did not originate concepts so much as extend and refine methods that had been applied by philanthropic societies already in the eighteenth century.

When it proved difficult to find recruits from among the clergy of the church, the CMS was forced to follow the precedent of the SPCK and accept German missionaries. Venn termed this lack of recruits a "reproach." In 1825 the Society founded the Church Missionary Institution at Islington to assure a regular supply of missionary candidates. In retelling history, Venn reported that the CMS's example inspired other societies to organize similar schools. He overlooked the fact that the Berlin and Basel mission institutions had long been in existence and, indeed, trained nearly all CMS missionaries in the first fifteen years. The CMS got *its* pattern from the Germans and the Swiss.

The growth of the CMS from a plan in the hands of the founding fathers to a place of preeminence among missionary societies fifty years later moved Venn deeply. The success of the CMS, he believed, proved that its fundamental principles enjoyed divine favor.

Venn and the Church Missionary Society at Midcentury

By 1850 the Evangelical machine was extensive and well organized. Its nerve center was the annual "May Meetings" at Exeter Hall in the Strand. When Exeter Hall opened in 1831, the main auditorium could accommodate more than three thousand people. The larger societies soon found this inadequate and the facilities were enlarged. The ability to attract crowds in such numbers gave the Evangelicals influence. J. C. Ryle remarked that Exeter Hall was one of the main estates of the realm: "There are Queen, Lords, and Commons, and the *Times* newspaper, and the fifth estate is Exeter Hall."[16] The CMS was recognized as one of the leading Evangelical societies, and Venn exerted considerable influence in Evangelical circles.

Venn was keenly aware of the CMS's position and jealously guarded it against all encroachments.[17] He refused to allow his name to be used in support of other causes lest this detract from the Society. He enjoyed respect as the CMS secretary; but he was not without his critics, even among Evangelicals. Upon the death of Dandeson Coates in 1846, *The Record* extolled Coates's qualities as lay secretary. The editor pointedly urged the Society to appoint another strong lay secretary like Coates as a safeguard against Tractarianism. The editor argued that clergymen were subject to temptations to compromise their Evangelical principles that laymen did not face.[18] That was one view. The other was that Evangelicals enjoyed a position of influence in the church and should exploit it. In 1848 the elevation to Canterbury of the Evangelical bishop of Chester, J. B. Sumner, bode well for the CMS. Venn soon became a confidant of the archbishop. On one occasion he sent his regrets to his children on holiday because he had been detained in London so Archbishop Sumner could consult him on the appointment of the new bishop of Sydney. Venn justified himself, saying, "It is a most high honour put upon your father to have any part in it."[19]

Venn's life had become completely identified with the Society. Even his physical well-being seemed to benefit from his work. His brother-in-law, Sir James Stephen, wrote to their mutual friend, Bishop Daniel Wilson of Calcutta, that Venn was keeping steadily at his work in spite of the effects of his old malady "which still occasionally distresses him . . . but he thrives and improves in spirits and strength upon his labour."[20]

NOTES

1. Venn MSS F13.
2. Knight, 1882, pp. 120–23.
3. *Life of Sir James Fitzjames Stephen,* p. 38.
4. Venn MSS C34, July 19, 1856.
5. Knight, 1880.
6. Venn MSS C34, July 19, 1854.
7. G/AC1/16, June 14, 1866, to Rev. D. Miller.
8. Venn MSS C36. Cf. Knight, 1880, p. 395, which omits Chichester's remarks about Venn's bluntness and his self-awareness of this trait.
9. Venn MSS C36.
10. Venn MSS F13.
11. Ibid.
12. VB 19, VB 32, VB 130. Our purpose here is only to present Venn's view of CMS history, which Charles Hole and Eugene Stock subsequently adopted for their official histories.
13. The "fundamental principle" of the LMS says: "As the union of Christians of various denominations in carrying on this great work is a most desirable object, so, to prevent, if possible, any cause of future dissensions, it is declared to be a *fundamental principle of The Missionary Society* that its design is not to send Presbyterian,

Independency, of any other form of Church Order and Government (about which there may be difference of opinion among serious persons) but the glorious Gospel of the Blessed God, to the heathen; and that it shall be left (as it ought to be left) to the minds of the persons whom God may call into the fellowship of His Son from among them to assume for themselves such form of Church Government as to them shall appear most agreeable to the Word of God." *The Plan and Constitution of the Society* (1796).

14. VB 32:7, 10–15.
15. VB 130:173.
16. In Charles Bridges (ed.), *The Church.*
17. G/AC1/14, Dec. 15, 1859.
18. *The Record,* no. 1,939, April 30, 1846, 4; no. 1,944, May 11, 1846, 4.
19. Venn MSS C34, July 21 and 23, 1854.
20. *The Right Honourable Sir James Stephen,* p. 156 (letter dated April 18, 1852).

3
Theorist

Although missions were no longer a novelty by the time Venn became CMS secretary in 1841, no one had yet conceived a formal theoretical framework of mission. Venn became a central figure in the forging of mission theory. He was convinced that missions were in an era of experimentation. Mission supporters during the previous fifty years had naively believed that a few missionaries would enter a country, overwhelm the enemy, and establish Christ's kingdom. Experience had proved the contrary.

In the previous era missionaries went as pioneers, knowing little of the geography or peoples to whom they went. Their experience laid a valuable foundation. The present generation now was in a position to discover basic missionary principles. Indeed, what distinguished modern missions from the old era was this consciousness of fundamental principles by which missionary work was to be prosecuted.

The problems and questions of missions became Venn's meat. "While the present era is one for the development of missionary principles," he wrote in 1858, "it is also one of incompetent theorising with a tinge of missionary romance."[1] Venn became both student and teacher in clarifying the missionary task. His written Instructions to Missionaries consistently show Venn playing this dual role.[2]

He first of all made the work of his own society a field of continual investigation and reflection, urging missionaries to write frequent and full accounts of their work. No sentimentalist, Venn asked for the truth. In his correspondence with individual missionaries he raised questions, solicited information, challenged performance, and applied principles to particular situations.

A second source for study was missionary history. Venn knew the course taken by Protestant missions since the time of John Eliot in New England. He observed the basic assumptions that had guided missions during the past two centuries. Alongside the Protestant experience, he studied the Roman Catholic story, focusing on Saint Francis Xavier.[3] Convinced that romanticism stifled true missionary spirituality, Venn sought to strip the myth from the man. Legends about missionaries like Xavier, he believed, reinforced the "romance of missions." Such tales pictured the missionary as an ascetic, self-denying hero. They put the missionary, rather than the gospel and the influence of the Holy Spirit, at center stage.

The continuing debate within Anglicanism, centering around the question of episcopacy, furnished a third stimulus to the development of missionary principles. The issues arose in concrete field situations. Solutions did not depend simply on settling questions with the hierarchy. Often legal questions were at stake and the government was party to the problems.

In his struggle to identify and codify missionary principles, Venn worked inductively. He was not a venturesome theological thinker. Indeed, theology seldom intrudes in his reflections on the missionary task. Instead Venn focused his search for principles on practical application. He was a pragmatist.

What then were the problems with which Venn had to wrestle? In short, the problems revolved around ecclesiology. What form does the missionary church take? What is the ultimate goal of missionary labors? But the nineteenth-century missionary movement was a product of the eighteenth-century Evangelical Revival, which concentrated on the doctrine of salvation. All missionary societies claimed to be extending the church, but they focused on salvation for the individual. The doctrine that they avoided discussing was ecclesiology.

The Baptist Missionary Society, of which William Carey was the leading mind, did not ask questions about the church in the missionary setting. Converts were baptized into the church, not the mission. Church and mission were integrated from the outset.

The London Missionary Society decided from the start not to export a particular ecclesiology. They encouraged converts to study the Word and determine what form the church would take, thus avoiding the divisive issue. The Church Missionary Society rejected this LMS fundamental principle. Based on the "church principle," the CMS sent its missionaries out to establish churches according to Anglican church order and with episcopal support. They made it clear, however, that spiritual principles were more important than church principles.[4]

The CMS financial crisis in 1841 sparked further questioning of the nature of the missionary church. How is a native church founded? Venn asked. He observed weaknesses in a missionary-founded, missionary-led church. What, he asked, gave a church integrity? The financial crisis emphasized the importance of freeing young churches from dependence on the missionary society. Evidence suggested that the present system made the local church dependent on the missionary society. By 1841 the CMS had established schools and trained many people in Sierra Leone; but few Africans exercised leadership in the church. Where would the present system lead?

The problem had two foci: the integrity of the missionary society and the integrity of the local church. In 1841 the CMS issued a statement announcing that they intended to place greater responsibility on local resources. They would expect local Christian friends and churches to raise needed resources.[5] Venn could not be content with the assumptions of first-generation CMS leaders. These had been good, but did not go far enough. How do you get beyond the missionary stage to an independent, fully competent church? he asked. In order to define the goal, criteria had to be established.

Venn's Theological Assumptions

Although Venn devoted most of his attention to principles of missionary action rather than the theology of mission, he had definite theological presuppositions that provided the fixed and unchanging part of his system. "The missionary's work is flexible and his course is variously directed but the polestar of it is unchangeable,"[6] he told outgoing missionaries. For Venn the Christ-event held the solution to the human condition. The missionary task is to make two realities clear to people: that they are sinners and that Jesus Christ is savior.

Venn shuddered at the prospect of propagating a cheap Christianity. He was not interested in simply giving people new religious forms or swelling membership statistics. He criticized Xavier's work on the ground that it promoted a nominal Christianity. Protestant missions, too, were tempted to accept form without substance.[7] With his roots in the eighteenth-century Evangelical Revival, Venn believed churches could be founded in Asia and Africa based on living faith. In reality he wanted to achieve with the new churches what was impossible in the mother church—a disciplined and committed membership.

This standard could be reached only if people came to the church by way of conversion. "The visible and the true Church each consists of a *company* of believers, banded together by a common faith, whether that faith be of intellectual or of deeper origin; but the real foundation of association in the true church is *conversion* of the sinner to Christ, the radical renewal of the individual, and his mystical incorporation into the body of Christ."[8]

This emphasis on conversion, however, did not overlook the fact that salvation had a present and temporal dimension. Venn did not set word against deed. His heroes were the Clapham Sect. Their tradition combined a vigorous and plain proclamation of the gospel with practical measures to relieve humanity's present sufferings. Venn approved founding schools in most CMS missions and promoting the development of commerce and industry in West Africa. He threw himself into the struggle to root out the remnants of slave trade in Africa. The missionary could not avoid involvement in the converts' temporal welfare.[9] But these were penultimate—not ultimate.

Venn rejected the long-held assumption that civilization was the precursor of Christianity. "Commerce, civilization, and Christianity" was still a powerful slogan among nineteenth-century mission supporters. Venn never used it. He believed the three elements went together, but concluded that Christianity neither rose nor fell with civilization. In 1856 he made a spirited comment on the question to the missionaries. "The principle that men must be civilized in order to embrace Christianity is untenable; for civilization, though favorable to the development of Christianity, so far from being essential for its initiation, is, on the contrary, the consequence, not the forerunner, of the gospel."[10]

For Venn it was the politician's task in the divine economy to improve people's material welfare. The missionary applauds all that is done to mitigate misery and enrich human life, but knows such improvements are only temporary. The mission call to present the gospel of salvation to sinners moves beyond the temporary to the eternal. Whatever the issue at hand, Venn invariably returned to the doctrine of salvation as the basis of mission.

Venn declined to take a position on certain theological questions such as the final state of the heathen.[11] He turned to first-generation CMS leader Thomas Scott, who argued that even if we do not know the final condition of the heathen with certainty, Christian love compels action on their behalf. If we have no definite knowledge of their true state, then our duty is to act toward the heathen on the basis of what we do know: because of divine love Christ died for them. That is motive enough.[12]

Intrinsic to Venn's theological foundation was his belief that God is present and active in history, guiding human affairs according to his plan. Christian mission interprets the acts of God and calls people to obedience. He believed his own Evangelical heritage was in continuity with biblical history.[13] Through world mission the church was extending the tradition of faith in time and space. The present was in dialogue with the past. Both looked ahead to the time when all would be "gathered up into Jesus Christ." This is as close as Venn comes to a statement of eschatology.

The providential design could be discerned in history. The missionary should understand that design and align himself with it. Repeatedly, Venn's Instructions described the providences connected with particular missions. He traced the hand of Providence in past events. He also pointed out that the historical view calls for patience. The first CMS report designated Africa and China as the fields of labor. The door to Africa opened early; but the Society entered China only after fifty years. For some nations the hour had not yet come and Providence could not be hurried—only followed.

These, then, were the theological assumptions undergirding Venn's search for mission principles. He did not base his interpretations on certain biblical texts. He did not exegete, for example, the Great Commission. His theology rested on certain fixed propostions. He felt no need for its development, but directed his energies to application. For foundation principles of mission he turned to the book of Acts, appealing to the primitive church as an example of method. Acts depicted not a set of general rules, but an account of particular experiences. He conjectured that apostolic writers purposely did not describe specific principles. Each generation had to discover these afresh in the progress of their work.

The Primitive Church: A Pattern

The Antioch church presented a pattern for modern missions.[14] It emerged in the midst of persecution following the martyrdom of Stephen. The small group of Christians in Jerusalem were "scattered abroad" as the result of intense opposition, but as they were dispersed, they preached the Word. This incident and its aftermath provide a paradigm of the missionary church.

The emergence of the Antioch church suggested to Venn a first principle: "that the preaching of the Gospel to all nations, and to every creature, is a paramount duty of the Church of Christ."[15] These first Christians accepted the conversion of the world as their chief duty. They lived and died for this cause. Venn pointed out that the primitive Christians did not succumb to the temptation to concentrate on fully winning their own nation before going to other peoples. They immediately began to implement the command of Christ to go to all the world. As the church's concern and understanding grow, Venn asserted, the means are also found to do the tasks at home. The church receives a reflex benefit as it obeys Christ's command to go to the nations.

The Antioch church experience revealed a second principle. All Christians are witnesses to the gospel[16]—laymen from the Catechetical School in Alexandria, one of whom took a missionary tour as far east as India; a Christian slave-girl carried off by the Iberians; the church of Ethiopia founded by two shipwrecked sailors. Venn did not conclude that no special missionary office existed, but rather, used this history to attack the notion that only the missionary was responsible for sharing the gospel and extending the church.

The third principle demonstrated by the Antioch church was that God honors his word when Christ is preached as the only means of salvation.[17] The missionary should share the fruits of civilization and expose false systems of religion. But the highest task is to declare the Word of God, Venn argued. Most missionaries in modern times have been men of simple faith and single-minded devotion. Not theologians, they have been intent on one thing: preaching Christ. The success of modern missions has resulted from this preaching. It has touched peoples of all ranks and classes in all parts of the world. By contrast, Venn noted the inefficiency of other methods. The conquest of India by Britain (a Christian nation), the presence of British merchants and scholars of Hindu literature and religion, the educators who introduced the fruits of Western science—all failed to win an interest in the Christian faith. Only dissemination of the Word has proved efficacious.

Venn also studied the rapid growth of the Antioch church, which soon became the mother church of many branch churches. He cited several reasons for this growth, which furnished useful insights for modern missions. First, and most important, the church grew because God's grace was upon the converts. "God's providence must be followed, not anticipated," Venn's father had said. For Venn too the church in mission must respect both the opening and the closing of doors.

Second, the Antioch church grew because it responded immediately to God's grace at work in the community.[18] Antioch freely sent men to and fro to facilitate the work. Leaders of the church did not stand on rank, but accepted appointment according to their qualifications. Venn contrasted this to the later pattern in the church where the most experienced and effective leaders maintain the established church rather than moving to the frontiers.

A third reason for the rapid growth of the Antioch church was its close relationship with the Jerusalem church. The stability and strength of the younger church was enhanced by its ties to the older one.

This relationship was not without tensions. Nonetheless, the churches needed each other. While political colonization produced a strong desire for independence, stemming from human pride and selfishness, the church of Christ has another foundation. Within the established church a legal relationship bound the parent stem to each branch. The spirit of the mother church determined whether there would be real interdependence. If that spirit was moderate, wise, and evangelical, a natural identity of interests emerged between the parent church and the branches. The church would become a true commonwealth.

Fourth, the Antioch church grew because it appointed a chief minister as overseer. Modern missionary experience shows the importance of proper superintendence. Missionaries could do the initial work of preaching and gathering converts best. Once this initial phase had been completed, the supervision of a bishop was of help. When the church had a native ministry and a second generation of Christians was added to the church, a resident bishop was essential.

Venn argued that the Antioch experience did not demonstrate that a bishop was the mainstay of a mission.[19] The personal qualifications of the man rather than the office determined his effectiveness. The bishop must evidence the fruits of the Spirit. He sustained others by his example and faith.

The spirituality of the apostles advanced the work of the Antioch church. The Acts account is silent concerning the form of ecclesiastical order and discipline. Venn noted, "The single recorded thesis of the preaching of Barnabas is the essence of experimental religion—'cleaving unto the Lord with purpose of heart.' "[20] Paul and Barnabas spent an entire year teaching and training the Antioch church. A bishop's true work was promoting the growth of grace in the hearts of the people. Venn compared this grace with a jewel, and ecclesiastical order with the jewelbox. A box without the jewel was "a cause of reproach and sorrow." A bishop proved his missionary leadership by his own spirituality, by promoting spiritual growth in his people, and by encouraging those specially commissioned for missionary work.

Venn thus proposed that the New Testament church provided a normative pattern that was binding on the church in all ages. The Holy Spirit had selected Paul and Barnabas as special instruments of divine purpose. They were released from the duties of the home ministry and sent out to preach to people who had never heard the gospel. "Missions are pre-eminently the work of the Holy Spirit," Venn said. As the primary agent of mission, the Spirit called, taught, qualified, and guided the missionary in doing the work. "We send you not forth to a work of which we can only hope that the Holy Spirit may . . . bless your labours," he told missionaries, "but we send you forth because the Holy Spirit is doing a work among the heathen."[21]

Working Principles

Venn used the term "principle" in several ways. In some cases he treated a principle as both axiom and goal. He established no ranking of principles. He did, however, make a distinction between basic biblical-theological principles, which we have already discussed, and functional principles to which we now turn.

Venn expected that "working" principles would be modified by time and place. His well-defined sense of what missionary work was helped to provide a clear sense of the role of the missionary. Communicating Christ as Savior was an infinitely varied and complex process. Questions of system had to be decided case by case. This did not mean Venn pursued new principles faddishly but he regarded all principles as valid only as long as they served the missionary cause.

Venn's working principles were in many ways interrelated. The first of these was preaching. Venn saw preaching as the engine of mission, but not to be misused.[22] The preacher could cheapen the gospel by proclaiming it in the wrong manner or place. The cross of Christ was the center of Christian preaching. Wherever it was proclaimed, Christ's messenger was sure to be countered by the enemy.

Venn saw preaching not only in the narrower sense of standing before a crowd. "This work is to be accomplished, not only in the pulpit, or when preaching in the bazaar," he said, "but in the streets and lanes of the city, in the native cottage, in the school-room class, or in the Missionary's study, whether natives come to seek advice or information, or to discharge the usual civilities of society."[23] Preaching was witnessing with a variety of methods.

The second of Venn's working principles was that the missionary master the vernacular languages. Venn felt so strongly about this that he would recall a missionary who failed to pass the language examination. He insisted that preaching through an interpreter was not missionary work.[24]

Third, Venn stressed the importance of giving the people the Scriptures in their own language as early as possible. This was important because all Christians need to be people of the Book if they are to be properly nurtured. The written word provides a source of authority. This may prove decisive particularly among people whose language is reduced to writing for the first time. Giving them the Scriptures in their own language releases in them a sense of pride and respect that is salutary for their development.

Fourth, Venn emphasized that the Bible should be given a prominent place in mission work. This point is related, but separate from the previous one. Venn wanted his missionaries to be known as people of the Book. The Bible should be physically exhibited and made prominent. All CMS schools used the Bible as a classroom text and required students to participate in Bible classes.[25] India missionaries took advantage of the provision to offer Bible instruction in government schools. "You may be silent on points of difference which are really unessential," Venn told missionaries, "but the basis of your teaching will be the Bible, the whole Bible, and nothing but the Bible. . . ."[26] For Venn the Bible was efficacious apart from the ministrations of the missionary. It possessed a "living energy."[27]

Venn's fifth principle was that education is basic to missionary work. If translation and use of the Scriptures in the vernacular were important, then it followed that education was needed. Education bulked large as a part of the missionary task. Venn looked to the educational program to train future leaders and to serve as a means of evangelism. He often felt uneasy about educational programs, not because of the principle, but because of difficulties in implementing it. Perhaps more than with other principles, nonmissionary purposes subverted it.

Venn enunciated his sixth principle—continuous advance in mission—in 1849, at the end of the Society's fifth decade, a period of slow growth. Besides the usual call for additional men and money from the supporting churches, Venn believed the solution lay in stirring up the missionaries. "The watchword of the present occasion must be—Enlarged expectations abroad, and enlarged exertions at home."[28] The older stations were encouraged to break up and move out. Those who remain in the original community should be as zealous in evangelism as those who go to start elsewhere. Each missionary and mission must maintain this larger view of the total task in order to avoid stagnation.

According to the seventh principle, native agency is basic to the development of the mission. From the very beginning the CMS set as a goal the training of indigenous leadersip. Venn deepened and broadened the concept. Indeed, it was out of this insight that he finally formulated the "three-selfs" criteria. As early as possible, local leadership should replace the missionary.[29] In 1846 Venn wrote to the teachers in Sierra Leone in straightforward language. "It has been our constant aim and prayer," he said, "that we might be enabled to train up a body of Native Teachers to whom we may turn over the pastoral charge of those of your countrymen who have embraced the Gospel of Christ."[30] He went on to emphasize the unique task of the Society as pioneering rather than pastoring. He told the teachers that they were those "upon whom the hopes of an African Church are fixed." In this statement he intertwined the principles of native agency, education, self-reliance, and continuous advance.

His eighth missionary principle was to inculcate self-reliance rather than dependence. Native agency developed only if there was self-reliance. "Do not let them lean too much on the Society," Venn said. "Draw out their native resources. Let them feel their own powers and responsibilities."[31] This admonition was given as much for the benefit of the missionary as for the young church. The missionary was too inclined to take the lead. Venn insisted that "prompting to self-action is more important than inducing men to follow a leader."[32] In a paternalistic age, which assumed Western nations were trustees of the welfare of the rest of the world, Venn saw how this attitude inhibited self-respect and self-reliance in the young church. His insight and conviction grew over time. He was less successful in working out the problems or in changing the institutions that fostered paternalism. He did succeed in describing the problem and in awakening others to it.

The ninth missionary principle was to kindle missionary zeal among the young church from the beginning. One might reasonably expect a people who have just discovered the blessings of faith in Christ to evangelize automatically. But Venn observed that this generally was not the case. Instead the young church got the idea that evangelism was the province of the missionary. Some exceptional cases offered hope. "Wherever great success has been vouchsafed in modern missionary annals, it will be found to have arisen in a large degree from the zealous efforts of private individual native Christians —men who have not been the salaried agents of a foreign Missionary Society."[33]

Venn's tenth principle was to "preach" only where Christ has not yet been named. He intended that his society should extend itself only into areas that had no church or mission. This principle stemmed in part from the distinction drawn in 1799 between the CMS and the Society for the Propagation of the Gospel. The latter society was specially responsible for founding churches in British colonies overseas. The CMS was devoted to sending missions to non-Western, non-Christian areas.[34] But the principle took on greater importance as more and more societies sent missionaries overseas. It was especially difficult to observe when each mission wished to have a center in the major cities of a country. The principle had another aspect. It continually reminded the missionary not to settle down.

The CMS founding document set forth the eleventh principle. All CMS missionaries were to maintain friendly relations with other Protestant missionary societies.[35] Venn put the regulation succinctly when he wrote, "God grant that unity of spirit may ever exist, but unity of operations we are not prepared for except where the object is so definite as in the Bible Society."[36] CMS missionaries were to have cordial relations but not to unite with others. The CMS would enter an area where another society was working, as in the case of Madagascar, only if invited to do so. Venn believed that cooperation with other societies was easier overseas. "The union in foreign missions is more easy than at home. But may a blessed reflex of that spirit also return into our own bosoms."[37] Venn rejoiced when his missionaries participated in a monthly meeting with missionaries from other societies in Ceylon. He gratefully acknowledged the assistance of the American Mission in Syria. And it was partly in response to the invitation of American Presbyterians that the CMS entered the Punjab in 1851. The latter event so moved Venn that he termed it a "providential token that a new order of things is established, when the nations of Christendom shall forget their ancient jealousies, and unite in a holy brotherhood for the evangelization of the earth."[38]

The twelfth principle also came from the Society's regulations: "Every missionary is strictly charged to abstain from interfering in the political affairs of the country or place in which he may be situated."[39] Venn was realistic about this matter. He knew the missionary could not ignore or remain aloof from social and political affairs. This regulation encouraged the missionary to avoid acting in a political spirit or deliberately meddling in political affairs. Venn dealt with problem cases continually.

The thirteenth principle identified the fundamental importance of culture. The prevailing nineteenth-century view was that the world's cultures were ranged along a continuum from the primitive to the advanced. Western culture represented the most advanced point on the line. Venn accepted this idea, but only in part.

His early interest in languages and the complexities of translation helped open the realm of cultures to him. When a prospective missionary candidate wrote concerning his ability to learn a language, Venn replied: "You speak with confidence of your acquiring languages readily; but this is a different faculty from that of adapting the organs of speech and the ideas of the mind to the vernacular style and habits of a people."[40]

He urged missionaries to take a positive view of indigenous institutions. "Many of the modes of exercising authority may appear at first, to the eyes of a European, absurd. Some of their governmental institutions are connected with idolatry: nevertheless, they are the framework of society; and, till they are replaced by a more enlightened system, they must be respected."[41]

Venn based his counsel on both theological and practical grounds. Social institutions were a part of the order of creation and existed for the welfare of the people. Even though they did not yet recognize the lordship of Christ, they had a positive function. From a practical viewpoint, the friendship of a people should be won before attempting to evangelize. To do this the missionary must observe and appreciate the customs of the people.

Venn's View of Culture

While the British believed that destiny had called their nation to be trustee of the less advanced peoples of the world, incidents from time to time showed that not all Asians, Africans, or North Americans were happy subjects of the British crown. Venn recognized that self-respect and dignity cannot be built through subjugation. He was on guard against tendencies in missionary schools to Westernize young people, because this would destroy pride in their own culture. When the CMS missionary J. C. Taylor, himself an African, was about to return to West Africa from a visit to England, Venn admonished him to "let all European habits, European tastes, European ideas, be left behind you. Let no other change be visible in your tone of mind or behaviour than that of a growth in grace and in the knowledge and love of God."[42] Venn did not, however, instruct Taylor also to live in an African-style house and cease wearing European clothes.

The problem went deeper than clothes and customs. In an 1867 letter to the bishop of Kingston, Venn explained why the West Africans had made greater progress than the emancipated slaves of Jamaica. The church in Jamaica had failed to provide teachers from among the people themselves. "It may be said to have been only lately discovered in the science of Missions," Venn wrote, "that when the Missionary is of another and superior race than his converts he must not attempt to be their *Pastor.*"[43] Venn was familiar with the almost universal attitude among missionaries that a group of people were not yet capable of providing their own leadership because they had not advanced far enough in the civilized arts or in spirituality. Venn challenged this, claiming that the absence of missionary efforts to devolve responsibilities in the young church was the cause, rather than the consequence, of the low spiritual condition referred to.[44] Paternalism, racialism, and dependency were all a part of the same problem. They were a hindrance to missionary work. The first step toward solution was recognition of the condition.

Out of his background of experience, Venn suggested five principles of "national distinctions."[45] First, "study the national character of the people among whom you labor, and show the utmost respect for national peculiarities." Venn made the unflattering assertion that the Englishman's besetting sin was to disdain the "peculiarities" of other peoples, but it was far worse when such an attitude marked the missionary.

Second, Venn showed considerable prescience when he warned that racism was likely to grow with mission expansion. He saw this as the natural product of a process that began with the missionary in sole charge and ended with a growing and maturing church struggling against missionary paternalism for self-determination. Nevertheless he urged, in the third place, that the church "be organized as a national institution." The "native" Christian should feel bound to his nation, by birth and by Christian responsibility. The possibility that being a Christian made a person less authentic in his environment was totally at odds with Venn's vision.

Fourth, Venn envisaged the time when denominational differences which missions introduced would be overcome in a truly national church. A CMS missionary was duty-bound to found churches according to the discipline and polity of the Church of England. But Venn was quick to point out that the Anglican Prayer Book allowed for adaptations according to national preferences (Article 34). The Christians of a nation would have the freedom to evolve forms of church life most suited to their circumstances.

Venn's fifth point emphasized again that missionaries are a temporary part of the local church. Their first calling was to be pioneer evangelists. If they did this, their true character would be kept clear to all, and they would not be diverted from their primary vocation.

To sum up the meaning of culture for Venn, two principles applied to every missionary.[46] First, the missionary could win the respect of the people and bring them to Christ only by thoroughly identifying with them. Second, the missionary should identify even more fully with local Christians. Missionary failure to accept and be accepted in the local church was a denial of the power of the gospel message.

While Venn affirmed other peoples, he viewed other religions critically. In fact, he took the negative view typical of Christians of the period—that other religions possessed no salvific value. A widespread view in the nineteenth century was that other religions were archaic and would soon collapse. Venn put forward this view repeatedly. He ended his annual report for 1843–44 with these words: "The Lord is carrying on a wonderful work in the midst of the Heathen world—chiefly, indeed, a work of preparation, but one which bespeaks some coming change. The power of Heathenism is failing—the native mind of Africa and the East is awakening—the Agents of infidelity and of apostate Christianity are gathering around to seize upon the minds detached from their ancient superstition—and the preachers of the Gospel are animated by fresh hopes."[47] Such rhetoric might arouse support for his cause but it hardly squared with his demands of his missionaries to listen and study carefully other peoples in their situations.

Venn's missionary principles reflect the period in which he lived, the object of mission that he set forth, and the means he employed for achieving that object. He held his theological presuppositions firmly, while he subjected his practical principles to modification in the light of experience. What is more, he was always on the alert for new insights and stimulated his colleagues to join in the search. His philosophy was that "missionary principles are worked out, like all great principles in social questions, by a process of slow induction, amidst many mistakes and disappointments."[48] Venn was a pioneer at heart.

Episcopacy and Mission

Venn was thoroughly indoctrinated in his father's philosophy of episcopacy as it related to mission. The CMS stood for the "church principle" and not the "high-church principle." But his own position was forged in the crucible of intense negotiations between the hierarchy and the CMS in the late 1830s when the Society wanted to gain official sanction for its work and the hierarchy was disposed to come to terms with the largest Anglican missionary society.[49]

The Society's ecclesiastical relations had to be regularized on two counts: obstacles which prevented bishops from joining, and episcopal supervision of missionaries and young churches overseas. Removal of these obstacles involved complex legal and ecclesiastical issues. This was a time when the British empire was growing rapidly and events did not move in an orderly or logical fashion. It was Venn's genius to see the issues at stake in these situations that stood outside ecclesiastical and civil law and argue for a course of action appropriate to the Anglican communion as he understood it. In the process he helped bring the CMS and the hierarchy together.

In the contrast to the SPG, the CMS deployed missionaries to areas not under the British crown. How could they enjoy episcopal superintendence in such instances? In 1836 Venn, as a committee member, assisted the secretariat in drafting a resolution that recognized "a Colonial Bishop cannot grant Licenses in extra-diocesan Stations."[50] He had no jurisdiction outside his diocese. Yet the resolution went on to suggest that a bishop did, by virtue of office, have responsibility for spiritual oversight of members of the church living outside a recognized diocese.

On the home front the debate between the CMS and high-church critics was intensifying. With his bent toward law, Venn undertook a defense of the CMS position in a document that became "Appendix II to the Thirty-Ninth Report," and was appended to each annual report thereafter until 1877. It demonstrated that "the constitution and practice of the Church Missionary Society are in strict conformity with Ecclesiastical Principles."[51] Venn argued that the Anglican system of government rested on a duality of temporal and spiritual functions. Clergy and laity had distinct spheres of responsibility within the church but cooperated in order to accomplish ecclesiastical objects. Bishops and clergy carried responsibility in the spiritual realm; laity were responsible in the temporal. But the two areas overlapped and this made cooperation necessary.

With the founders of the CMS, Venn held that the Society was "strictly a Lay Institution: it exercises, as a Society, no spiritual functions whatsoever."[52] What was clear to Venn in theory proved far from tidy in practice.

Venn's position on the episcopate involved a major missiological point as well. In the 1843 Bampton Lectures, Anthony Grant developed a theory of mission based on the ecclesio-centric approach. According to this school, a church came into being only when the bishop was present to head it. Only a bishop, therefore, should head a mission—that which was sent with the express purpose of founding the church.[53]

During the next thirty years Venn's archopponent in this debate was Bishop Samuel Wilberforce. Wilberforce was no mere theorist either. He expounded the ecclesio-centric theory with a passion. He was also a man of action—an ardent advocate of missions. But he was identified with the Tractarians' views on bishops. Anything Tractarian set Evangelical teeth on edge.

Against the proponents of the "church" approach to missions, Venn insisted—with history as his defense—that if the church had waited for the bishops to organize a missionary program, it would never have had one at all.[54]

Venn was a loyal Anglican. As a parish minister he had attempted to develop in his parishioners an appreciation for the established church and its form of government.[55] Small wonder he wearied of needing constantly to prove his fundamental loyalty. For him the crux of the matter lay elsewhere. Venn espoused a theory of episcopacy that differed from the "high" Anglican view. His theory was tested and developed in the missionary situation, which both revealed the archaic condition of traditional ecclesiastical law and the restrictions on missionary action that adherence to high-church theory entailed. His theory of missions and of the episcopate proceeded from the same premise. Every organism and every movement should begin from the ground and develop outward and upward. In the development of the church the evangelist preceded the bishop.

This was not quite the full story. Venn also disliked prelacy intensely. He used his study of Francis Xavier to point out the evils of authoritarianism. An authoritarian leader placed a blight on the church. What Venn wanted was a bishop who saw his role as that of servant and shepherd.[56]

No Anglican leader in the nineteenth century played a greater role in establishing the Anglican episcopate round the world than did Venn. In 1837 there were only nine Anglican bishops overseas. By 1867 the number had increased to fifty-one. A good deal of Venn's official correspondence was with colonial and missionary bishops. The fact that these exchanges were often strained reflects the strength both of bishops and of Henry Venn, who were operating in a field for which neither civil nor ecclesiastical law provided guidance.

NOTES

1. G/AC/17/2, Sept. 6, 1858.
2. Cf. Wilbert R. Shenk, "Henry Venn's Instructions to Missionaries."
3. He published *Missionary Life and Labours of Francis Xavier* in 1862.
4. VB 102:339.
5. VB 10.
6. VB 124:186.
7. VB 131:323f.
8. VB 124:187.
9. VB 118:5f.
10. VB 87:153.
11. C/AC1/8, Feb. 23, 1850.
12. See Scott's sermon in CMS *Proceedings,* 1800–1801.
13. Joseph Milner influenced Evangelical historiography through his multi-volume *History of the Church of Christ* (published between 1797 and 1806).
14. VB 37.
15. Ibid., p. 6.
16. Ibid., p. 7.
17. Ibid., p. 11.
18. Ibid., p. 19.
19. Ibid., p. 24.
20. Ibid., p. 26.
21. Instructions, C.A1/L7, Oct. 16, 1863.
22. VB 129:52.
23. VB 49:428.
24. VB 129:52.
25. G/AC1/15, Sept. 6, 1861; G/AC1/15, April 7 and 10, 1862.
26. VB 85:509.
27. VB 134:111.
28. VB 40:167.

29. VB 129:50.

30. C.A1/L3, July 10, 1846.

31. VB 33:10.

32. 114:90.

33. VB 178:243.

34. VB 118:5.

35. *Laws and Regulations of the CMS,* XXXI: "A friendly intercourse shall be maintained with other Protestant Societies engaged in the same benevolent design of propagating the Gospel of Jesus Christ."

36. C.CH/L1, Dec. 8, 1845.

37. VB 54:187

38. Ibid.

39. *Laws and Regulations of the CMS,* sect. VI, no. 9.

40. G/AC1/9, May 12, 1852.

41. VB 90:20.

42. VB 114:89.

43. VB 163:5.

44. VB 178:244.

45. VB 170.

46. VB 187.

47. *Proceedings,* 1843–44, p. 113.

48. *Proceedings,* 1861–62, P. 230.

49. For a full-scale investigation of Venn and episcopacy, see T.E. Yates, *Venn and Victorian Bishops Abroad* (London: SPCK, 1978).

50. CMS Minutes, 15:485, Dec. 6, 1836, and 15:507f, Dec. 27, 1836.

51. VB 8.

52. Ibid.

53. *The Past and Prospective Extension of the Gospel by Missions to the Heathen* (London, 1844), p. 372.

54. VB 130:178ff. Cf. VB 19, Appendix II:37, and VB 32:15f.

55. Venn MSS C31 pt. 2, Oct. 29, 1828.

56. Venn instructed missionaries to respect their diocesan even when they disagreed. See CCH/L1, March 23, 1852, C/CE/L3, Jan. 23, 1852, CN/L6, June 17, 1853; VB 37:24.

4

Strategist

Venn devoted less energy to considering methods than to principles of mission. Some missionary methods followed so logically from principles that they required little discussion. Venn dealt with untried or inadequate methods. We shall identify the various methods used in Venn's period, pausing to examine only those that he treated.

We cannot speak of a general method for preaching the gospel, said Venn. For certain classes of people another means of communication than preaching was more effective. In presenting the Christian message to the high-caste Hindu, the Muslim, or other educated peoples, the approved method was "controversy" or disputation. Venn recognized the innate hostility of the ancient faiths to Christianity. The Christian faith had to be presented in a form that would win a hearing. Through "controversy" comparisons were drawn between Christianity and the other faith with the intention of demonstrating the errors of the latter and the truth of the former. Venn held up CMS missionary C. G. Pfander as an exemplary practitioner of controversy with Muslims. Pfander combined persistence with a meek, gentle, and humble spirit. He attempted to understand the Muslim's world-view and prepared treatises on the Christian faith that the Muslim could understand.[1]

In 1851 Venn mentioned briefly in an Instruction that missionaries to India found conversations and daily religious instruction more effective than preaching.[2] Twenty years later he reported that the London Secretaries' Association (LSA) had recently discussed and approved a new method.[3] This method called the missionary to "cultivate direct personal intercourse with leading men amongst the non-Christian population." This opened up direct communication on a personal basis. Dialogue was beginning to replace "controversy."

The institution as a missionary method consistently raised questions for Venn, as well it might. The CMS made a substantial commitment to various kinds of education but Venn was frequently disappointed at the lack of missionary results. Schools proved ineffective as means of evangelization and were a heavy financial drain on a missionary society.[4]

Female education was a pioneering venture in societies that traditionally did not give girls formal training. According to Venn, "Female Education as a means of training Christian mothers and female native teachers presents at the present time one of the most important fields of missionary labor."[5] He was content, in some instances, to have the Christian Female Education Society formed in 1834 carry on as much of this work as they could.

Missionary societies at various times attempted to establish Christian villages. Venn discounted this method. "Beautiful as the theory of Christian villages appears, in practice they have generally proved a hindrance to missionary progress: because they confine the missionary to one place and the quality of life in the village did not attract the surrounding people."[6]

Orphanages were also well accepted as a necessary missionary method. Venn, however, judged them even more unsatisfactory than Christian villages. "They have failed in North India as aids to Missions. The converts derived from them have proved sickly specimens of native Christians."[7]

As Venn grew increasingly dissatisfied with institutional methods, he sought alternatives. He took early interest in itineration even though he saw weaknesses in the touring system. When a missionary wrote about a plan to visit systematically 285 villages in western India, Venn urged that he not tie himself to a schedule so firmly that he could not follow the Spirit. Venn found in T. G. Ragland the man who caught the vision for itineration which combined flexibility and mobility with responsiveness. The "Ragland Plan" required the evangelists to live in tents and move from village to village. Missionaries and local evangelists comprised the teams.[8]

Medical missions were still in their infancy in 1850. The medical profession had not yet won public confidence. It was another generation before medical missions were accepted among missionary societies. Venn was among those who had little enthusiasm for medical missions. Except for doctors for West Africa, the CMS did not accept applications from missionary doctors until 1864. Venn justified doctors for West Africa largely on the grounds that there would be no other medical service available to the missionaries. He also expected the doctors there to give training to young Africans. Otherwise he took the position that "except in some peculiar fields of labour, it is questionable whether a missionary does not lose rather than gain influence with the natives by the exercise of medical knowledge."[9]

As late as 1864 Venn reported that the CMS had had a uniformly unsuccessful experience with medical missionaries.[10] The problem seemed to center in the Society's expectation that a medical missionary should be first of all an evangelist and secondarily a doctor.[11] In explaining to a correspondent why the Society would not send a doctor to Benares, Venn said the CMS considered preachers its responsibility rather than doctors.[12]

A request from India in 1864 for a medical missionary to open a mission in Kashmir set a new direction. With the help of the Edinburgh Medical Missionary Society, the CMS sent Dr. William Elmslie to Kashmir. This was the third attempt by a missionary society to establish work in Kashmir. Contrary to what Venn had been saying, the doctor's services helped them to gain acceptance among the Kashmiris.[13]

The Role of the Missionary Society

Venn saw the missionary agency as the "heart of the system."[14] The sending church dispatched missionaries to the far corners of the earth. The agency facilitated the vital flow of funds and workers to the field, as well as ensuring proper reporting in order to stimulate the sending church's continued support.

The missionary agency enhanced the missionary's effectiveness by assuming responsibility for the physical, emotional, and spiritual well-being of field staff. The agency gave the missionary basic instructions and policy guidance and coordinated the individual's work with colleagues in order to maintain a unity in purpose and direction.[15] It provided a continuity for the tradition which it represented and brought that tradition to bear on the programs being carried out. In short, the missionary agency gave leadership to the total mission both at home and to the various missions abroad.

The missionary agency headquarters carried out its administrative work in the same spirit and according to the same principles as in the field. It took decisions in an attitude of prayer after careful deliberation.[16] The main task of the Board of Directors was to establish basic principles and overall strategy.

Because a missionary is vulnerable to pursuing activities that are legitimate but not primary, it falls to the agency to maintain a sense of priorities at home and abroad. Frequent evaluation of work on the field and at headquarters was a must.

Venn was in no sense apologetic about the missionary agency as the "scaffolding" of mission. It filled an indispensable purpose and played a constructive role in the life of both the sending church and the developing church.

The Role of the Missionary

CMS founding fathers often cited the dictum that only a spiritual person could do a spiritual work. Venn's ideal missionary embodied the spiritual principles on which the society was based. The missionary, under the Holy Spirit, was the agent of mission.

The first mark of the missionary character is to be *fixed in purpose.*[17] The apostle Paul was the missionary's model in this respect.[18] The great apostle took an interest in many aspects of his converts' welfare, but he never allowed himself to be long detained from his primary calling. Second, the missionary is *a visionary and pioneer.* "He ceases to be a Missionary when he loses this characteristic,"[19] Venn insisted. The missionary was not to stop to shepherd sheep that could feed themselves while others perished in helplessness.[20]

Third, the missionary's character and calling differed from that of any other in the church. The missionary's unique vocation is to cross cultural boundaries in order to preach the gospel of Jesus Christ and extend the church. Never a regular part of the local church, the missionary is appointed to continue founding churches.

Finally, although the missionary's calling is unique, many kinds of people are called to the missionary vocation—from the highly trained university graduate to the individual with more humble credentials.[21]

Only a vital spirituality can sustain the missionary vocation. The missionary must personally exemplify the gospel. A disparity between doctrine and practice discredited the gospel.[22] The missionary maintained this spirituality by practicing the presence of Christ daily.[23]

Missionary spirituality was not solitary. Venn urged the missionaries to meet regularly for prayer. The Christian graces were best cultivated in the give-and-take of church life. Venn disliked any suggestion that the missionary was an ascetic. This image ran counter to his vision of a full-bodied community life that worshiped and served Christ.

Early Goals of Mission

Venn's earliest references to mission goals were stated in individualistic terms. The ideal of the "indigenous church" had not yet emerged. The social scientist used the word "indigenous" to refer to the original culture, social institutions, and people of a particular place. A mutation occurred when the missionary theorist appropriated this term. According to the conventional wisdom of the day, indigenous cultures were less advanced and refined than European culture.

The missionary theorist thus assumed that an "indigenous" church was one in which indigenous peoples had become competent to lead an institution that met European standards. Venn reported to his brother in 1858 that the CMS Committee had just received heartening proof of progress in South India. Nine trained native teachers were being presented to the bishop for ordination. These men had theological training as well as long experience as catechists. "Their examination papers before our missionaries . . . would have satisfied any of our English bishops."[24] These Indians had met European standards.

Yet Venn respected other peoples and taught appreciation for their cultures. In 1843 he opposed a proposal to bring Indians to Great Britain for training because it would denationalize them.[25] Venn's anxiety about educational institutions centered on their disruptive influence, especially in pastoral training. "The question which presents itself to our minds," he wrote the bishop of Bombay, "is whether the present institution is not too much in advance of real Mission work—the error will be seen in the character of the students. If they affect European habits and feelings, we should consider that the institution had failed—that it was not preparing a Native Ministry, but a kind of Indo-European agency which experience has shown us is not a desirable agency for us to employ."[26]

In 1855 Venn entertained in his home a Sierra Leonean merchant who had traveled with his family on the Continent as well as throughout England. Knowing that the man had considerable means, Venn said, "Well now, if you can spend so much money on your travels, you ought surely to be able to do more towards the support of your own clergymen in Sierra Leone." The African responded immediately: "Of course we could, Mr. Venn; but so long as you treat us like children we shall behave like children. Treat us like men and we shall behave like men. We spend our money upon ourselves because you don't invite us to support our clergy."[27] Venn did not need plainer proof to convince him of the evils of paternalism.

This represents one of the major points of tension in Venn's thought. On the one hand, he assumed that the superiority of Western culture meant the European was trustee of the less advanced peoples of the world. On the other hand, he strongly believed that all people were created equal and were worthy of full respect. The problem was not easily solved. The missionary went out from the powerful and wealthy West to the less technologically advanced peoples of the world, committed to transforming both the individuals and their civilization. The missionary found it difficult to be free of feelings of cultural superiority. Paternalism was woven into the very fabric of missions. Against this background, Venn worked out his ideas about self-responsibility.

Two maxims guided Venn during the first twenty years of his administration. First, a native ministry is the crown of native agency. Second, native agency must be under European superintendence. Training produced native agency. Primary schools in the vernacular laid the basis for intermediate and secondary schools. From these came the teachers trained in the normal schools. The teacher's group furnished catechists and evangelists. Finally, pastors were chosen from among the catechists and evangelists. In this sense native ministry was the crown of native agency. The CMS supported the native agency. Teachers taught in mission schools and the Society employed the catechists and evangelists. The Society insisted that it must retain control of any program for which it provided salaries or subsidies. It insisted on European superintendence for both financial and moral reasons. Venn said, "Let it be remembered that the great principle of Protestant Missions is *Native Agency under European superintendence.* Hence our large and expensive Educational Establishments to raise up an educated class."[28] At all costs genuine conversion was to be the standard—not nominal converts. European superintendence was essential to maintain that standard. But Venn eventually, after observing the evils of missionary paternalism, rejected this dictum in favor of mutuality in relationship and equality in status. Experience had changed Venn's mind substantially.

Goals of Mission Clarified

Although Venn's earlier understanding of mission goals was stated in individualistic terms, his thinking underwent changes that were finally to bring him to the self-supporting, self-governing, and self-propagating indigenous church for which he is known today.[29] He continued to speak of the salvation of souls; but this aim was intermediate. The ultimate object of mission had become the establishment of the indigenous church. Let us trace the steps Venn took to arrive at this insight.

In 1841 Venn urged missionaries to place greater stress on developing local resources. He had already identified the principle of self-support. Why, he asked, could not the native ministry be locally supported? Experience had shown, according to prevailing views, that native agency could be effective only with European superintendence. When someone challenged Venn by lifting up the apostolic model, he argued that the apostles appointed to leadership converts from Judaism or the higher classes of pagan society. Modern missions worked among primitive peoples. So despite Venn's recognition that the grand aim of mission work is native ministry, self-governance remained a distant ideal.[30]

Self-support, however, became the key to Venn's whole system of missions. He insisted on local support for pastors as a condition for ordination. Thus at this early stage he subsumed self-government under self-support.

Venn's policies on the development of an indigenous church appeared in papers released in 1851, 1861, and 1866.[31] These were collated and published as a pamphlet in 1866. His 1851 perspectives are reflected in his instructions to a group of missionaries about to set out for Yorubaland. "Keep in mind the importance of introducing, from the first, the principles of self-support and self-government among converts," he said.

"Never let them imagine that the Society is to do all and to pay all. Remind them daily and hourly that you only come amongst them to put them in the way of doing all for themselves."[32] Applying the principles to institutions as well as churches, Venn suggested that the local people should build new schools and pay teachers' salaries out of local funds. While pleased that the Church of England liturgy was being used happily in Yorubaland, Venn urged the missionaries to remember that the church must become independent and adapt liturgy and discipline to fit the circumstances.

Venn could be philosophical about slow progress and weakness in the young church. To a missionary in China who was discouraged with the small results, Venn wrote: "You should bear in mind the advantage of leaving a native church to feel its weakness, and to struggle for its own establishment, by occasional promptings from without, rather than by the constant presence of a strong arm to lean upon."[33]

In 1852 Venn addressed the problem of the larger "station" church and "its tendency to occupy the energy of a Missionary in pastoral, instead of Mission work."[34] He wrote that the committee opposed building large mission churches and advocated instead the use of "cottage lectures" as a means of getting into the community and out of the large center.

By 1859 he observed that the mission station and education of the masses were on the way out. The greatest success had been among adults—not children. The missionary could train adults to engage in evangelism after conversion.[35] Children required many years of training before they could become responsible members of the Christian church.

In spite of his best efforts to show missionaries the problems and defects of the present system, Venn was discouraged by their lack of response. In 1861 he issued a second paper to call attention to the principles he outlined ten years before.[36] He began by stating that the work of modern missions was twofold: winning converts to Christ, and forming converts into Christian churches. This distinction had only recently been made, he said, but on this basis missionaries were not being appointed specially for evangelism.

The present system was based on the mission station concept. A missionary was appointed to a locality, won converts, catechised them, and admitted them into church membership. As the work grew the missionary would hire a catechist to assist. "But all is dependent upon the missionary, and all the agency is provided for at the cost of the Society."[37] This system produced three evils. First, the character of the missionary undergoes a complete change so that he or she no longer has time for evangelism. Second, the converts become inured to the idea of dependency on the foreign agency rather than feeling responsible for their own church. "The principles of self-support, self-government, and self-extension are wanting; on which depends the breath of life in a native Church."[38] The missionary society, in the third place, becomes burdened with growing responsibilities for its oldest missions until it is incapable of moving to "the regions beyond." Venn urged study of recent examples of spontaneous development: the Karens of Burma, the Armenians, and the Hovas of Madagascar.

To remedy the present deficiencies, Venn wanted to introduce an elementary organization into the native churches, based on four principles: train converts as early as possible in self-government and self-support; make converts responsible for the cost of their own Christian education and that of their children through contributions to the Native Church Fund; divide native teachers into two classes—evangelists working with the missionary and pastors supported through the Native Church Fund; and at each step in the formation of a new church keep in view the ultimate establishment of the native church on a settled ecclesiastical basis with an "indigenous" episcopate independent of foreign aid.

Venn's key concept was to build up an ecclesiastical structure from the simplest unit of a Christian "company" to a full-fledged church consisting of districts. He inveighed against the fallacy of importing a complete church system, which missionaries imposed on a group of people without consider-ing their resources. The system must grow upwards rather than being im-posed from outside.

Nowhere did Venn state more clearly the ideal that he had in mind than in Instructions handed to missionaries going to Madagascar in 1863. The great object of a mission, he said, was "the raising up of a Native Church—self-supporting, self-governing, self-extending. The Mission is the scaffolding; the Native Church is the edifice. The removal of the scaffolding is the proof that the building is completed. You will have achieved the greatest success when you have taught your converts to do without you and can leave them, for fresh inroads into the 'regions beyond.' "[39] Here Venn summarized his mature thought tempered by experience.

Venn thus conceived the growth of the church as a series of stages, begin-ning with the period when the missionary laid the foundation and progressing to the point where a self-responsible and indigenous church had emerged. When this process was completed, Venn said, the "euthanasia of the mission" had occurred.[40] Critics have charged Venn with advocating the eventual end of *mission*. Nothing could be further from the truth. What he intended this phrase to describe was the completion of the cycle from the time when a mission had full charge to the final stage with the church itself being self-reliant and engaged in missionary outreach. Venn called for the phasing out of a foreign-controlled mission to a particular place as a prod and an en-couragement to the local church to become a missionary church. He believed that the mission of the church was always imperiled by missions that domi-nated and stifled the young church, missions that turned themselves into ends rather than remaining the grand means of mission.

NOTES

1. VB 154:529.
2. VB 54:189.
3. VB 192:446. The London Secretaries' Association Minutes do not record this method being discussed. For the first sixty years the Minutes rarely included more than a list of participants, the place and date of meeting, and the topics discussed. Venn was no longer able to attend association meetings by 1871 so the idea had to be reported to him by his colleagues. It illustrates the cross-fertilization of ideas that went on among the various societies.
4. VB 62:285f.
5. G/AC1/9, Sept. 25, 1852.
6. CI3/L2, March 25, 1847. Cf. Venn's letter to Mrs. Kruse, Jaffa: "A female school is an important branch of Missionary work, *in connection with other branches;* but where these languish, a female school can produce little comparative good" (CM/L4, March 15, 1858).

7. CI3/L2, Feb. 24, 1854.

8. Ibid.

9. See Venn's account of the "Plan" in the memorial to Ragland (VB 105) and comments in a letter to his son (Venn MSS C34, July 19, 1856). He commented enthusiastically on the method in correspondence (C13/L3, April 28, 1856).

10. G/AC1/9, Dec. 11, 1851. See Christopher Fyfe, *Africanus Horton* (New York: Oxford University Press, 1972), for an account of the first African trained as a medical doctor. Horton's benefactor was Henry Venn.

11. CI1/L6, April 11, 1864.

12. CI1/L3, July 7, 1849.

13. G/AC1/11, Nov. 27, 1854.

14. G/AC1/16, Nov. 27, 1863, and April 7, 1864.

15. VB 18a:4.

16. VB 90:22.

17. CN/L6, June 8, 1860.

18. VB 154.

19. VB 124:186.

20. VB 40:167.

21. VB 124:187.

22. VB 54:186.

23. VB 93:157-60.

24. Knight, 1882, p. 313.

25. CI3/L2, Feb. 27, 1843.

26. CI3/L2, Oct. 17, 1851.

27. Knight, 1880, p. 546.

28. *Proceedings,* 1850-51, p. 240.

29. For a discussion of the influence of Rufus Anderson and Henry Venn on each other in arriving at the three-selfs formula, see Wilbert R. Shenk, "Rufus Anderson and Henry Venn: A Special Relationship?"

30. CI3/L2, Feb. 1842.

31. Appendix 1 reproduces these statements.

32. VB 57:20. Cf. C/MA/L1, Nov. 5, 1860.

33. C.CH/L2, Jan. 11, 1864.

34. C/CE/L3, Jan. 8, 1852.

35. CI3/L3, March 4, 1859. C/MA/L1, March 17, 1860.

36. VB 125.

37. Ibid.

38. Ibid.

39. VB 134:112.

40. Venn did not originate the phrase "euthanasia of the mission" but appropriated it from someone else (VB 44:2). Other Venn references to the term: VB 102:339; 124:187; 134:112; 157:307; 163; 164:4.

5

Administrator

Venn considered the directorate of a missionary society as the "heart of the system."[1] While missions sent to various parts of the world were temporary, the society itself furnished continuous missionary agency. The work of the directorate was no less spiritual than that of the missionary on the field.

Venn saw the CMS as a tradition. The directors' task was not only to defend the tradition, but to keep it vital by constant interaction with current issues and challenges. The interplay of the Society's past, present, and future runs throughout Venn's work. Under Venn's leadership CMS administration was based on tradition rather than bureaucracy.[2] This is the key to understanding Venn as missionary administrator.

The CMS was comprised of members who paid an annual subscription. All subscribing clergy and twenty-four annually elected laypeople formed the General Committee. The General Committee appointed four subcommittees: Patronage, Funds, Accounts, and Correspondence. The most important committee was the Correspondence Committee, which met weekly with the secretaries to oversee administration of missionary operations.[3] The other committees were concerned with constituency relations and raising and disbursing funds.

The General Committee also appointed the secretariat. Although Venn did not ask that the position of general secretary be created, in an 1856 statement he emphasized the importance of charging someone to oversee the total work. The undisputed leader of the secretariat since 1846, he was merely describing current practice. Venn was sensitive to the need for both clear administrative lines and good working relationships among secretaries. Individual secretaries were responsible for finance, missionary candidates, or publications. But one secretary, Venn said, should be finally responsible over every department, "and especially over the drafting of the Committee Minutes, Resolutions, and Despatches."[4] "Minutes and Despatches Secretary" became Venn's euphemism for the general secretary.

Venn strongly held to the principle that decisions should be made by consensus. This might involve modifying and changing a proposal to fit diverse views, but the resulting unity and goodwill was worth it. Venn also insisted that minutes not merely record discussions, but place in bold relief the decisions and ground on which each one was taken. The minute record placed limits on the powers of the secretary.

Continuity and control in administration were augmented by the type of individuals elected to the committees. CMS laws required that eighteen of twenty-four of the lay members of the General Committee be chosen from among those who had already served. Frequently, missionaries who had retired from service abroad were also enlisted to serve on the committees.

As a voluntary society, the CMS had to organize its own system to raise financial support for its program. When reliance on direct contributions in the early years proved inadequate, the committee developed a plan for Church Missionary Associations. By 1849 Venn reported that approximately 80 percent of all income for the first fifty years had been raised through the associations. The CMS worked closely with the associations, providing speakers and literature and giving counsel, but did not control the associations.[5]

CMS home organization was a model of its kind, which Venn jealously guarded. Repeated suggestions that an association raise support for both the CMS and the SPG threatened him greatly. Venn feared such a step would dilute supporters' interest. He refused to allow official CMS representatives to participate in meetings to discuss such proposals.[6]

Field Organization

The CMS constitution did not prescribe a field organization. It was understood that a field committee, usually appointed by the parent committee in London, managed the work of each mission. The parent committee exercised close control over general policies and principles followed locally, but it granted considerable discretionary powers on day-to-day program operation. Once missionaries arrived in their field of service, they were responsible to CMS local committees.[7]

The field committee's role was to provide supervision and counsel to missionaries through a body not directly involved in program. It also served as liaison with the diocesan. The bishop normally presided over the committee and was always represented in its deliberations.

Official correspondence passed through the secretary of the local committee to London. For confidential matters, however, or if the local committee's decision did not meet an individual's approval, a missionary had direct access to the parent committee.

Early in the Society's history field committees, particularly those in India, with members drawn from officials of the East India Company, became citadels of lay control. Dandeson Coates fostered this, especially in disputes between the CMS and a bishop, by invariably backing the lay members. In 1859 the CMS issued regulations stipulating that a field committee consist of nine members, of which six were to be laypeople. Although Venn brought the lay members of field committees under greater control,[8] he nevertheless valued the lay character of field committees. In his polemic against "church missions" he asserted that the lay field committees were more flexible in adapting the mission system to diverse situations because they concentrated efforts on basic mission work rather than on ecclesiastical organization.[9]

Another important part of field management was the missionary conference. Venn urged local conferences to hold meetings twice a year to foster unity in fellowship and to bring information, experience, and judgment to bear upon the general management of the mission. Venn placed all missionaries on equal footing—in responsibility for work and the right to question any aspect of program.

Personnel

One of the axioms laid down by John Venn at the founding of the CMS was that the success of missionary work depended on the quality of people sent. A tension runs throughout the CMS story between the need for more recruits and the insistence on maintaining certain standards. The committee held to high standards and their critics scored them for their rigid adherence to them. The Society was embarrassed at the number of applications they had to reject. Out of sixty or seventy offers annually, Venn estimated that they accepted not more than one in ten.[10] He insisted, however, that the Society never rejected a qualified candidate.

Among rejected applicants were a fifty-eight-year-old man (experience showed that such people had difficulty in learning a new language and faced greater health hazards), a former Roman Catholic priest,[11] and children born out of wedlock. The latter Venn justified weakly on the grounds the Society wished to testify against immorality.[12]

Venn usually summarized missionary qualifications in four points. First, candidates must have sound health. Second, they must be able to acquire a foreign language. Third, they must have the disposition and mental powers that qualify a person for home ministry. Fourth, they must have firmness of purpose and the ability to meet any crisis.[13]

Believing that universities were responsible to train missionaries, Venn made special efforts to arouse missionary interest at Cambridge and Oxford. One of the outstanding graduates of the 1840s, T. G. Ragland, responded to Venn's appeal during a visit.[14] Venn saw mission work as the highest expression of the Christian calling, which demanded the best minds the church had. He did not, however, make academic qualifications an absolute condition.[15]

Since the idea of lay missionaries was not well accepted, CMS policy indicated that a missionary should be either ordained or eligible for ordination.[16] The Society did, however, send out mechanics and qualified teachers who were unordained and had no intention of proceeding to ordination.[17] These were not recognized as missionaries in the strict sense.

Behind this seeming ambivalence was a deeper issue. Early caution in CMS circles over the use of catechists stemmed from fear of censure by bishops and high-church critics. Venn himself was not always clear on this issue. He believed in the value of service ministries. Sometimes he used the term "missionary" inclusively, to indicate everyone sent out; other times he used the term in a stricter sense to mean only those doing direct evangelism and church planting.

A Society rule said that a missionary candidate had to be either a university graduate or take the course at Islington.[18] The Islington program offered training to five different groups: returned catechists; English nongraduates; graduates; Germans; and Africans and other non-Europeans. The largest group was the English nongraduates for whom the institution was originally intended.

The number of missionary recruits declined in the 1860s partly because offers from Europe virtually dried up. Venn had earlier become a personal friend of Dr. Wilhelm Hoffmann, Basel director, and vigorously defended his missionaries from the Continent. In spite of this fruitful collaboration, the question of the status of Lutheran orders was never resolved.[19] Increasingly the CMS had taken a stricter view and insisted on Anglican ordination for all missionaries. Understandably some Europeans objected. But the more powerful reason for the change was the growing fear among British Evangelicals of German biblical criticism.

Relationship to Missionaries

If Venn's ideal of missionary vocation made some of his missionaries tremble with fear, his sane and commonsense approach to practical problems was reassuring. Venn appreciated and was generous with missionaries. He entertained many in his home. His preoccupation with the "missionary character" was simply part of his overall effort to define the task of modern missions and the role of the missionary.

He saw three elements comprising the ideal missionary character—strength of personality, compatibility, and spirituality. He elaborated much on these three features. He believed that the missionary should have come to terms with self, accepting one's own deficiencies and inadequacies in the confidence that as God called he also enabled. One could relax self-doubts into the hand of God. Venn was a foe of missionary asceticism as he saw it in Francis Xavier, but he believed missionaries should be willing to forego desirable living accommodations in order to live among the people with whom they worked. To live self-sacrifice without self-pity, he believed, required personal strength.

Venn recognized that strength of personality was often in itself a detriment to harmony within a mission. His instructions to missionaries touch frequently on this theme.[20] Disharmony and division he believed grow where "men connect their own particular work too much with themselves and too little with Christ." All had to guard against actions and attitudes that destroyed the fabric of fellowship. The counsel of Matthew 18 applied to the missionary community.

According to Venn's philosophy of financial support for missionaries, allowances should be adequate to maintain the missionaries but nothing more.[21] The children of missionaries were supported up to age fifteen. Because of the debilitating climate, missionaries posted to West Africa could return home before four years' service. Otherwise only a medical certificate, family circumstances, or a request by the committee entitled a missionary to return home at Society expense before twelve years' service.

Missionaries were barred from receiving any other salaries than that paid to them by the CMS.[22] Behind this policy lay experience with the East India Company and colonial government, which frequently wished to secure chaplaincy services from local missionaries. Venn held the line against "sharing the support of CMS agents with any other society or with the Government."[23] This extended to the home scene as well. When a local Church Missionary Association proposed that they should raise the support for a particular missionary, Venn demurred. He argued that missionaries wished to feel that they were missionaries of the whole church and not a local group. He further suggested that an association would be inclined to judge missionaries' worth by their success. His third reason was the weighty one: the members of the association might feel they ought to exercise some control over the missionaries.[24] Venn would not consider any plan that might lead to a shared administration.

Venn was sensitive to the welfare of missionaries. A chief concern of missionary families was their children. For many families this meant eventually sending the children home to England for schooling. A portion of the Josiah Pratt Memorial Fund was devoted to founding a home for the daughters of missionaries.[25] In early 1850 a Missionaries' Children's Home was opened. Venn also boarded some missionary sons in his home over the years, and his letters to missionaries frequently contain references to their children with whom he had contact. He took a similar interest in the well-being of the missionaries themselves. In 1864 he wrote to the missionaries in China that the committee "have lately determined to secure for their Missionaries a sanatorium of easy access wherever it is possible, and they will grudge no expense to secure this. Other societies are doing the same—a few weeks retirement each year would save many years in the long run."[26]

Venn's commitment to provide for the missionary's welfare was combined with his insistence that the missionary had definite responsibilities to the sending church. It was important to sustain a partnership between sending and mission churches as exemplified in the Antiochene church. Such a relationship required regular and faithful reporting. Regulations required all missionaries to keep a journal from the time of departure from England until they returned home again. These journals became the property of the Society.[27] By this means the committee hoped to enter into the work of the missionary and the journals were a source of information to the supporting church.

Few missionaries lived up to such requirements. It was difficult to obtain even annual letters from some of the most diligent, Venn admitted. He asserted nonetheless that the missionary's duty was to give an account of what God was doing. Honest reporting at least annually was helpful to both the sending church and the missionary. The home church needed to be educated to the true situation—not fed on fables. And the missionary could benefit from careful self-analysis and evaluation.

Those missionaries who did write received warm acknowledgment. Venn found in these exchanges a sense of fellowship and release from the problems of home administration. From the tone of his correspondence with individual missionaries, he emerges as a person of sympathy and pastoral concern. He consistently tried to combine practical and pastoral perspectives in resolving personnel problems.

Finances

Although he could hold his own in any discussion of fiscal matters, Venn was not intimately involved with financial management of the CMS. His approach to finances was not the usual business viewpoint in one respect. He believed the work of the CMS was a spiritual enterprise based on faith. The work was God's, and the money to do it would be provided. This was the basic assumption on which he attempted to operate.

Financial stringency, however, frequently influenced decisions. In response to an application for a grant toward purchase of a church site in Colombo in 1854, Venn stressed that funds were limited because of a general expansion of the missions. Since Ceylon had been a difficult and unresponsive area, the Society was placing priority on those places where there was response.

Other Societies

According to CMS Law XXXI, "a friendly intercourse shall be maintained with other Protestant Societies engaged in the same benevolent design of propagating the Gospel of Jesus Christ."[28] This obligation was enjoined on the missionary in the field as well as on the Society at home. For the secretariat this involved relations with both other Protestant societies and sister Anglican societies.

The CMS was one of four founding members of the London Secretaries' Association in 1819. This group of London-based mission secretaries met primarily for counsel and fellowship and took no administrative decisions. Occasionally members of the group cooperated in presenting a memorial to the government as at the time of the Indian crisis in 1857. Venn became active in the LSA when he joined the secretariat full-time in 1846, and he remained a key figure until 1867. The sparse minutes of these meetings show that Venn was often called on to formulate position papers on policy questions.

Venn did not use the term "comity," and he did not refer missionaries to written policies, but he had a clear sense of the conventions governing relations among missionary societies. When a question arose, he merely cited the appropriate guideline. Three principles were observed. In the first place, the society that first occupied an area had premier rights, and no other society was to work there unless invited by the first one. On this basis, the CMS did not enter the Punjab until the American mission already there invited them to come. The same thing happened in Syria and Turkey.[29] The second principle held that the rural areas should be worked by a single agency rather than by several societies.[30] According to the third principle, capital cities and metropolitan areas were open to all.[31]

In addition to these formal principles, Venn counseled his missionaries to avoid controversial theological questions in relation to other missions, and especially warned against making ecclesiastical form a point of contention.[32] Such a policy enabled CMS to enjoy good relations with other Protestant societies, but it intensified suspicion of the Society among high churchmen. When three CMS missionaries attended the opening of a Methodist chapel in Ceylon, Venn received a letter from the bishop of Colombo charging them with giving their countenance to schism.[33] He brushed the matter aside. This did not mean relations were always amicable with other Protestants. When the Methodists proposed to establish a new mission in South India adjacent to CMS work, Venn challenged them for failing to consult with the Society.[34] In North India an unpleasant dispute erupted in Meerut between the Baptists and the CMS over the question of baptism. In this instance, Venn declined to become involved in the controversy.[35]

For Venn, two underlying considerations governed ecumenical relations. He believed that the gospel, rather than ecclesiastical form or particular doctrines, was the basis of Christian unity and cooperation. The British and Foreign Bible Society had been a notable instrument of cooperation and goodwill because it represented "a centre of union among the various Missionary Societies and exercises a moderating and binding influence among them all."[36] The missionary societies individually had to deal with ecclesiastical questions. He also believed that the new church ought to be left as free as possible to adapt ecclesiastical forms inherited from the missions to the indigenous culture. He foresaw the day when the denominational distinctives brought by the missionary societies would be superseded by a more truly national church form.[37] This attitude ran counter to the views of those who had strong convictions about church policy.

In 1859 sponsors of the Calcutta and Central Normal School sought Venn's counsel concerning their proposal to reorganize in order to serve all missions. The bishop of Calcutta was cool to the idea, but Venn urged the principal of the school to seize the opportunity. "The Church Missionary Society would give these measures their most hearty countenance and cooperation: and while other parties are waiting and discussing, you might at once exhibit the system in operation."[38] In this instance Venn demonstrated both his ecumenical spirit and his adherence to the voluntary principle.

The CMS venture into Madagascar tested Venn's principles and policies at several points. Before 1862 the London Missionary Society had been the only mission at work in Madagascar. In the face of expanding opportunity, the LMS invited the CMS also to establish a mission on the island. At the same time, the bishop of Mauritius urged both the CMS and the Society for the Propagation of the Gospel to found missions on Madagascar. Venn was unwilling to proceed apart from the counsel of the LMS.[39] The SPG felt less bound by this consideration. The real test came when the SPG decided to establish a bishopric in the capital city against the express wishes of the LMS. Venn and the CMS sided with the LMS out of respect for their seniority on the island and a desire to minimize ecclesiastical differences through introducing the episcopal form of church government into an area where only congregational polity had been found. When the SPG persisted in their plan, the CMS felt they could not cooperate with integrity. Either move would give offense. Unwillingness to cooperate in founding a new bishopric was interpreted as lack of commitment to "Church principles"; but the LMS wanted them to observe the usual rules of cooperation. In a confused situation, the CMS tried to carry out a strategic retreat.[40]

As has just been noted, the relationship to other Anglican Societies, particularly the SPG, proved to be sensitive and complex. Relations were never easy. The CMS was the larger society, but the SPG enjoyed official favor to a degree never achieved by the CMS. Venn adhered to the traditional CMS position with regard to church societies. According to this interpretation, each society had its peculiar purposes. In order to maintain individual integrity, Venn insisted that there should be "independence of action upon our distinctive principles."[41]

On the basis of this principle, Venn resisted all attempts to draw the societies together for common efforts in fund raising or joint administration. When someone inquired whether the SPG and CMS looked for the same qualifications in missionary candidates, Venn's stock answer was that each society had its unique requirements.[42] Another person had heard a rumor that steps were being taken to amalgamate the two societies. Venn replied impatiently that he knew of no such plans, and added, "nor do I know any true friend of the CMS who would regard such an event otherwise than as a fatal catastrophe." He concluded ominously that "the idea may have been entertained by parties who wish to keep it from the CMS in the first instance."[43] So reluctant was he to get involved with the SPG that he even refused to support a joint request to the Bishops to sponsor an annual mission day sermon.[44]

On a few occasions joint initiative was possible. In 1852 the two societies formed a committee in order to make representation to government when the renewal of the East India Company charter came up for debate.[45] The two societies usually cooperated more amicably overseas than in London. Occasionally one society reassigned workers to the other, and they exchanged information.[46] Officially, Venn discouraged CMS supporters from any public criticism of SPG,[47] but Venn was himself charged with having unfairly criticized the SPG,[48] and the SPG complained that he was discourteous to them in correspondence.[49] Evangelicals, however, suspected Venn at times of being too favorable to the SPG.[50] As a CMS leader, Venn had to walk carefully between various parties and interests. Not least of his problems was the intense and sometimes unfair attacks on the CMS by the SPG and its supporters. Both Bishop Wilberforce and SPG Secretary Ernest Hawkins, through the *Colonial Church Chronicle*, did not spare Venn and the Society.[51]

Other Activities

It is impossible to give anything like a complete account of the non-missionary societies, committees, and institutions (other than strictly missionary) in which Venn took part. The records are scanty; presumably this can be explained in terms of his practice of not giving public support to other agencies or causes.

In connection with the Crystal Palace Exhibit of 1851, Protestants cooperated in setting up exhibits and special services to visitors from other countries. The missionary societies worked together in producing their own exhibit as well as in encouraging that a Christian witness be given in various ways at the exhibition.[52]

Another activity which Venn carried on across denominational lines was orthography. Chevalier Bunsen, envoy of the King of Prussia, shared this interest, and they frequently consulted.[53] Venn acted as editor of a small pamphlet of "Rules for reducing unwritten languages to alphabetical writings in Roman characters with reference especially to the languages spoken in Africa."[54] Venn had no special training in linguistics, but he was convinced that literacy was fundamental to the advance of the gospel. He promoted the work of Professor Lepsius of Berlin, a German expert who attempted to develop an alphabet that would be suitable for all languages.[55] Venn took part in attempts to settle the controversy among missionaries in China over a proper term in Chinese for "god."[56] In this instance he sought to mediate in a situation where the Bible Society lacked the courage to take a position.

Because of his long association with the Islington district, he devoted some of his interests to parochial programs. The Highbury Training Institution prepared schoolmasters and supplied a number of educationists for the CMS schools overseas. Venn was on the board of directors. In the early 1850s Islington Church Home Mission was founded with the object of providing more clergy and Scripture-readers in the district. In 1856 a group created the Islington Church Extension Society to sponsor the building of new church buildings. Venn was a founding member of both of these associations and an honorary secretary of the latter.[57] These early ventures in home mission stimulated emulation elsewhere.

Venn took primary responsibility in another home mission. This was the "Strangers' Home" established in 1855. The need for a service to non-European shiphands who frequently got stranded in London was long recognized. The mission secretaries discussed this concern in the London Secretaries' Association on several occasions. Colonel R. M. Hughes, who had served in India, became concerned about the problem in 1854 and was advised to talk it over with Venn. Hughes remarked later that he had discussed the proposal with many others, all of whom endorsed the idea. But nothing happened "until it was taken up by the Rev. Henry Venn, Honorary Clerical Secretary of the CMS, through whose powerful influence and exertions the Society was formed."[58] Venn personally purchased the site on which a facility was to be built until the association was formed to assume responsibility for it.[59] He called the founding meeting and helped organize the association. The last piece Venn wrote for publication was a preface to the book by Joseph Salter, *The Asiatic in England*, in which Salter described the work of this mission during the first seventeen years.

Venn was also involved in several church patronage trusts, patterned on the Thornton and Simeon trusts.

Following the Indian Mutiny in 1857, amid public outcry against the missionary societies, Venn seized the initiative and proposed the formation of the Christian Vernacular Education Society for India. He wanted this society to "establish in the great towns of India Christian Vernacular Training Institutions, Male and Female, and to supply, as far as possible, in each of the native languages of India, School Books and other Educational Works, prepared on Christian principles. Each Training Institution to comprise a Vernacular Model School."[60] Venn envisaged this as a non-denominational society dedicated to a specialized function which Venn believed was beyond the responsibility of the missionary societies.[61] He was convinced that the rising expectations of the Indian peoples had to be met by mass education. Christians could contribute by leading the way in emphasizing vernacular language schools and training teachers and headmasters for these schools.

In 1834 the Rev. Baptist Noel and his niece, Mrs. Arthur Kinnaird, founded the Society for Promoting Female Education in the East. This society opened the Calcutta Normal School in 1852, the beginning of the Zenana Mission. In 1864 the directors renamed it Indian Female Normal School and Instruction Society. Mrs. Kinnaird wished to open the society to all Christians, but the Calcutta Normal School remained attached to the Church of England. In 1867 the Society asked Venn to draft a basis of association which would allow participating groups to maintain ties with their denominational traditions. His document, which demonstrated to the full Venn's pragmatic approach in administration, proved to be a breakthrough. It said, "In the constitution and management of Missionary Societies each section of the Church must conduct its operations upon its own distinctive denominational principles." But he also made it possible for schoolmasters to move easily from one Society to another. "No questions need arise to prevent the members of different Churches from uniting to support a vernacular school, normal school or training institution."[62] The Zenana Mission, though largely supported by members of the Church of England who remained loyal to their church, nonetheless pledged itself to cooperation with other churches. This constitution was a new development. It was not a society based on cooperation as were the British and Foreign Bible Society and Religious Tract Society. It was not simply a fellowship like the Evangelical Alliance. Nor did it ask members to leave their denominational loyalties behind. It aimed at comprehension of all participating traditions.[63]

In spite of his stern injunctions against romanticizing missions, Venn felt exhilarated when he contemplated the far horizons. Geographical exploration fascinated him. The vision of opening new territory to the gospel caused him to lend his every assistance to explorers. Venn saw a direct relationship between geographical exploration and missionary expansion. When the discovery of a large lake in East Africa was announced in 1850, Venn immediately saw the implications this would have for missionary advance.[64] When Dr. Heinrich Barth, the explorer, took an expedition to Africa in 1849–50, Venn furnished letters of introduction for members of the party to CMS missionaries.[65] In explaining the attitude of the CMS toward scientific exploration, he said, "The missionaries of our Society are instructed to collect and communicate every information of a scientific interest which comes in their way, and we shall always be ready to make a free communication of it to any society or parties, willing to turn it to a profitable account. We have no ambition besides our simple object of extending the knowledge of our blessed Saviour."[66] He encouraged the missionaries in their scientific interests by arranging publication of their findings.[67] And he lobbied to get men like Dr. Baikie to lead expeditions.[68] During this period the *Intelligencer* reported the results of expeditions, thus bringing before missions supporters linguistic and anthropological information which opened up new worlds of understanding and concern.

Constituency Relations

Venn's philosophy of program promotion was simple. He was convinced that support for the Society's work was best developed by regular, consistent, and frequent presentations. He did not believe in annual or occasional appeals made with fanfare.[69]

The CMS communicated with its constituency in several ways. The anniversary meetings each May drew large crowds and were an important platform. Church Missionary associations sponsored deputations to the parishes to interpret the Society's work. Missionaries on furlough also itinerated; but the most extensive means of reaching the constituency was the printed page.

In 1849 the CMS launched the *Church Missionary Intelligencer,* which learned respect both at home and abroad. The *Intelligencer* was Venn's mouthpiece even without his by-line.

The one CMS publication for which Venn assumed personal responsibility was the annual report. This was largely a compilation from correspondence, journals, and other reports submitted by missionaries in the field. Venn wanted an honest and balanced report. On occasion he deliberately omitted some more positive and hopeful passages in order to avoid giving his public an unduly optimistic impression.[70] His method was to cull from incoming dispatches throughout the year materials he felt might become a part of the report. He attempted to relate the report to program policy.[71] This made the report an instrument of accountability. But he also kept in mind the situation in the home church, at times merely mirroring the fears that agitated the public mind, as during the height of anti-Roman Catholic feelings in the early 1850s.

The task of responding to adverse criticism of the Society fell largely to Venn. The criticisms tended to concentrate on a small range of themes. One of these was the unfavorable comparison of the CMS to the SPG: this might involve financial management or the CMS's lack of church loyalty. Another line of attack was on the CMS management compared with that of other missionary societies. Critics reproached the CMS for its unwillingness to enter into a union of Church of England missionary societies. To each of these criticisms Venn had a well-honed answer.

Policy and Strategy

In administering a society based on tradition, Venn followed well-defined principles and policies, emphasizing their continuity with the founder's vision. Innovation was not prized except as it made the tradition more effective.

Venn never visited any CMS mission abroad. Edward Bickersteth went to West Africa on behalf of the CMS in 1815. Venn also sent his colleague William Knight to the Mediterranean, India, and Ceylon missions in 1853–54 to deal with several difficult problems. But Venn himself relied on missionary letters and journals, the reporting of corresponding secretaries, interviews with missionaries on home leave, reports from colonial civil servants visiting London, personal contacts and correspondence with African and Asian leaders, and privileged communications from government ministries. As secretary of the preeminent missionary society with headquarters in the capital of the major world power, he did not lack information. Yet he continually asked for more.

Venn possessed a clear sense of strategy. His interest in geographical exploration was dictated by the conviction that this contributed to missionary penetration. On the other hand, he challenged the widely accepted strategy that missionary societies concentrate their efforts on the lower classes of society,[72] to the neglect of the influential classes.[73] He insisted that one person from the leadership class could advance Christianity more than many converts from the lower classes.

Venn urged the CMS China Mission to adopt a different strategy from that followed in India. Chinese converts came from the educated class and could more readily be trained for leadership in the church. A missionary would accomplish far more by training these leaders than by attempting to teach the masses. In other countries the missionary had to begin with the masses. But for China, Venn advised starting at the top.[74]

Missions and the Social Order

To understand Venn's mission strategy we need also to understand his approach to relating mission to the social order. By the time he came to the CMS secretariat in 1841, the Society had had much experience in collaborating with government. Venn looked on the government's colonial policies as means of achieving humanitarian objects. He responded to those policies as critic, advocate, and collaborator.

An important influence on Venn's thinking was another son of Clapham: James Stephen (1789–1859), Venn's brother-in-law and permanent under-secretary for the colonies, 1839–1847. It was Stephen who drafted the bill that legally abolished slavery in 1833. A controversial figure in the civil service, Stephen opposed schemes for colonization and expansion of the empire that he felt were unsound, and used his position to further humanitarian objectives. He did not oppose colonization, but accepted the prevailing concept of trusteeship. To him the British empire was a positive means of controlling the abuses of unprincipled exploiters, thereby turning expansionist impulses to constructive ends.

Stephen stood by his principles that colonists control their local affairs and move toward political autonomy. Although he took pride in the British legal system, he sought to allow latitude in the development of the legal system for each colony. Rather than insisting on a straight transplant of British forms, he helped guide the colonies as they evolved their own institutions. He sought continually to ensure that colonies were administered without exploitation and with special regard for the weak.[75]

These themes of Stephen's political ideals are present both in Venn's theory of the indigenous church and in his social and economic development schemes. The imperialistic spirit of the next generation had not yet been born. Stephen's generation believed that Britain's trusteeship on behalf of less advanced peoples was a temporary task that should be carried out with a view toward self-determination.

In Venn's thought mission and politics were dynamically related, but the relationship was marked by tensions. These conflicts had a theological basis. There were two orders in history, each seeking supremacy. One order recognized the lordship of Jesus Christ and was characterized by love, righteousness, justice, and peace. The other was set in opposition to Christ and was the source of disorder, injustice, and sin. Mission work, to Venn, was an act of aggression against the kingdom of the world, and could thus not escape the consequences of conflict.

Constituted political powers were also divided into two classes: Christian and non-Christian. One could not demand the same moral commitments of a non-Christian government as of a Christian government, yet God was present in all nations and had established government to maintain order among people. Missionaries were to respect both Christian and non-Christian governments. Although not everything they did was right, Christian governments had moral responsibilities that went beyond anything required of a non-Christian state. Venn demanded that the British government espouse the Christian cause by identifying with the church and giving legal protection.

Church Missionary Society Policy: Politics and Missions

Missionaries continually faced questions in relationship to civil authorities. In 1860 Venn issued his most complete statement on politics and missions.[76] He based his policy on two considerations: the Society's object and the specific regulation. The Christian message awakened new Christians to questions of justice and equality, enabling them to evaluate instances of oppression or misgovernment. As Christians they learned obedience to properly constituted authorities, but not an unconditional obedience. New faith introduced a new basis of measurement. Government institutions and social customs that conflicted with the Bible had to be rejected. By introducing a message that had revolutionary implications, missionaries were agents of change.[77]

Missionaries had a special responsibility to converts. They could not restrict themselves to spiritual matters without attention to their physical and social well-being. Missionaries identified with the people. They would live among the local peoples and avoid fraternizing with other expatriates. As missionaries showed loyalty and respect for people, the people placed confidence in them and sought counsel. The Christian community could claim moral support and guidance from the missionary when faced with persecution or questions of conscience. The missionary could not turn away from such difficult problems, but would accept the responsibility of leadership.

The missionary's duty extended beyond the immediate Christian community. Occasions arise when a missionary must address those in authority. For that moment in that circumstance the missionary becomes the prophet who declares the Word of God. Venn did not offer such advice lightly. The Society's history contained many cases when others did so at considerable cost. The Society gave this counsel only because it was prepared to stand with the missionary in bearing any consequences.

Even when dealing with a complex situation the missionary was to keep the primary object clear. This in no way shielded the missionary from social and political involvements. All missionaries must be prepared to bear reproach for taking a position against the powers that be. To withdraw by "spiritualizing" the task was not an acceptable solution.

Crisis situations brought tensions and problems to the surface. These became moments of opportunity as well as peril. When a national emergency arose, the Christian community needed leadership and reassurance. The missionary's aim was nothing less than establishment of the kingdom of God.[78] The missionary was always to act according to the standards and modes of the kingdom of God.

The other focus for Venn's policy was the CMS regulation that tersely states: "Every Missionary is strictly charged to abstain from interfering in the political affairs of the country or place in which he may be situated."[79] This regulation requires interpretation.

Venn argued for a stricter definition of the term "political." The problem was that politicians, careless in their use of terms, were apt to sweep everything into the political category. National education, state support of religious institutions, slavery, treatment of aborigines, the private actions of a government official—all these were treated by some politicians as purely political issues. A Christian minister who raised these same issues for discussion was accused of meddling in politics. Venn wanted to establish the fact that certain areas overlapped and some questions were of a mixed character.

Venn divided the issues into three categories: political questions, to be resolved by politicians; religious questions, which were the province of the church and its ministers; and issues that touched more than one area. Venn devoted most of his policy statement to this last category because the "mixed" issues led to most of the conflict between missionary and government.

Consistent with his view of order in creation, Venn saw distinct spheres of responsibility. The missionary, as a servant of the church, was responsible for the spiritual and moral welfare of the people. The politician, as a servant of a divinely appointed institution, the government, was charged with managing the temporal affairs of the community or the state. The missionary was not to play the part of the politician, nor was the politician competent as a religious adviser. The missionary was to remind the politicians that they too were servants of God and had moral responsibilities.[80]

Venn offered several practical guidelines for dealing with political situations. First, a missionary should not act hastily or alone. Missionaries should consult with the Christian leaders and establish the facts of the situation. "Remember that these 'mixed' questions form the exceptions to the general rule of strict abstinence from interfering in political affairs." Common sense should be the guide in determining whether moral issues were involved.

Second, if the missionary becomes involved in an issue, he or she should avoid acting in a "political" spirit. Partisanship was unbecoming to a Christian minister. A missionary was to address the issue and avoid attacking the personalities leading the debate. Should this approach fail to win a hearing, the missionary was to transmit a statement to the home office, and the Society would submit the matter to the court of public opinion.

Third, in all cases the missionary should avoid being drawn into political discussions. Venn warned against becoming preoccupied with politics and devoting to political affairs energies that ought to be directed elsewhere. Such preoccupation confounded the missionary's vocation with the politician's.

Fourth, any missionary who took part in a "mixed" question, did so fully conscious of the Society's regulation; and all missionaries were to observe conscientiously this regulation in other circumstances. The missionary was careful to respect those in authority and to be proper in all relations with government officials. A readiness to pay respect would result in a reciprocal respect being shown to the Christian church and its minister.

A fifth guideline stated that when missionaries faced a crisis situation, they were to rely on their own best judgment.[81] In an emergency decisions had to be taken quickly. The Society had confidence in its workers to act discreetly.

NOTES

1. VB 18a. For Rufus Anderson's views of the missionary society, see R. Pierce Beaver (ed.), *To Advance the Gospel,* pp. 64–66.

2. Peter F. Rudge divides ecclesiastical administration into five types: traditional, charismatic, classical, human relations, and systemic. The focus of a traditional organization is a historical institution designed to maintain the status quo. The source of momentum is the strength of the heritage. It is a coherent and stable system attuned to or embedded in a static society. The main business transacted is recurrent items. The organization is operated nonreflectively and decisions are based on the precedent of custom. The leadership centers in the elders who are the voice of tradition, albeit wise and paternal (*Ministry and Management,* p. 32). Some aspects of this description border on caricature; nor is it fair to take a twentieth-century typology and apply it wholesale to the nineteenth century when most organizations were, by definition, traditional but could be conducted dynamically.

3. The CMS Laws and Regulations define membership, committees, etc. The purpose here is to identify the line of decision and administration rather than the organization per se.

4. VB 89:1.

5. VB 53.

6. G/AC1/6, Jan. 6, 1848, and May 5, 1848. Cf. T.C.F. Stunt, "John Henry Newman and the Evangelicals." Stunt describes a disagreement within the Oxford Church Missionary Association in the 1830s involving Newman.

7. CI3/L3, Oct. 4, 1863: strong criticism of a missionary who wrote directly to the government rather than through the Correspondence Committee.

8. VB 112:2; and CI3/L2, July 4, 1843: diocesan officials excluded from membership in local committee to avoid friction. The bishop or his representative alone was eligible.

9. VB 84.

10. G/AC1/7, Jan. 24, 1849.

11. Ibid.

12. G/AC1/8, Oct. 15, 1850. Cf. G/AC1/17, March 17, 1871, in which Venn regrets being unable to accept an applicant of illegitimate birth because of precarious public relations.

13. G/AC1/11, Feb. 6, 1854. Cf. letter by Coates and Jowett, 1837, reprinted in

Jubilee Volume, 1848–49, pp. 31–37, giving a comprehensive statement of personnel qualifications.

14. VB 105:6.

15. G/AC1/11, March 17, 1854.

16. G/AC1/14, July 2, 1860.

17. G/AC1/7, Sept. 27, 1849.

18. C/C1/L3, May 27, 1867.

19. Cnattingius, *Bishops and Societies,* pp. 172ff., and J. Pinnington, "Church principles in the early years of the Church Missionary Society: the problem of the 'German' missionaries."

20. VB 93:156–60.

21. G/AC1/9, Jan. 13, 1851. Cf. G/AC1/14, July 2, 1860: In reply to a request for an increase in the stipend, Venn said: "The principle on which all our salaries—whether missionaries, secretaries, or clerks—are based is that of giving the most moderate compensation for which the work may be done rather than following the scale which may prevail in other employments."

22. G/AC1/11, Nov. 9, 1853.

23. G/AC1/16, May 20, 1865.

24. G/AC1/16, June 8, 1865.

25. VB 21.

26. C.CH/12, Jan. 11, 1864. This is another example of Venn working out his personnel and program policies in the broader context of current practice among missionary societies generally. The London Secretaries' Association was a prime forum for discussion.

27. Regulations, sect. VI, nos. 6 and 7.

28. CMS Laws and Regulations.

29. VB 54:187.

30. G/AC1/16, Nov. 29, 1864, and Jan. 5, 1865.

31. Ibid.; VB 173:74.

32. VB 114:91.

33. C/CE/L3, Dec. 22, 1854. Cf. Jan. 8, 1855.

34. G/AC1/16, Feb. 2, 1865 (to W. J. Edmonds), Feb. 2, 1865 (to Secretaries, Wesleyan Methodist Missionary Society), and Feb. 28, 1865.

35. G/AC1/15, April 3, 1862, Aug. 25, 1862, and Dec. 31, 1862.

36. VB 123:250.

37. VB 170:317.

38. G/AC1/14, Dec. 14, 1859.

39. G/AC1/15, Nov. 12, 1862.

40. C/MA/L1, April 11, 1870; VB 190, 191, 193, 194, 195. Cf. Stock, II:472–81.

41. G/AC1/16, Jan. 17, 1866.

42. G/AC1/16, Oct. 2, 1863.

43. G/AC1/16, Dec. 29, 1865.

44. G/AC1/12, Jan. 16, 1856. Cf. G/AC1/17, Sept. 1, 1871.

45. CI3/L2, April 7, 1852.

46. G/AC1/8, Feb. 8, 1850; G/AC1/14, March 4, 1859; G/AC1/16, Feb. 12, 1866, and March 23, 1866.

47. G/AC1/13, March 4, 1858.

48. G/AC1/14, Nov. 4, 1858.

49. Ibid., Nov. 9, 1858.

50. Ibid., March 4, 1859.

51. G/AC1/15, Dec. 5, 1860; Dec. 5, 1860; Nov. 12, 1862.

52. London Secretaries' Association, Minutes, April 10, 1850; CCH/L1, March 24, 1851.

53. Private Journal, Oct. 11, 1850; Jan. 30, 1854; Feb. 1 and 4, 1854, Knight, 1880, p. 118ff. These citations refer only to discussions of orthography.

54. VB 34.

55. Venn MSS C34. July 19, 1854. "Prof. Lepsius one of the most learned men in Germany wishes to put forth his system in England under my sanction, and I am to write a preface—a work very far beyond my ability or my line of study—but yet forced upon me because I have stood in a kind of middle position and tried to reconcile contending parties in their literary disputes." Venn came to realize the limitations of Lepsius' work. He wrote to Rufus Anderson in 1860 that "although very usable for West African languages, scholars of Indian languages are not as pleased with it. Dr. Lepsius is writing a second edition which may be improved" (G/AC/17/3, April 23, 1860).

56. Concerning the controversy in China see: CCH/L1, June 24, 1848, Nov. 25, 1850, Dec. 19, 1850, Sept. 24, 1851. For the BFBS responses see: BFBS Foreign Correspondence, Inward, 1848, no. 1, p. 183, Venn to Brandram, June 2, 1848 (communicating a resolution of the CMS); Minutes of Editorial Sub-Committee, no. 3, Aug. 24, 1848; F.C. Inward, 1850, no. 1, Jan. 24, 1850, p. 51; no. 2, 1850, Nov. 30, 1850, pp. 178 and 197, Dec. 17, 1850.

57. Stock, II:27.

58. R.M. Hughes, Introduction to Joseph Salter, *The Asiatic in England*, p. 8. Cf. G/AC1/12, April 3, 1855, in which Venn reports on developments and the cooperation among the various missionary societies and urges the SPG to also participate.

59. Private Journal, Feb. 25 and 29, 1856; Knight, 1880, p. 133. Cf. VB 79.

60. Occasional Paper, CVESI, II, July 1858, gives the Laws and Regulations of the Society.

61. Ibid. Report of public meeting (i.e., the founding meeting) includes Venn's speech in which he set forth the rationale for the society. VB 102a.

62. J. C. Pollock, *Shadows Fall Apart—the story of the Zenana Bible and Medical Mission*, p. 45. Cf. J. K. H. Denny, *Toward the Sunrising: a history of work for the women of India done by women from England, 1852-1901*, p. 8. Neither Pollock nor Denny gives the complete Venn statement and their extracts are not parallel.

63. Pollock, p. 48, reports on the dispute among the participating denominations a decade later which led to a separation with the Church of England Zenana Bible and Medical Mission being formed by Anglicans unwilling to cooperate with the rest of the ZBMM.

64. CI3/L2, Feb. 25, 1850. Cf. VB 158a, a review of Livingstone's *The Zambesi and its tributaries*.

65. G/AC1/8, Nov. 26, 1849. Venn also met with Barth later. Private Journal 1, Knight, 1880, p. 133, Feb. 2, 1856.

66. G/AC1/8, Dec. 20, 1849.

67. E.g., Rebmann's map of East Africa (G/AC1/12, Aug. 11, 1855) and Koelle's *Polyglotta Africana*.

68. G/AC1/12, April 8, 1856.

69. G/AC1/13, July 31, 1856.

70. Cf. *Proceedings*, 1856-57, p. 204: caveat about overestimating progress of the

work. "Forty-five years are spent in Sierra Leone, yet at last there is a Native Church established, with an indigenous ministry." The conclusion to be drawn: "That the conversion of the world is a great work, as yet scarcely commenced. That the agencies now in operation are able, if adequately enlarged, and accompanied by the Spirit from on high, to accomplish that work. And, that if the Church of Christ desires to prosecute the work in *earnest*, it must put forth a far larger amount of effort, and of self-sacrifice, and of persevering prayer, than it has hitherto done."

71. Stock, II:100.

72. VB 192:442.

73. C.CH/L1, Dec. 29, 1849.

74. C.CH/L1, Dec. 10, 1863; C.CH/L2, Dec. 10, 1863. Cf. C.CH/L2, Feb. 26, 1864.

75. Bell and Morrell, *Select Documents on British Colonial Policy, 1830–1860,* p. xxiii.

76. Appendix 2 reproduces this statement. For a fuller study, see Wilbert R. Shenk, "Politics and Missions: Henry Venn's Guidelines."

77.For background on the period, see Max Warren, *Social History and Christian Mission*, pp. 82–95, and J. F. A. Ajayi, "Henry Venn and the Policy of Development," *Journal of the Historical Society of Nigeria*, pp. 331–42.

78. Instructions to Missionaries, CN/L6, June 8, 1860.

79. CMS Regulation, VI, 9.

80. VB 87:153f.

81. CI3/L3, Sept. 25, 1857, to J. S. S. Robertson.

6
Advocate for Africa

In his interpretation of CMS history, Venn emphasized the close connection between the antislavery movement and Society origins. Both in West Africa and the West Indies the CMS and other missionary societies worked to end slavery. Although slavery was officially abolished in 1833, it continued to thrive. By 1839 the slave trade was, if anything, flourishing more than ever.

Sir Thomas Fowell Buxton led the abolition forces in Parliament to victory in 1833, and proposed to end the slave trade by developing legitimate trade.[1] He argued that whatever help and encouragement outside powers might give, the solution finally had to come from Africa itself. "It is in our power to encourage her commerce," wrote Buxton, "—to improve the cultivation of her soil;—and to raise the morals, and the mind of her inhabitants. This is all that we can do; but this done, the Slave Trade cannot continue."[2] The true remedy was Christianity. The Bible must accompany the plow.

Buxton took the offensive by organizing the first Niger Expedition, which was carried out in 1841. The sponsors hoped to open trade routes to the interior, establish agricultural settlements and trading centers, make treaties with African chiefs, and prepare the way for the entry of Christian missions. Buxton envisaged a grand collaboration between government and voluntary philanthropic, commercial, and missionary agencies to achieve these objects.

The expedition was a disaster in the short run, and brought public humiliation on Buxton. From a longer perspective, it made an important contribution.[3] The "Bible and plough" slogan caught the imagination of the next generation. Venn became an energetic exponent of the Buxton doctrine.

In 1842 the CMS proposed to introduce a higher level of training in Sierra Leone. In his appeal for funds Venn cited the CMS's commitment to train Africans from the earliest days of the mission. The West African climate was inhospitable to Europeans, and heavy mortality among European members of the Niger Expedition added new urgency to the training of Africans for leadership.[4] The expedition also confirmed the existence of missionary opportunities in the interior. Africans were needed for missionary advance.

The new program would continue the old one. Demand for trained people was growing. Not all of those trained for service in the church remained there. Some were employed in government offices and commercial firms; others had taken positions as schoolmasters with the government. The CMS investment in training people benefited society in general.

The basic course Venn described was the classical English curriculum. "The main object will be the sound Theological training of the Youths and the diligent use of the means best calculated to promote, under the Divine Blessing, personal Religion."[5] The proposed course comprised both general and theological subjects. Venn added the practical arts; according to his concept of development, sound growth worked from the ground upward. The principle applied to the church as well as to institutions or individuals. He often recurred to this emphasis on the practical arts.

By 1844 Venn was buoyant concerning prospects in West Africa.[6] The CMS was making plans to establish a mission in Yorubaland. Liberated Africans, particularly the Yoruba, were leaving Sierra Leone Colony to return to their homelands. Some of them were Christians whom Venn hoped might be the vanguard of the church in Nigeria. When the first CMS missionaries were dispatched to Yorubaland in late 1844, Venn outlined the means to be used in social development. First and most important was the Christian gospel. This was the foundation for everything else. The second means was agriculture because it contributed to the necessities of life and provided a constructive occupation. In the third place, he advocated commerce to stimulate local production and create demand for imports. Venn also warned missionaries against personal involvement in agriculture and commerce except on a marginal basis, since these would distract them from their primary task.

In 1845 Venn set up the African Native Agency Committee to encourage "the social and religious improvement of Africa by means of her own sons." The patrons were prominent humanitarians committed to helping Africa develop. Venn planned to bring young Africans to England for training in commerce and the professions. Through this effort young men developed skills in producing and marketing cotton, brick- and tile-making, building, medicine, printing, agriculture, and navigation.[7] In 1848 the scope of the committee's interests changed, and their emphasis shifted to training in the practical arts. After 1850 the committee also encouraged African initiative in Africa.

The 1824 agreement between Lord Bathurst and the CMS had provided that the Society would undertake the education of Liberated Africans. By 1842 the Society had become dissatisfied with the government's performance of its part of the contract. In 1846 a new agreement placed effective control in the Society's hands, with the government giving an annual grant.[8] This official relationship allowed for give-and-take. In 1846 Lord Grey, colonial secretary, informed the CMS of a vacancy in the chaplaincy at Cape Coast Castle and inquired whether the committee could nominate an African clergyman for the position. Although pleased at the proposal the committee had no applicant to recommend.

Grey's office encouraged the Society to expand its educational program in Sierra Leone, offering to assist the Society in establishing an Industrial and Training School,[9] and urging the CMS to consider ways of improving agriculture.[10]

In the meantime Venn became absorbed in the problem of making all programs self-supporting. In 1846, when the government began to turn over the schools for liberated Africans, tensions emerged between the missionaries and local teachers over salary scales. Venn argued that the teachers should prepare themselves for the day when they would be supported from local sources, not from England. He opposed setting salary scales that exceeded the capacity of the local community.[11]

In 1847 Venn drew up "Suggestions for the improvement of the social and intellectual condition of the native Africans at Sierra Leone."[12] It reviewed the progress that had been made toward Christianizing the colony and in raising the social and economic conditions. The problem of unemployment, however, disturbed him because of the deleterious effect it would have on community morals and spirit. What was the point of teaching people to read if there was no way of putting this skill to practical use?

The statement also presented a comprehensive program for social development. He appealed for voluntary action in establishing a savings bank, benefit clubs, clothing clubs, dispensary, reading rooms, lending libraries, and lecture series. He wanted a means of promoting agriculture and trade.

Venn's "Suggestions" also defined spheres of responsibility. The CMS did not wish to initiate development. This ought to be the responsibility of a specially organized society. The CMS would, however, train several young men each year as teachers, tradesmen, and agriculturalists. They would send an agriculturalist to Sierra Leone to found model farms. Venn proposed that the Sierra Leonean catechists be given more responsibility as pastors.

Thus Venn tried early to alter missionary patterns that were not producing the results he wanted. He not only affirmed "native agency" but proposed a series of steps that might equip native agency to be self-reliant. In trying to convince the Sierra Leonean teachers to accept a salary scale that the local economy could support, he had recognized that the community had to be strengthened in order to assume this responsibility. He broadened his concept of training to encompass a variety of activities besides the formal school program.

One of the next steps was to organize the African Improvement Committee (AIC) in Sierra Leone, as the counterpart to the African Native Agency Committee in London. The Reverend J. U. Graf, a CMS missionary in Sierra Leone, was secretary of the AIC.[13] Venn began promoting African products for the European market. He asked missionaries and Africans to send him "specimens of medicinal plants, leaves, or roots, with descriptions of the properties."[14] He took these samples to the experts at Kew Botanical Gardens for analysis, and then tried to interest manufacturers in Manchester and London in the commercial potential of these products. By the end of 1850 he had made some progress, but something more was needed.[15]

Venn and his friends believed that production of a major cash crop for export was required. They selected cotton.[16] To introduce cotton production in West Africa, they brought Africans to England for training in the manufacture and marketing of cotton and bought machinery for processing the raw materials in Sierra Leone and Yorubaland. The group eventually built warehouses at the ports to expedite shipment from Lagos and Freetown. Regular shipping started between West Africa and Manchester.

One of Venn's closest allies was the Manchester merchant Thomas Clegg. Venn wrote to him asking for help to procure the best quality cotton seeds, practical instructions in cultivation, and working capital. "I adopted this course in arrowroot five or six years ago," Venn said, "but cotton is beyond my sphere. . . . We have now nearly 20,000 Christian natives in Sierra Leone; when they shall be once placed in an independent position, and shall be enabled to accumulate wealth, they will support their own ministers, and European missionaries will remove to the regions beyond them."[17]

Clegg took up the challenge. He furnished ideas for other new products such as indigo, cochineal, and silkworms; and he invested capital (including some of his own) in these enterprises. Others, too, supported the efforts to develop African commerce. When Venn's Quaker friend Samuel Gurney discovered that Venn had sent out a press and machinery for the cotton industry on his own costing £200, Gurney queried him: "Is it paid for?" Venn answered that it was only half paid for. Gurney replied: "Then I will give the remainder, Henry Venn, on one condition, that thou wilt apply to me for another £100 whenever thou wantest it."[18]

Venn rested his hopes for developing an export trade for Africa on cotton. The African Native Agency Committee brought Henry Robbin to England in 1853 for training in the cotton industry under Clegg at Manchester.[19] Samuel Crowther, Jr., joined Robbin in developing the cotton industry.

For several years the cotton industry made progress. The experiment in Sierra Leone had failed for lack of suitable land, but by 1859 the Abeokuta Institution in Yorubaland was shipping more than one hundred bales a month to England. As a result of this increased income, the Yoruba producers were beginning to demand more consumer products. Venn reported one instance where a chief ordered a moderator lamp from England. When it arrived along with other goods from England, the chief invited other chiefs to see his acquisitions and to harangue them on the advantages of trading with Great Britain. His peroration: "All England is at my feet."

Nevertheless, Venn's dream that West Africa should become a major cotton producer was doomed to fail. Things had gone well with Robbin and Crowther for a time, but in 1858 the first of a series of crises erupted.[20] For the next several years the Yoruba Mission, Clegg, and the Industrial Institution were embroiled in one misunderstanding after another.[21] Venn tried to mediate and sort out the problems. He was humiliated by Robbin's apparent lack of integrity,[22] and Clegg had proved inept as a businessman.[23] The CMS severed its ties with the institution in 1860 and turned it over to Clegg and his agents. In the 1860s cotton production went into decline.

Venn was philosophical about the results of the painful experiment: "We can now only console ourselves with the testimony we receive from all parties that the CMS gave the first impulse to the cotton trade which must eventually raise the social position of the Yoruba Nation to the first rank amongst African tribes."[24] Even if the cotton venture failed, he believed the experience itself had been valuable. Venn continued to take a close interest in the development of Africa and helped Clegg carry on the cotton business for several years. However, he did not attempt to sponsor new initiatives through the CMS or special committees.

Although the emphasis on the cotton industry in West Africa tended to overshadow other efforts, CMS involvement in various education programs no doubt proved more important for future development. The Victorians attributed Britain's recent economic and social change to a rising middle class.[25] Venn geared his development strategy for West Africa to this assumption. He aimed to create a middle class in African society. This strategy was not to be applied naively. While confident of Africa's potential to equal Europe culturally, economically, and politically, Venn knew Africa was starting from a different point.

The cultural change Venn envisaged for Africa depended on education, which had to begin with reducing unwritten vernacular languages to writing. Several CMS missionaries in West Africa devoted themselves to linguistic work. The science of linguistics was still in its infancy. Despite lack of training in this field, Venn worked closely with missionaries engaged in linguistic work. He entered into the technical problems and offered advice. Each missionary translator working with an unwritten language developed his own system of orthography. Someone had to formulate basic principles. Venn took part in discussions aimed at producing a single orthography suitable for all languages. Secretaries of the several missionary societies and the British and Foreign Bible Society developed a system and published their work in 1848 in a small pamphlet edited by Venn.[26]

Preeminent among CMS linguists was S. W. Koelle. In March 1853 Venn assisted Koelle in preparing his award-winning *Polyglotta Africana* for publication.[27] The interest and approval of the experts were cheering, but Venn's basic purpose was the opening up of new opportunity.

An important new step in education had been taken with the decision in 1849 to establish an industrial and training institution in Sierra Leone. Although government paid the training master's salary and passage, he was a CMS agent. In his instructions to Master John Johnson, Venn said, "The great principle which you must keep in view is that of teaching and encouraging the natives to act for themselves, and to carry forward their own social improvements."[28]

By 1852 the CMS appointed W. C. Hensman as medical adviser and industrial agent to Abeokuta Industrial and Training Institution. Venn insisted that the Abeokuta Institution was not to be patterned after either Islington or Fourah Bay. "We must begin at Abeokuta with laying the basis of elementary education."[29]

The industrial institution concept suited Venn's idea of development. Separation of training into scholastic and practical categories might be justified in

Europe, but it was ill-suited to Africa. In the early stages of economic development training geared to the native culture and economy was more effective.

Abeokuta combined training with industrial and commercial activity. It had workshops for carpentry, joinery, sawing, and preparing indigo, and a smithery for repairing machinery.

With his concern to make all institutions self-supporting, Venn urged that pupils at Abeokuta be charged for their tuition. They should do some manual labor each day. "The paying a price, however small, for the teaching can alone convince the people that they are not doing us a favour by sending their children, and that we are not bound to provide for those who grew up under our teaching."[30]

Also as a part of his self-support policy Venn began in 1854 to phase out Fourah Bay Institution in order to let the local mission redevelop it. Gradually the mission formulated a policy for the institution. When a principal was appointed by the mission in 1866 regular courses began again.

Both Venn's strategy for developing the commerce of West Africa and missionary prospects depended on British military presence. The CMS thus became politically involved in efforts to ensure continued military presence. Of major concern was the government's running debate whether to maintain the antislave ship naval patrol on the coast of West Africa. The CMS and other antislavery forces believed that even though the squadron had been ineffective in eliminating the slave trade, it had liberated thousands of Africans and by its presence had a positive moral effect on other nations.

Before the squadron issue came up for review in Parliament in 1850 Venn formed the West Africa Party, which asked that the squadron be not only maintained, but strengthened. Yorubaland missionaries Henry Townsend and C. A. Gollmer testified before the House of Lords Select Committee. The missionaries wanted to see the squadron patrol maintained until legitimate trade could be introduced and the incentive to engage in slave trading eliminated. Legitimate trade and slave trade could not coexist; unless it was restrained, slave trade would defeat legitimate trade. Townsend admitted that as missionaries they had personal interest in controlling slave trade. The traders made the missionary a particular object of abuse. Withdrawing the squadron could endanger missionary work.

CMS efforts to establish commercial relations with inland tribes of Yorubaland were hindered by the insecurity of the area due to attacks from Dahomians and slave traders. Traders were known to have recaptured liberated Africans after they returned to Abeokuta. The Egba nation was eager for British protection. Tension mounted the summer of 1849 as rumors circulated that the king of Dahomey was plotting another attack on the Egba at Abeokuta.

The CMS took the cause of the Egba people to both Foreign Minister Lord Palmerston and Earl Grey, secretary for the colonies. They asked the British government to station a military force in the area reinforced by forts along the coast and gunboats at Lagos. Efforts to arouse public support were proving fruitful. Venn reported to John Warburton in Sierra Leone that the "improvement and civilization of Africa is becoming an every day subject of greater interest at home."[31] The West Africa Party continued to push for antislave support as the day of the debate in Parliament approached. A second deputation visited Lord Palmerston. In addition the CMS petitioned the House of Commons to continue the patrol squadron on the coast of Africa. The petition emphasized the squadron's important role in restraining illegitimate trade until legitimate trade could develop.

The following day, March 19, the House of Commons voted 232 to 154 to continue the squadron.[32] Venn wrote the joyful news to James Beale, missionary to Sierra Leone. He requested that missionaries assess the effectiveness of the squadron in checking slave trade, and investigate the ill-famed "middle passage." The debate had actually benefited missions by placing them in a favorable light.

Another Dahomian attack on Abeokuta became imminent in early 1851. Consul Beecroft gave supplies of ammunition to Henry Townsend, which were distributed to the Egba. Confident of an Egba victory, the missionaries declined any personal assistance from British cruisers.[33] When the Egba won the war in early March, the missionaries were rewarded with new status in the community.[34] Townsend became the principal architect of the Egba policy toward the British, calculated to maintain the peace and allow the missionary and other civilizing influences to flourish.

This episode hastened a decision by the British government to establish regular command posts on the coast. Venn did what he could to facilitate it. He invited missionary Samuel Adjai Crowther to visit England in the autumn of 1851 to meet the CMS committee concerning mission affairs and to publicize missions.[35] With his firsthand account of the Dahomey–Egba war, Crowther was a sought-after speaker. Venn arranged for him to meet Lord Palmerston and Sir Francis Baring to discuss the possibility of opening navigation on the Ogun River and future relations with Abeokuta.[36] Brazilian slave traders were attempting to bribe local chiefs to attack and destroy Abeokuta in retaliation for the curbs the British had placed on their activities. Crowther made the case for stronger British forces.

When Crowther returned to West Africa at the end of December, he carried with him a letter from Palmerston assuring that Great Britain "takes a lively interest in the welfare of the Egba nation."[37] Venn sent along five clocks from the CMS as gifts for the chiefs.

On January 10, 1852, James White, a Yoruba catechist, conducted the first Christian services at Lagos. Commodore Bruce had just ousted the chief, Kosoko, in order to secure the area against slave traders. The CMS sent C. A. Gollmer to Lagos to establish the mission there. Venn encouraged him to "believe that God designs thus to open to us inland Africa."

Already in the aftermath of the Egba–Dahomey war the missionaries had come into conflict with the British consul. The consul accused the missionaries of meddling in politics, and these accusations were publicized in London. The plot was thickening. More than military or political considerations were at stake. Venn informed Sir Francis Baring that the naval officers reporting to him did not understand that the war was more than an internal contest; it was rooted in the slave trade. Lagos, Porto Novo, and Dahomey were devoted entirely to the revival of the slave trade whereas the Egba defended both the English and English interests against the trade. Yet when a top Egba leader asked for British protection for Badagry, he was rewarded with a treaty suppressing trade with the Egba chiefs.[38] This was only the beginning of missionary difficulties with consuls.

Parliament discussed the political involvement of missionaries, especially at Lagos, the spring of 1852.[39] Not all British officials and military men were pleased with the Yoruba Mission. A CMS member was asked in the House of Commons if the missionaries did not control all the warfare in Lagos. This matter erupted into a public dispute between Gollmer and merchants in Lagos in 1853. The merchants claimed that the CMS headquarters were improperly located and that the missionaries were interfering with trade. The problem drew newspaper coverage in London and finally led to an official investigation, which fully exonerated the mission.[40]

Meanwhile continued attacks and counterattacks led to war between Ado and Abeokuta. In January 1853 the officer of the squadron and the vice consul tried in vain to mediate between the two sides. In desperation they called in the missionaries. Townsend and Crowther succeeded in getting the two groups to settle their differences.[41]

Later that year there was insurrection in Lagos and Portuguese slave-traders in league with certain chiefs tried to take control. Gollmer, located in Lagos, refused to leave when war became imminent because local people begged him not to abandon them. The mission house was besieged until armed forces finally came and freed the Gollmer family and a host of Africans.[42] This display of courage and loyalty won Gollmer the appreciation of the local people and warm commendation from British officials.

While Venn was trying to secure from the government military protection for West Africa, he also campaigned for government assistance in economic development. One of the recognized needs was for better shipping service between West Africa and Europe. In a memorandum to Earl Grey in 1851, Macgregor Laird proposed opening regular steam communication with West Africa. In a statement to Grey, the CMS supported Laird.[43] Early in 1854 Laird announced plans for a Second Niger Expedition. He invited the Society to send Crowther along with the expedition, which was to explore the Benue River. Venn's only request was that Crowther be given ample opportunity to investigate the languages of the people and their moral conditions. The object of the expedition was to develop commerce and establish regular steamer service. The expedition was a success in many ways, but it failed in its primary object.

Mission involvement in West Africa continued to be anything but smooth sailing. The decade of the 1850s saw some dark days and complicated struggles among missionaries, government officials, and Africans. In 1852 Palmerston moved from the Foreign Ministry to the Home Ministry, leaving the CMS without his good offices. The government had also recalled Admiral Bruce, another staunch ally, because of the threat of war with Russia.

Venn attempted to relieve missionaries Gollmer and Townsend of their commercial and political connections by appointing Dr. Edward Irving to Lagos and Abeokuta as lay agent. Having served as a physician with the squadron, Irving had impressed Venn with suggestions concerning the economic and political relations of Lagos and Abeokuta missionaries. He was assigned to cooperate with missionaries in improving the social, political, and commercial conditions of the peoples.

Irving was free to involve himself in nonecclesiastical concerns in which Venn himself was much interested: fostering an alliance between Lagos and Abeokuta, checking the amount of cotton grown and marketed, encouraging local traders to produce for sale to foreign traders.

From the start Irving encountered difficulties with missionary colleagues who were not ready to relinquish nonecclesiastical duties. Local chiefs had learned to trust the missionaries. Both missionaries and local people felt the tension in the process of training for independence. Irving advocated stricter control of native agents.

Equally serious, relationships with the British consul were going from bad to worse. Consul Campbell claimed that Gollmer tried to get him ousted by agitating Africans against him. Instead of averting political problems, as Venn had hoped, Irving himself became part of them, antagonizing the consul at Lagos and writing in intemperate language to Lord Clarendon. Irving died before things were resolved, after only a year and a half in office. He had served too short a time to achieve much, but Venn did not pronounce his work a failure.

Trouble continued to stalk the Yoruba Mission, with European traders circulating charges that the missionaries were engaged in trade. Venn believed that the crux of the matter was that in elevating the social and economic level of Africans the missionaries posed a threat. Ultimately Africans would compete with Europeans.

The CMS welcomed the development of the Third Niger Expedition by interrupting a committee meeting to thank God on their knees. They had urged the government to establish regular shipping on the Niger and were concerned that the expedition include a number of Africans. They wanted to keep white traders from reaching the interior.[44] Laird would again sponsor the expedition , with Dr. Baikie serving as leader. The CMS appointed Samuel Crowther to accompany the expedition, along with six African teachers.

Mission enthusiasts saw the 1857 Niger Expedition as indispensable in opening the way to Buxton's Bible-and-plow doctrine. The CMS was eager to exploit such exploration for mission. Crowther selected six sites on the river for mission stations. "It is clear that we must fill up the distance between

Lagos and the Niger with civilization, through missionary operations and lawful commerce," Venn said.[45]

Notwithstanding the step taken toward opening the Niger to civilization, commerce, and Christianity, progress was in jeopardy. The government wavered in its commitment to West Africa, terminating Laird's five-year contract for shipping on the Niger. The Niger Mission also faced difficulties from Muslims along the Upper Niger and the Delta peoples in the south.[46] Again the CMS struggled with the government and again was given assurance of support. A new three-year contract for shipping on the Niger was signed.

Venn had special hopes for the new Niger Mission. It was headed by an African, Crowther, and the first missionaries and teachers were all African. The fundamental principle of the Niger Mission, said Venn, was not to be "Native agency and European superintendence: or European agency and Native Superintendency; but Native and European Association."[47]

Nevertheless, further frustrations and delays lay ahead. Laird's death and the disintegration of his company destroyed hopes of steamboat trade on the Niger. By September 1861 the Niger Mission seemed stalemated. The CMS began pulling back. Venn mentioned to Crowther the burden of the work on his "tired, old, shoulders." The CMS assigned primary responsibility for developing the Niger Mission's economic and social services to a separate committee. Venn now concentrated his energies elsewhere.

Early in 1860 the smoldering differences between the Egba people and other peoples came to the surface. War erupted. Townsend at Abeokuta was involved as an adviser to the Egba leaders. Convinced of the rightness of the Egba cause, Townsend urged the CMS to appropriate funds for their defense.[48] The mission at Abeokuta was the most popular of all CMS missions at that time. Venn had a paternal affection for all of West Africa. But the situation was not as simple as Townsend's interpretation of it. David Hinderer at Ibadan was working among a people who were sworn enemies of the Egba.[49] The Yoruba Christians were not united in their views of the dispute.[50] Venn refused to take a position on the merits of the Egba case. He deplored that local Christians had been drawn into the fighting and suggested that they should have declined participation if that option was open to them.[51] Worst of all, the mission was divided over these local political issues. In a private letter to Crowther, Venn sharply criticized the partisanship among the missionaries and the compromise this brought on the mission.[52]

Politics in West Africa continued to be unsettled. Missionary relationships with British consuls were strained. Lagos missionaries disliked the way Consul H. Stanhope Freeman handled relations with local chiefs. When a Dahomean attack on Abeokuta became imminent in late 1862, Freeman ordered all British subjects to leave. The missionaries refused; Venn approved: "I am more and more convinced that the policy of the mission is to be separate as possible from the government, and to look as little as possible for government countenance and protection."[53]

The CMS protested Freeman's policies to the colonial secretary, stating that the good relations established with Yoruba chiefs during Palmerston's time as foreign secretary had been sadly destroyed. The Society wanted a return to Palmerstonian policies, the dismissal of Freeman. He was recalled, but then reappointed to Lagos.

Venn was growing less sanguine about the value of lobbying with government. "I have learnt therefore to be less eager than I once was to protest against official violence and injustice and to trust more to prayer to Him who turneth the hearts of kings whithersoever he wills."[54] From this time on he launched no new official initiatives on behalf of West Africa.

When Parliament sent Colonel Henry Ord on a fact-finding mission to West Africa, however, Venn showed some enthusiasm. He introduced Ord to missionaries and prepared a long briefing prior to Ord's visit. He again voiced the familiar questions: How can British trade with West Africa be strengthened and how can the squadron be made effective in suppressing the slave trade?

Ord returned from West Africa in February and the commission conducted public hearings in April. Meanwhile Venn published a pamphlet, *West-African Colonies.*[55] The line of argument was familiar. He brought forward no new evidence. He showed his mastery of the literature on West Africa, including earlier government commissions and published reports. But he stated his case with a new forcefulness and cogency, outlining Sir T. F. Buxton's 1840 government policy for British colonies in West Africa. First, the colonial governments were responsible to educate the local people and train them for government employment. Second, the Admiralty should enlist Africans in the West African Squadron. Third, the colonial governments had neglected to promote agriculture and to develop Africa's natural resources. Fourth, the policy of taking liberated Africans from Africa to the West Indies was wrong. Fifth, colonial governments had not followed wise or consistent policies with respect to the native chiefs.

Venn spent several days attending the Ord Commission hearings.[56] The final report and recommendations that the commission presented to Parliament fell far short of his expectations. The report did highlight the need to train Africans for self-reliance and self-government.[57]

By 1866 it became clear that the slave trade in West Africa had been ended. The campaign against the slave trade now entered a new round. In 1868 the bishop of Mauritius appealed to the CMS to make representation against the slave trade of East Africa. In the spring a pamphlet was published exposing the trade.[58] The sultan of Zanzibar visited London in the autumn to review his treaty with the British government for the control of the slave trade on the East Africa coast. At that point the Foreign Office urged the CMS to send a deputation to the secretary for India to ask for a new agreement, which would allow for strict control of the slave trade outside the sultan's own territory.[59] The deputation was carried out in February 1869. The memorial asked for "measures as will effectually terminate this remaining relic of that infamous traffic which it is the pride of England to have swept from the Atlantic."[60] This was Venn's final attack on slavery.

NOTES

1. T. F. Buxton, *The African Slave Trade and Its Remedy,* pp. 436ff.

2. Ibid., p. 310.

3. Ifemesia, "The 'Civilizing' Mission of 1841: Aspects of an Episode in Anglo-Nigerian Relations," pp. 291–310.

4. VB 17a.

5. VB 13.

6. VB 18a.

7. Cf. VB 68:29f. for the practical advice Venn gave a young African.

8. These negotiations extended over a period of at least eight years. This was a case where Dandeson Coates had antagonized the Colonial Office. Venn and Straith reopened negotiations after Coates's death and brought them to a satisfactory, if slow, conclusion.

9. CMS Minutes, Nov. 16, 1847, 26:206f.

10. Ibid., Jan. 30, 1849, 26:671.

11. CA1/L3.

12. VB 28.

13. CA1/L4, Nov. 1, 1849, to J. U. Graf.

14. CA1/L4, March 5, 1850, to T. Macaulay.

15. CA1/L4, Nov. 14, 1850, to T. McCormack.

16. G/AC1/1, March 6, 1850, to Sir E. N. Buxton.

17. CA1/L4, April 14, 1851, to T. Peyton; Knight, 1880, pp. 541f.

18. Private Journal, Dec. 9, 1851 (Knight, 1882, p. 219).

19. CA2/L1, Dec. 22, 1855, to H. Robbin.

20. CA2/L2, April 23, 1858, to H. Robbin.

21. CA2/L2, June 22, 1858, to S. Crowther, Jr., same date to H. Robbin; ibid., July 22, 1858, to H. Townsend; Sept. 23, 1858, to H. Robbin; same date, H. Townsend; ibid., Oct. 22, 1858, to Yoruba Finance Committee; Oct. 23, 1858, to H. Robbin; Dec. 21, 1858, to H. Townsend; Dec. 23, 1858, to B. Campbell.

22. CA2/L2, March 23, 1859, to H. Robbin. Cf. G/AC1/14, May 18, 1860, to F. Fenn, and June 20, 1860, to G. F. Buhler.

23. CA2/L2, Feb. 23, 1860, to C. A. Gollmer.

24. CA2/L2, March 23, 1860, to C. A. Gollmer.

25. Kitson Clark, *The Making of Victorian England,* pp. 5–7, 118–23, discusses problems associated with the term "middle class."

26. VB 34.

27. For this Koelle received the French Institute's Volney Prize as the outstanding linguistic work in 1854. It contained samples from 150 languages and dialects, most of which Koelle collected within Sierra Leone Colony. Cf. Stock, II:102.

28. CA1/L4, Jan. 4, 1850, to John Johnson.

29. CA2/L1, Dec. 2, 1852, to T. Macaulay.

30. CA2/L2, Jan. 29, 1856, to W. Kirkham. Cf. Instructions to Missionaries going to West Africa in 1851 (VB 57:20).

31. CA1/L4, Feb. 28, 1850.

32. *Hansard,* 1850, CIX, pp. 1093–1186.

33. CMS Minutes, 28:259, extract from dispatch of Capt. Adams, HMS Gladiator, Dec. 5, 1851, transmitted by Sir F. Baring, First Lord of the Admiralty.

34. *Proceedings,* 1851–52, pp. xcv–vi, and 1852–53, pp. 47f., 50.

35. CA2/L1, June 14, 1851, to S. A. Crowther.

36. CA2/L1, Sept. 9, 1851, to C. A. Gollmer; Private Journal, Nov. 22, 1851 (Knight, 1880, p. 122).

37. Stock, II:114.

38. G/AC1/9, Dec. 10, 1851, to Sir F. Baring.

39. CA2/L1, March 15, 1852, to S. A. Crowther.

40. Feb. 28, 1853, Com. R. D. White to Rear-Admiral Bruce; March 3, 1853, Bruce to Sec. of Admiralty—compiled in G/AZ1/1, 72; CMS Minutes, June 21, 1853, vol. 29.

41. July 21, 1853, Townsend to Venn.

42. Sept. 8, 1853, Gollmer to Venn.

43. CMS Minutes, May 1, 1851, 28:129.

44. CA2/L2, Oct. 22, 1856, to S. A. Crowther.

45. CA2/L2, April 20, 1858, to S. Crowther, Jr.

46. CA1/L7, Jan. 23, 1860, to C. F. Ehemann; CA3/L1, Dec. 22, 1859, to S. A. Crowther.

47. CA3/L1, May 23, 1860, to S. A. Crowther (Private). Cf. Instructions to Missionaries, CN/L6, June 8, 1860.

48. Oct. 4, 1860, to Venn.

49. CA1/L2, June 23, 1860, to D. Hinderer, and, same date, to H. Townsend.

50. See Venn's comments on the report of a Yoruba catechist, T. King, CA2/L2, July 19, 1860.

51. CA2/L2, Sept. 24, 1860, to H. Townsend. Venn received a letter from a group of Abeokuta Christians asking for guidance on whether to participate in war. Venn replied (CA2/L3, Dec. 20, 1861): 1) If Abeokuta and/or villages are attacked by an enemy, then they should join in defense; but the Committee would not advise them whether to fight against Ibadan or Dahomey; if they are not compelled to join the army, they must decide where they can best serve Christ; if they decline joining the army, they must explain to the King that they are governed by the "book." 2) In Africa war is fought to regain their native land. In Europe the victor keeps the land conquered. The Committee feels the same should apply in Africa as well.

52. CA3/L1, Dec. 24, 1860, to S. A. Crowther.

53. CA2/L3, Jan. 23, 1863, to H. Townsend; VB 139.

54. CA2/L3, Nov. 23, 1863, to Dr. Harrison.

55. VB 155.

56. CA2/L3, April 25, 1865, to H. Townsend.

57. CA2/L3, Aug. 23, 1865, to H. Townsend. Cf. Resolutions of the Select Committee of the House of Commons, June 26, 1865, *Parliamentary Papers,* 1865, V (412) iii, reprinted in H. S. Wilson (ed.), *Origins of West African Nationalism,* pp. 151f.

58. VB 172.

59. G/AC1/17, Nov. 24, 1868, to Earl of Chichester.

60. VB 175 and 176.

7

Critic of Colonial Policies: India and New Zealand

India

As we have seen, Venn's policy in West Africa called forth vigorous inter-action between the mission and the political realm. He did not hesitate to press the government to provide guarantees and services that advanced the Christian cause. Neither did he hesitate to oppose government policies and actions that he deemed detrimental to missions. Although he acted within a theological framework, Venn's policies reflected the prevailing secular as-sumptions of the day. In India again we shall see how he worked within these currents, exploiting them when possible in the cause of missions.

In the first half of the nineteenth century, British policy for India was inspired by the myth that British greatness was founded on Indian happi-ness.[1] The popular British impression of India was dominated by the "Black Hole of Calcutta" and the Vellore Mutiny of 1808.[2] The "orientalists" found merit in the Indian literary tradition and advocated the translation and study of the Indian classics. Evangelicals saw India as engulfed in darkness, which could only be dispelled through enlightenment. The light of the gospel was the source of all truth, but Western learning in general was part of the anti-dote to heathen darkness. Education became basic to all missionary policy for India.

In 1835 the governor-general of India, Lord William Bentinck, announced a new educational policy, which set the course of educational developments for the next three generations. Western literature and science were to be the core content of higher education. The medium of instruction would be Eng-lish. A key concept for educational policy was the "percolation" principle: ideas and influence are communicated from the elite to the masses. There-fore, government would concentrate its funds on educating this elite. Educa-tion in the vernacular languages for the masses at the lower levels was af-firmed, but government assistance was applied to higher education for the select few.

Bentinck's policy was the product of various influences. The "anglicists" and missionary educationists like Alexander Duff had triumphed over the "orientalists." Lord Macaulay in his famous "Minute" predicted the early

80

collapse of traditional Indian civilization as Western education was introduced. The enlightened young Indian would find it impossible not to repudiate his father's faith and superstitions when he saw the truth.[3]

The debate concerning educational policy took place within a wider discussion of the development of India. All parties recognized the need to train Indians to share in governing the country.[4] Natural resources were to be developed and Indians were to be trained in Western technology for this purpose.[5] The policy included a vision for introducing Western medicine by training Indian medical doctors.[6]

The CMS, like other missionary societies, operated educational institutions in India almost from the first. But from the early days of Venn's secretariat he worried lest education become an end in itself, drawing the missionary away from church extension. In 1843, for example, he encouraged James Long, a leading CMS educationist, to concentrate on educational work provided he did not neglect his preaching ministry.[7]

In 1845 the general CMS policy on education met a test. Government was encouraging the expansion of educational programs, and Indians wanted education in English. The governor-general had given official impetus to education in 1844 by declaring that the government was prepared to offer employment to people trained in private institutions. The missions saw this as an opportunity to train future civil servants who would understand and espouse Christian values and who would influence the future course of Indian government and society. The CMS South India Mission proposed a major enlargement of the CMS school system. Knowing that the Society might be reluctant to undertake this work, the Madras Corresponding Committee suggested organizing a separate society for this purpose.[8] Although the CMS expressed interest in the proposal, they took no action. When the Madras Corresponding Committee proposed to request the East India Company to make a grant for schools, Venn demurred.[9]

At this time Venn stressed the importance of European superintendence in the development of native agency. Education for the masses was not the responsibility of a missionary society, he claimed. The peculiar duty of the mission was to train Christian leadership. To do this on an increasing scale required a corresponding increase in the number of missionaries. India particularly needed the "European mind and intelligence, to regulate, mature, and discipline the congregations of Native Converts,"[10] according to Venn.

CMS policy in 1846 was geared to train native teachers.[11] One of the first things a mission did was to establish day schools and boarding schools for children. Later another level was added to receive those students who had done well in primary school. A select group was admitted into a course of theological education. The lack of moral and intellectual background made educational progress slow. Close supervision had to be given.

In contrast to the policy for Africa, Venn opposed suggestions that Indians should come to Europe for further training.[12] The main argument against the idea was that such education would denationalize the individual. In contrast to Africa at that time, other training was available in India, and the Society offered assistance to students wishing to get advanced training for the ministry.

The CMS educational policy of the 1840s was rather precisely defined. Education was an auxiliary to missions and not a program carried on as a service in its own right. Venn put a positive construction on the lack of "actual results" in North India by drawing attention to the "indirect effects" of missionary labors: "A general knowledge of the elementary truths of revelation—the cessation of violent opposition to the preaching of the Gospel—a wide-spread respect for the Missionary office, as one of good-will to the Natives—an undefined expectation that Christianity will prevail in the second or third generation from the present time—and the weakening of the hold of the native superstitions upon the minds of the people."[13]

The CMS attempted a fresh start in the autumn of 1850. Two missionaries were sent to Agra, India, to open St. John's College with a view to serving the upper classes of society. The college was to offer a superior level of instruction, which was at the same time thoroughly Christian.[14] This venture, based on the Duff concept, had been under consideration for several years. Venn was eager to develop a program that combined high academic standards with evangelism.

In 1851 Venn authorized the reorganization of the Cottayam Institution in Ceylon. This institution was at the top level in the usual CMS educational pyramid and offered theological training for teachers and catechists. But the system was not satisfactory. To tackle the problems, the school became a general educational institution. Students were enrolled in general education with a view to employment in government or the community. Only those who elected theological training were admitted for that course. Venn insisted that the object remained the same as before, but in fact, the mission provided only what the community demanded—general education instead of theological.[15]

The charter of the East India Company was due to be renewed in 1853. The previous year the SPG and the CMS formed a joint committee to prepare recommendations to the government concerning the East India Company's religious policies.[16] Each of the societies then presented its own memorial to the government. Bishops and missionaries in India furnished reports and recommendations of changes they wished to see made. The memorial made three key points: the company should appoint more chaplains; education (with higher standards) should be extended to many more people; and the government of India should separate itself completely from idolatry.[17] The Bengal Calcutta Missionary Conference called attention to the social disorganization and general chaos of the Bengal presidency, and asserted the need for judicial and administrative reforms.

The CMS memorial laid three concerns before the government. First, it requested the government of India to end all connection with Hinduism and Islam through endowments or other official countenance. Lord Bentinck had abolished most official involvements with the traditional religions in

1833 but vestiges remained. The CMS also wanted restrictions lifted against East India Company employees who participated in Christian missionary activities. At issue here was the policy of neutrality, which the company had followed for many years. The missionary societies charged that it was a bad policy, enforced in a way that discriminated against Christians, individually and institutionally.

The second point requested that the government allow Indian Christians to share in government education funds. This referred to a specific grievance against the neutrality policy. Only government institutions had hitherto been given allocations out of government funds. Government schools were operated on a strictly secular basis. The Society insisted that there was discrimination against Christian Indians who applied for admission to a government college. Furthermore, government schools enrolled only one-fourth as many pupils as did mission schools. The solution was either to allow Christian teaching to be offered in government schools, or to give government subsidy to private schools. It specifically called for a system of grants-in-aid.

In the third place, the memorial asked the government of India to adhere to the Charter Act of 1833, which provided "that no Native of India shall be ineligible to office on account of his religion." This was another protest against a specific aspect of the much criticized policy of neutrality. It was precisely the Christians who were penalized by the "Christian" government's desire not to offend adherents of the traditional religions.

Government responded to CMS recommendations with a new policy drawn largely from memoranda submitted by Duff, J. C. Marshman, and CMS committee member J. M. Strachan. The despatch declared that the object of the policy was to inculcate European education. It was known as the Educational Despatch of 1854, and as for the language of instruction, it called for a dual approach. At the higher levels English was to be mandatory, but it recognized that vernacular languages were important for the masses. English was not to supplant the vernaculars but to supplement them at the advanced level where science and Western learning were taught. The 1854 Despatch did not repudiate the "filtration" theory, which had figured so prominently in the 1835 Policy; but it introduced a more democratic emphasis through its commitment to education for far more people at all levels.

Issuance of the Despatch of 1854 culminated many years of debate among missionaries over educational policy. In 1846 the Madras Corresponding Committee requested government assistance for education, only to have Venn oppose it.[18] But Venn had had a change of mind by 1854. Duff's philosophy had gradually gained ground so that by 1850 most missionaries in India and the societies at home had adopted it.

In some cases, however, a missionary had moved beyond acceptance of Duff's ideas to a more critical position. CMS missionary James Long was one such critic.[19] An early "convert" to Duff's concept, Long had observed that in spite of official sanction for vernacular-language schools, they were losing ground to English-medium institutions. He also insisted that it was impossible to learn well through the medium of a foreign language. Long was interested in helping the peasants and he doubted that instruction in a foreign language produced teachers for village schools. The "filtration" theory was not working in practice. The Duff policy, argued Long, led to an elitism that left untouched the problem of mass illiteracy.

Missionaries also opposed the grants-in-aid system because it involved further cooperation with government. But supporters of the new policy saw it as a bridge between government and private education. It recognized the work of the missionary societies and acknowledged that the government acting alone would not be able to provide all the schools needed. Private initiative was to be welcomed and supported. Duff had urged the government of India to adopt the same system of grants-in-aid to private education as was followed in England.[20] This policy pledged government grants-in-aid to all schools regardless of religious affiliation, and an official inspection system was to be instituted to maintain standards. Duff and Strachan had proposed that the Bible be made the basic textbook for the schools, but the Despatch of 1854 adhered to the policy of government neutrality.

Venn welcomed the Despatch of 1854 as a "foundation for missionary schools which would accomplish more towards the evangelization of India than any public measure which has yet been adopted."[21] In polite but firm language, he urged missionaries to cooperate with these new measures. The new policy would enable expansion of missions and they could continue to operate without any change in religious emphasis. One of the most important prospects arising out of the new measures was that people from the lower castes were now to be given opportunity for government employment. "Education presents the most obvious means of relaxing the dominion of caste," Venn wrote. Education was a socially desirable goal apart from its missionary purpose.[22] He encouraged the missionaries to hold periodic conferences on education in order to raise standards.

The grants-in-aid scheme set off vigorous debate among the India missionaries. Most CMS missionaries sided with the independents, who wanted nothing to do with government support for education. As a part of the established church, the CMS was naturally less suspicious of receiving government aid. In India the CMS had the largest educational system of any of the missions and thus stood to gain most from grants-in-aid. James Long was the first CMS missionary to accept government aid in 1855.[23]

The Bengal missionaries communicated their criticism of the government scheme in a July 9 minute.[24] Venn responded with another statement.[25] He tried to allay missionary fears that acceptance of government grants was tantamount to placing mission schools under government control. The CMS was not abrogating its evangelistic intention or altering the policy of required Bible instruction in all mission schools. Venn insisted that the intent of the Despatch of 1854 was to give government support to secular education and not Muslim, Hindu, or Christian education. The Despatch of 1854 placed Christianity on an equal footing with other religious groups for the first time.

Furthermore, Venn reminded the missionaries that nearly all Christian groups in Great Britain had no scruples against accepting government aid for education. That logic should now be applied to India.

Venn went on the offensive. It was widely acknowledged that the mission schools maintained high academic standards and offered the best secular education. Missions should continue with the same program. Most important, education sponsored by the CMS remained *missionary.* "The Society are willing to accept the aid of Government, so far as they will give it. But they consider themselves as doing their own work, and not as standing in the position of Schoolmasters to the Government." It was up to the missionaries to thwart any secularizing tendencies.

In May 1857 the Indian Mutiny erupted at Meerut. Slow and inadequate means of communication made it difficult to assess the situation even in India. By early June word reached the CMS in London.[26] The Reverend Arthur Medland, CMS missionary at Meerut, had narrowly escaped harm. All other missionaries were reported safe and the Reverend G.G. Cuthbert wrote Venn about the rumored "causes" of the mutiny. His real fear was that irreligious folk in England would claim that missionaries were to blame for the outbreak. The missionaries themselves were convinced that the trouble stemmed from poor British command over the troops and ill-advised government actions. It was Indians who protected the missionaries from attack at Benares and Jaunpore.[27] There was no evidence of hostility toward missionaries.

Venn saw the hand of Providence in these events. "The Lord is indeed teaching the Indian Government a lesson of terrible importance. May he enable us all to lay it to heart."[28] Events in India aroused the British public and Christians united in prayer on behalf of missionaries in India.[29]

Cuthbert's fears were early fulfilled. Critics blamed the missionaries for the uprising.[30] Venn met these charges in a brief statement published in August.[31] He scoffed at the notion that the cause was related to the work of missions. Nor could it be charged that the sepoys rebelled because the government was countenancing missions. If anything the government had been hostile to missions. He called the revolt a military affair.

In September the CMS released a statement on the mutiny and missionary operations in India in the future.[32] The Indian crisis was interpreted as a judgment on Great Britain. Britain had been entrusted by Providence with the government of India.[33] Yet Christian Britain had failed to bring Christian truth to the Indian people for a century. The statement called on the Indian government to "honour God by avowing itself a Christian Government." Full tolerance for all citizens of whatever religion should be guaranteed, but the government should be avowedly Christian. Religious toleration should be maintained without condoning antisocial or immoral practices. The Bible should be the basis of education in government schools. The statement also called for an expansion of missions in India and a new effort to "give Christian instruction in the vernacular language of India to the masses of the population, and to provide them with a vernacular, moral, and Christian literature."

Critics of Christian missions in India had the weight of prestige and experience on their side. A foremost spokesman was Lord Ellenborough, a former governor-general and secularist, who had no sympathy for missions.[34] Venn was just as intent on seizing the moment and furthering policies more favorable to missions as Ellenborough was desirous of restricting missions. Venn was confident public sympathies could be aroused in support of a more Christian policy.[35]

In December 1857 the CMS presented a memorial to Queen Victoria.[36] This was a comprehensive restatement of the criticisms the CMS had been making against official policies with respect to India. It discussed seven points. First, the government of India had, until recently, given support to false religions while discouraging Christianity. Even if the practice had been officially abolished, it continued to have influence. Second, the 1833 policy of neutrality in religious matters had not been carried out satisfactorily. The remaining vestiges of government involvement with traditional religions ought to be removed. Third, it was impossible to maintain a policy of neutrality between true and false religions. Even to attempt this was an affront to God and did not serve the social welfare of the native people. Fourth, the Educational Despatch of 1854 was dedicated to promoting the education of the Indian people. However, it retained the principle of neutrality. True education acknowledged spiritual values as the foundation of learning. Christianity ought to be made the basis of the educational system. Fifth, schools operated directly by government should have the Bible in the curriculum. The 1854 Despatch only allowed for it to be placed in the library of a school but it was not to be discussed. Venn termed the policy "perfectly nugatory."[37] This was the evil of neutrality. Sixth, grants-in-aid had on occasion been withdrawn from mission schools on orders of the home government, where it was feared neutrality had been violated. This again demonstrated the anti-Christian bias in the administration of official policies. Seventh, advocates of the policy of neutrality spoke of treaty obligations not to interfere with traditional religious practices. Such treaties did not exist and could not be appealed to.

The memorial called for three specific actions: (1) abrogate present policy of neutrality and make Christianity the official religion; (2) make the Bible "the only standard of moral rectitude, and the source of those Christian principles" upon which the government itself was conducted; (3) sever all remaining connections between the state and the traditional religions.

Following presentation of the memorial to the queen, the CMS launched a public appeal.[38] Believing that the upheaval in India indicated a new opportunity for evangelism, the Society was "prepared to revise the whole system of their Missions in Northern India." It viewed existing centers in the major cities as bases from which to launch new missions on a comprehensive scale. To do this the CMS appealed for "men to carry forward the work." The object was "nothing less than that in our own day and generation, by God's help and blessing, India may become Christian."

Around this time another Venn dream became reality with the formation of the Christian Vernacular Education Society for India. James Long impressed on Venn the need for education in the vernacular. Missionary education thus far had benefited only a small number of people. Venn was convinced that the mutiny was due in part to this neglect of the masses. The September 1857 Society statement had mooted the need for vernacular education.

In spite of the irritations involved in getting a large group of people to cooperate, the campaign was having effect. By the end of 1857 Venn believed that all of Britain was rallying to the task of Christianizing India. He was convinced that public pressure was so strong that the government would allow the Bible to be introduced in government schools. He was ready to see grants-in-aid to be given to all schools, whether Muslim, Hindu, or Christian. The missionary societies alone could not undertake education for the masses of India. Government had to provide schools. The aim was to make sure these government schools also taught the Bible.

Venn's campaign for India was threatened from several sides. The first issue taken up with the government was the question of official support for idolatry. To the dismay of the CMS, proponents of the policy of neutrality were in power. In spite of strong public support for policy change, Parliament remained indifferent.

There was opposition from another quarter. Sir Charles Trevelyan, respected civil servant in India and well-known Evangelical, published a series of letters in the (London) *Times* under the pseudonym "Indophilus" in opposition to Christianization programs.[39] Trevelyan was an ally of Venn and the CMS on most issues. His opposition in this case was a serious blow.

In January 1858 the CMS held a special meeting in Exeter Hall with Archbishop Sumner in the chair. The government was again asked to avow a Christian policy for India. The CMS urged supporters to petition Parliament on the question.

Objections to Venn's proposal concerning the Bible and public schools began to grow. Some people thought Venn was asking for official government sponsorship of proselytization.[40] Other people were offended that the Society was meddling in politics and passing sentence on the government of India.[41]

Venn based his views on the role of government in religious matters on several axioms. First, he maintained that the people have confidence in government when it allies itself with missions. Furthermore, government should not be neutral with respect to religion. As a Christian government, Britain must exercise "the sword of rule and justice" and this requires a standard. For Christians this standard is to be found only in God's Word. Third, missions should not be supported through endowments from government. Endowed missions become stagnant. Aggressive missions are carried out on the basis of the sympathy and prayers of a dedicated group of people. But, in the fourth place, government can assert its Christian responsibility by introducing the Bible into the schools and allowing this to become the standard for moral instruction.[42]

In spite of committee and constituency support for these views, Venn failed to carry the missionaries in India with him. There were not enough Christian teachers to lead the Bible classes, they said. Admittedly, there were practically no Christians to teach religion in government schools. But, Venn argued, "many of us think there is a special providence over God's own word which is well able to take care of it." He was willing to have non-Christians teach the Bible in government schools.

Late in 1858 Queen Victoria issued a proclamation that placed the government of India under the British crown rather than in the hands of the East India Company. The proclamation was sufficiently ambiguous that it could be interpreted in several ways, but it had identified the crown with Christianity. Venn took the position that it opened the way to press for all the Christian measures he had been advocating.[43]

He continued to press vigorously for the Bible in Indian schools, publishing pamphlets for public circulation, sending deputations to government officials, and finally petitioning the House of Lords. There was growing support for the action, including that of Bishop Wilberforce and other leading prelates. Yet for procedural reasons the resolution was not acted on.

Unwilling to give up, the CMS obtained a statement from Lord Palmerston that the present policy did not prevent the holding of voluntary Bible classes on school premises, provided these were conducted outside school hours. When Sir Herbert Edwardes returned to India in 1862, Venn appealed to him as a member of the government of India to act on the Palmerstonian principle and introduce Bible classes on this informal basis.

Missionaries, however, understandably feared that this appeared to be official proselytizing and would engender anti-Christian hostility. Some of them also clashed with Venn's philosophy that it was not the task of missionary societies to educate the masses of India. They did not want conversion of adults to be the primary test of a missionary's work. John Barton complained to Venn that it was discouraging when the parent committee did not place a primary value on schools. "Either let us give up on schools altogether, or let them be supported by the sympathy, the interest, and the contributions of friends at home."[44] Barton's philosophy was to maintain the highest standards in all mission schools so that eventually the government would cede to the missions management of government schools as well. Venn had no time for this idea. If nothing else, financial considerations ruled it out. The new system of grants-in-aid did not save the Society money. Instead, Society expenditures were increased and educational programs were costing more than ever.[45]

Venn turned his energies toward increasing grants for schools in India and promoting teacher-training institutions. In a deputation to the sympathetic Sir Charles Wood, he pointed out that grants established through the 1854 Despatch were not stimulating voluntary societies to enlarge their programs as was intended. Restrictive rules of regional Indian governments resulted in a rapid increase in Society expenditures on education. Venn requested increased grants with independent schools receiving them on the basis of a per-capita allowance determined by examination results.

For the next several years the CMS continued conversations with the government over details of problems with the grants-in-aid system. Despite initial hesitation to use such aid, the missionaries increasingly worked with the system. In the end the missions accepted it.

Many of the questions that had exercised Western Christians about Hinduism and Islam in the first decades of the nineteenth century, such as *sati* (widow-burning), had been dealt with by 1860. Government sanction for idolatry ended in 1841, although complete separation did not take place until 1863 under Earl Elgin. One of the remaining problems that converts to Christianity in India faced was civil disability in such areas as the marriage laws. The CMS Committee was divided on this issue. Venn submitted a position paper, which proved unacceptable.[46] He attempted to adduce biblical teaching on divorce and remarriage in such circumstances (cf. 1 Cor. 7:10–16) and concluded that remarriage is problematic. The committee's final statement reflected its failure to reach agreement.[47] In 1864 Sir Henry Maine introduced legislation before the Indian government that legalized the remarriage of an Indian convert to Christianity when the spouse had terminated the first marriage on religious grounds. The CMS found it convenient merely to acquiesce to what the Legislative Council had decided, since it had failed to find any alternative solution.

In India, as in Africa, missionaries often found themselves in precarious positions between government and the people they served. While most of this chapter has dealt with struggles with education, we might pause to look at one such instance.

Over a period of years, the missionaries in Bengal came to be highly critical of the indigo planting system.[48] By the early 1850s there was hostility between the missionaries and the planters. In 1854 the Bengal Missionary Conference discussed oppression of the ryots (peasants) by the zamindars (planters).[49] The zamindars exploited the ryots; they also opposed ryot conversions to Christianity. The following year the conference again dealt with the zamindari system and brought the matter to public notice. In 1856 the missionaries petitioned the Legislative Council to reform the zamindari system.

The missionaries were drawn ever more deeply into political and social issues. James Vaughn wrote to Venn in 1857 about his dilemma—he felt he had to speak out against injustice but was reluctant to act politically.[50] Venn responded with careful advice on how to proceed in cases where native Christians were discriminated against.[51] Another CMS missionary, James Long, became even more deeply involved.

In April 1860 Long wrote to Venn about an appeal fifty ryots made to him to help them escape oppression at the hands of a planter.[52] Other missionaries became involved in the problem. Tensions began to build between the missionaries and the planters, who enjoyed the favor of the government of India. In March 1861 Venn wrote to Long assuring him of the Society's interest in him and in the cause of the ryots. He also referred Long to the Society's policy statement on "Politics and Missions." About that time Long was employed by the government as translator for a Bengali play entitled *Nil Darpan*[53]. The play stung the indigo planters and they quickly preferred charges of libel against Long. In what was freely acknowledged to be a rigged trial, Long was convicted, fined 1,000 rupees, and sentenced to one month's imprisonment. The case backfired for the planters. Long became a popular hero among the common people in Bengal, and the British public rallied to his side. The CMS published a Minute on the case and expressed full support for Long.[54] In a letter of sympathy to Long following his trial and conviction, Venn commented on the growing problem white settlers were facing in the colonies because of racism.[55]

New Zealand

A year before Venn joined the CMS secretariat in 1841, the Treaty of Waitangi was signed. The British government reluctantly accepted New Zealand as a colony in order to keep the French out of the region and to protect the Maoris against the swelling tide of European settlers.

The Society opposed colonization of New Zealand; but when it became obvious that settlers were bound to come, the cession of the islands to the British crown seemed the only way to ensure the rights of the Maoris. The missionaries acted as intermediaries between the British representatives and the Maori chiefs.

The settlers soon found the Treaty of Waitangi too restrictive and began circumventing it. The missionaries and their friends immediately became champions of native rights, and thus implacable foes of the colonists. Bishop Selwyn fully supported the missionaries and the Maoris. The CMS printed and circulated his early reports on the progress of Christianity in the islands because "they are eminently calculated to vindicate the character of the Mission work in New Zealand, and to draw forth the Christian sympathy and earnest prayers of many in its behalf."[56] The colonists had advocates in the homeland, too.[57]

In 1844 Coates, on behalf of the CMS, submitted a statement to Lord Stanley, colonial secretary, in rebuttal to the report of a parliamentary committee that was sympathetic to the colonists.[58] The following year Stanley ordered the governor to enforce the treaty. Unfortunately, because of their land holdings, the CMS missionaries themselves became embroiled in the problem. In 1846 the Society submitted another memorial to Stanley calling for a peaceful settlement of the disputes and urging that the Treaty of Waitangi be upheld.

With the death of Coates in April 1846 affairs in New Zealand languished for the next six months.[59] Sir George Grey became governor in 1845, and under his administration conditions became stabilized. In March 1848 Venn rejoiced that the missionaries' land question had been settled, even if imperfectly.[60] How imperfectly became clear within the month. The dispute centered on Archdeacon Henry Williams, who was separated from the CMS in 1849 on the basis of confused facts and amid divided opinion. The question of native rights was largely forgotten for several years.

The conflict erupted again in 1860, in the Taranaki war. In 1853 New Zealand had been given a colonial legislature, and the following year Sir George Grey returned to England. Under Governor Browne native rights were eroded. When word of war reached London, the CMS made plans to appeal to the colonial secretary. They wanted Governor Browne recalled and intended to lobby against a bill then before Parliament, which would have taken away more of the Maoris' land.[61]

The memorial presented to the Duke of Newcastle, colonial secretary, runs to forty-six pages and includes detailed appendices.[62] It includes an extensive historical and legal review of developments in New Zealand from the time of the signing of the Treaty of Waitangi. Venn's attention to legal detail is in full display.

The memorial offered three suggestions. First, the home government was urged to make an authoritative declaration that tribal rights would be respected. Second, a way should be found to rescind the martial law placed in force by Governor Browne and at the same time conciliate the Maoris by a peaceful solution. Third, the Society asked for the home government to set up adjudication procedures for the most difficult of the land disputes, the Waitara case.

A second pamphlet three months later presented a further critique of the New Zealand government's policies and defended the rights of the Maoris.[63] The burden of argument throughout was that the Maori should be fully respected. The colonists held that the Maori was not worthy of full dignity. A treaty made with him was not as binding as one drawn up with a European. But the CMS wanted Maori claims honored in "their full integrity." The concept of trusteeship entered in as well. The Society resisted selling certain land because it was being held in trust for the Maoris.[64] The CMS was outraged that Maori land was being taken by unscrupulous whites. The Maoris had accepted Christianity from the missionaries. Now the missionaries were embarrassed and the Maoris perplexed as other Europeans inflicted hurt on them.

Bishop Selwyn stood firmly and courageously with the missionaries and the Maoris in the struggle. He tried to intervene during the war in order to bring about peace. For his efforts he incurred criticism.[65] Governor Grey replaced Governor Browne in 1861, and this marked the beginning of a new era. Grey was a friend and member of the CMS and committed to a policy of justice toward the Maoris.

Circumstances in New Zealand were quite different from those of West Africa or India. The indigenous peoples were actually declining in numbers during most of the period 1840–65. Rapid growth in the European population introduced European civilization, with the accompanying social and economic system. Aside from the question of "native rights," during Venn's tenure the CMS exerted little influence on New Zealand colonial policies.

NOTES

1. See J. Roselli, *Lord William Bentinck.*

2. P. Spear, "Bentinck and Education," p.78.

3. Contrasting interpretations of this debate and the issues are given in Paton, *Alexander Duff,* and A. Mayhew, *The Education of India.* Spear, "Bentinck," redresses the unbalanced emphasis on Macaulay's influence.

4. Mayhew, *Education,* p. 14.

5. Spear, "Bentinck," p. 97.

6. CI1/L3, July 11, 1843, J. Long. Cf. July 7, 1843, Instructions to Rev. and Mrs. E. Johnson.

7. VB 24.

8. CI1/L4, Jan. 19, 1846, to J. Tucker.

9. VB 25:17.

10. VB 26:81f.

11. CI3/L2, Feb. 27, 1843, to W. R. Fletcher and J. Vaupell. The principle was repeated, May 24, 1851, to C. W. Isenberg, with reference to the failure of an experiment in educating young Ethiopians. No details are given.

12. VB 42:231.

13. VB 49:429f. See M. E. Gibbs, *The Anglican Church in India,* for an account of the first years of St. John's College.

14. VB 54:189.

15. CI3/L2, April 7, 1852, G. Candy; CMS Minutes, April 11, 1853, 29:365–66; May 27, 1853, 29:417.

16. CI2/028(c) (d) (e) New OII, from Bishop Dealtry, Madras; CI1/016–17, August 1852, petition adopted by Calcutta Missionary Conference.

17. CI1/L4, Aug. 26, 1853, Instructions to Missionaries.

18. G. A. Oddie, *The Reverend James Long and Protestant Missionary Policy in Bengal, 1840–1872.*

19. See Duff's memorandum attached to the 1853 memorial, VB 65, appendix, 35f.

20. Knight, 1882, p. 231.

21. See, "Education in India," *CM Intelligencer,* Sept. 1854, pp. 205–12, for the Salisbury Square interpretation of the Despatch of 1854.

22. Oddie, *James Long,* p. 117.

23. CMS, Com. of Correspondence Minutes, Nov. 27, 1855, 31:72f, and Dec. 4, 1858, 31:77f. It is instructive to study developments in Ceylon during the same period. See K. M. DeSilva, *Social Policy and Missionary Organization in Ceylon, 1840–1855.*

24. VB 82.

25. CI1/0177/54, from C. B. Leupolt, May 21, 1857, July 15, 1857; CI1/079/273, May 19, 1857, from G. G. Cuthbert; CI1/L4, July 10, 1857, to Cuthbert.

26. CI1/079/270, June 19, 1857, from G. G. Cuthbert.

27. G/AC1/13, July 29(?), 1857, to C. W. Lepp.

28. CI1/L4, Aug. 26, 1857, to G. G. Cuthbert.

29. E.g., CI3/L3, Sept. 25, 1857, to J. S. S. Robertson; CI1/L4, Sept. 25, 1857, to G. G. Cuthbert; CI2/L5, Sept. 25, 1857, to P. S. Royston.

30. VB 95.

31. VB 96.

32. The first volume of the *CM Intellingencer* carried an article entitled "The true strength of empires—a lesson from history"(July 1849). The writer said, "Nor is there any single lesson written with greater emphasis on every page of history, than this— that God ever bestows great empires for the *truest and highest* good of the governed; and that wherever that good is not steadfastly pursued, such a kingdom carries within it the sure seed and element of decay."

33. CI1/L4, Oct. 10, 1857, to G. G. Cuthbert.

34. CI1/L4, Oct. 26, 1857, to G. G. Cuthbert.

35. VB 98.

36. G/AC1/13, Nov. 4, 1857, to S. M. Humbert.

37. VB 97.

38. CI1/L5, Jan. 2, 1858, to G. G. Cuthbert.

39. G/AC1/13, Jan. 9, 1858, to Maj. Horsely.

40. G/AC1/13, Feb. 11, 1858, to Hercules Scott; CMS *Proceedings*, 1857-58, pp. 210f., commented on the relationship between England and India as threefold: (1) "England stands related to India as exercising sovereignty over the people." Christians especially were concerned for religious and moral principles. (2) "Parents to uneducated children." England must provide education for the masses. Missionary societies should provide the religious instruction. (3) "A Christian towards a heathen country." The Christian country has a duty to impart the gospel of Christ.

41. G/AC1/14, Sept. 30, 1858, to W. Edwards.

42. Private Journal, Dec. 6, 1858 (Stock, II:253ff.). Cf. CI1/L5, Dec. 9, 1858, and Jan. 3, 1858, to G. G. Cuthbert. Venn reports that a "National Declaration" was in preparation—as a means of ensuring that the minister for India interpreted the Royal Proclamation in its "Christian"sense. Cf. also, "The Royal Proclamation," *CM Intelligencer,* Jan. 1859, pp. 1-10.

43. CI1/037/19, May 14, 1861, from J. Barton.

44. CI1/L5, July 8, 1861, to J. Barton.

45. VB 141.

46. VB 152.

47. For the background, see B. B. Kling, *The Bengal Indigo Disturbances, 1859-1862,* pp. 256-66.

48. Reported in *CM Intelligencer,* Dec. 1854, pp. 287f.

49. Sept. 7, 1857, from J. Vaughan.

50. CI1/L4, Oct. 26, 1859, to J. Vaughan.

51. April 9, 1860, and June 18, 1860, from J. Long. See Oddie, *James Long,* chap. 5, for a detailed account of the episode.

52. CI1/L5, March 7, 1861, to J. Long; VB 118.

53. *Nil Darpen* is translated as *Mirror of Indigo Planters.*

54. VB 126.

55. CI1/L5, Sept. 9, 1861, to J. Long.

56. CN/L4, June 23, 1843, to Bishop Selwyn.

57. CN/L4, July 14, 1845, to missionaries and catechists.

58. CN/L4, Nov. 28, 1844, to T. Chapman; Dandeson Coates, *The New Zealanders and Their Lands* (London, 1844).

59. CN/L5, May 23, 1846, to T. Chapman; Dec. 2, 1846, to W. Williams.

60. CN/L5, March 3, 1848, to R. Maunsell.

61. CN/L6, July 18, 1860, to Archdeacon Kissling, and, same date, to Archdeacon Hadfield.

62. VB 121.

63. VB 122.

64. CN/L7, Aug. 25, 1864, to Archdeacon Brown; and, same date, to R. Burrows.

65. H. W. Tucker, *Memoir of the Life of G. A. Selwyn,* chap. 4.

8
Evangelical Elder

The last years of Henry Venn's life were marked by his repeatedly unsuccessful attempts to retire. He first indicated his intent to leave the secretariat at the dedication of the new CMS offices in Salisbury Square, London, in March 1862. "I have already reached nearly the longest tenure of office of any of my predecessors," he said. "I desire to leave the mantle I wear—which I received from those who have gone up—for those whom He, whose prerogative it is to select men for His work, may call to be my colleagues and my successors."[1]

Apparently Venn's declared intention to retire received no official notice. In the spring of 1862 he employed his younger son, Henry, as his administrative assistant. For the next seven years Venn managed to continue doing the work of secretary with the help of his son.

The summer of 1860 Venn had moved from Highbury to Mortlake with his daughter Henrietta. That fall, son John became curate at Mortlake and the family was together again, except for the younger son, Henry, who was in his last year at Cambridge. The move forced Venn to sort through letters and packets, which he had packed up in the rectory at Clapham in 1813. He was filled with nostalgia for his family and their past. "All this will hardly be intelligible to the 'degenerate' rising generation who write short notes and destroy them as soon as read," he said. "When the postage was 8d. and 11d., we thought over our letters and threw our souls into them. Alas for the penny post!"[2]

In the old Salisbury Square office building Venn occupied a drab room from which he banned any sort of luxury. The desk, chairs, bookcases, and carpet were old and grimy with London soot. When the CMS occupied the new building they assigned the best room to Venn with two windows looking out on the square. But he refused to allow any new furniture to be installed. Always sensitive to the need for keeping costs as low as possible, he insisted on exercising economy in headquarters management.

Although his health was increasingly a concern, Venn did nothing to shield himself. His pattern of working twelve to fifteen hours a day and occasionally far into the night was not easily broken.[3] On days when he went to Salisbury Square, he arrived soon after nine for staff prayers. By ten o'clock he was at his desk. Many days he never left the desk until five.

After Venn declared his desire to retire from office, he often mentioned his difficulty in keeping up with the work. He apologized to correspondents that he could answer only a part of the letters he received.[4] In December 1862 another CMS secretary, John Chapman, died. At the same time Venn's longtime confidante, William Knight, decided to resign and leave office the following spring. Venn lamented that "at an advanced age I am again left at work while others are removed."[5] The summer of 1863 he took his last holiday trip to the Continent with Henrietta and Henry.[6] Holidays abroad gave him more complete respite from his duties than working vacations in Wales or Scotland.

Now in their fourth generation, Evangelicals were beginning to demonstrate a limited capacity for self-criticism. Various Evangelicals observed that the Evangelical outlook was toward the past and suggested that as a movement it had completed its work. The issue struck close home for Venn in son John's own struggle for religious identity. Considering himself naturally inclined to skepticism, John was disturbed by the inconsistency of his own position. He affirmed Evangelicalism only because he was born into the tradition; he could not claim to hold to unique Evangelical presuppositions out of personal conviction. His personal disquiet as well as the fact that the Mortlake rector "was a humbug" led him to resign his curacy at Mortlake and return to Cambridge.[7]

Wisely Venn did not take issue with his son. He continued to speak to him in the old terms. After preaching a missionary sermon at St. Paul's, Clapham, Venn told John of his feelings while standing in the pulpit where both his father and his grandfather once served, knowing that he was the third generation and remembering that his son was now the fourth generation "of those who have endeavoured to witness to the truths of the blessed gospel which brings salvation and peace to the soul of fallen man. Many an earnest prayer did I put up as I knelt at the communion table during the prayers that God might make your witness bright and strong."[8] Nevertheless he knew full well of John's doubts.

John made an intellectual break with Evangelicalism in 1864. He was still a priest but his heart was not in it. Venn saw the forces of nationalism and Roman Catholicism as important in shaping the church. "Certainly the present day appears to be more favourable than ever I knew it before. The very opposite opinions which exist apparently in equal force, the absence of any recognized standard of biblical composition, the liberty of private judgement, these and many other things leave a young man more free to the guidance of the divine counsel than was formerly the case."[9] Venn's comments show not only his capacity to put things in a positive light, but also his attempts to understand his son and draw him toward the church.

Venn took keen interest in the 1859 revival, seeking to evaluate its character and to give it missionary purpose. He believed the revival posed new possibilities and wanted these newly released energies properly channeled. At his suggestion, the CMS sent a deputation to visit revival centers in Ireland, both to learn about the movement and to challenge people to missionary service.

As he contemplated retirement, Venn repeatedly expressed the desire to prepare a summary of what he had learned from his years as secretary. His contemporaries both in the secretariat and outside were passing away. He was frequently reminded that his own tenure was limited and he wished to transmit to the next generation the fruit of his experience.[10] In the autumn of 1864 Venn fell seriously ill again. For an entire month he was unable to read or write.[11] Late in November he returned to work.

Venn's failing strength and the lack of continuity among other members of the secretariat meant that certain things were slighted. Correspondence with individual missionaries was one duty sacrificed to more pressing matters. "The 'cyclone' of ordinary and necessary business sweeps down all but our best resolutions."[12]

In 1865 Venn addressed the Islington Clerical Society on the "Retrospect and prospect of the operations of the Church Missionary Society."[13] The CMS had hit a plateau in the early 1860s after a period of rapid expansion during the 1850s. Some notable senior missionaries died during Venn's final decade. New recruits were not forthcoming. Also, income stopped expanding at the rapid rate of the 1850s. Mission supporters began asking about the future of missions. Why had the revival of 1859–60 failed to result in great missionary response?

Venn told the Islington meeting that even though Evangelical influence had grown, missionary zeal had in fact declined. Missionary meetings were not as well attended and were less interesting. The spirit of sacrifice that had marked the missionary movement in earlier years was missing. He could also have pointed to continuing controversy in the church and growth in home missions as reasons for the falling off. But he was in a philosophical mood and advised the church against assuming that evangelization of the whole world depended on the Church of England or even on Europe and North America. The important thing was to send out the right kind of people so that an indigenous church might emerge to carry forward the evangelistic task.

Venn showed his capacity for optimism in a letter to Archdeacon Henry Williams in New Zealand. He knew that the archdeacon received conflicting interpretations of the situation within the English church. Venn assured Williams, "as one of the aged clergy to an aged brother," that he had never known such a large and able group of younger men who were "sound in the good old evangelical doctrine" as there were in the church in 1865. The mood was entirely different now from what it was in 1820. "The old armament with which our Fathers fought the battle of the Truth will not serve now; but I am full of confident hope that the truth of the gospel will not only continue with us but will prevail more and more."[14] Venn was taking a longer view and he saw no need to panic.

While on holiday during the summer of 1865, Venn told his brother John that being away from his regular responsibilities allowed him to see more clearly what he still needed to do by way of gathering up the "fragments of my desultory labours" in order to pass along the lessons that might be of use to his successors. "I hope to devote myself to this as my primary, or rather final, employment."[15]

That autumn Venn gave serious thought to his plan to prepare a manual of principles and practices of the CMS.[16] It remained only a plan, however, as other duties pressed on him. During the winter he was in failing health. He wrote to John Thomas in India that "if the lameness in my lower limbs extends to my right arm, I shall soon be a cripple and laid aside."[17] But he managed to continue working.

The summer of 1866 he wrote to the Sierra Leone pastor, James Quaker, that at age seventy he now hoped to be released from his work. The Reverend John Mee, formerly on the staff of the British and Foreign Bible Society, joined the secretariat that year and Venn was hopeful that he would soon be able to retire.

Venn's physical condition continued to decline. His knee was becoming lame, "making me so long about everything."[18] He now spent only three days each week at Salisbury Square. By the end of 1866 he relinquished to John Mee the writing of the annual report. This was the first time since 1842 that he did not prepare the report.

At this time the London Secretaries' Association was preoccupied with the question of "native agency" and the role of the missionary society, and asked Venn to prepare a paper on the subject, which member societies might use in their work. This was an important opportunity to summarize his many years of experience. He first agreed but then reneged on the assignment. In the April meeting he proposed instead to use a paper recently drawn up by H. Carre Tucker, secretary of the Christian Vernacular Education Society. After reading the paper, the secretaries still wanted Venn to produce a paper for them on "the employment, management and support of native teachers."[19] This proved to be the last meeting of the LSA that Venn attended, and he never furnished them with the statement they wanted.

Throughout the spring and summer of 1867 Venn was in poor health. Edward Hutchison joined the secretariat as lay secretary.[20] Colonel Dawes, the senior lay secretary, was ill. The future of the secretariat was still not settled. A missionary on furlough saw Venn in June. He found him to be the "same old Mr. Venn—so brotherly, so warm, so affectionate, so confidential." Venn walked with great difficulty and had to use a walking stick. Physically he seemed to be a wreck; mentally he was as alert as ever. He had just read through the two-volume *Acts of the Apostles* by Baumgarten because he was studying again the principles of missionary work.[21]

By the fall of 1867 Venn's health improved and he threw himself into a new responsibility that claimed his attention in the next few years. In order to counteract the influence of the English Church Union, Evangelicals and moderate churchpeople established the Church Association in 1865. The association wanted to stir up the church to the dangers of ritualism and sought to ascertain the legal force of laws pertaining to ritual by instituting suits in the courts. Parliament finally took up the ritual controversy in early 1867 and the government appointed a Royal Commission rather than face legislation proposed by Lord Shaftesbury, which would have checked further ritual innovations. The purpose of the commission was to inquire into differences of practice in the church, which had resulted from "varying interpretations put upon the Rubrics, Orders, and Directions for regulating the course and conduct of Public Worship . . . more especially with respect to the ornaments used in the churches, etc., and the vestments worn by ministers during the time of their ministration."[22]

The government appointed twenty-eight commissioners, but Evangelicals were not included. Venn was named to remedy this gap.[23] He had no background on the history of English ecclesiastical law and felt he had to master it. Lord Chichester later recalled how astonished he was when Venn told him of the books he had read in order to qualify himself on the subject.[24] He tried to approach the matter from several angles. To be fair to those favoring ritualism, he read literature with that viewpoint.[25] He studied the question through the history of Dissent, asking whether the Reformation had to lead to Dissent or whether there might have been other alternatives. "One point is clearer than ever to me, that the question of 'habits, vestments,' etc., once raised in a Protestant Church, if not wisely suppressed, will inflame and ruin that Church."[26] Evangelicals suspected that the clamor for disestablishment was linked to the ritualist controversy.

In December 1867 Venn was confined to two rooms of his home because of his lame leg. Yet he insisted on attending the Ritual Commission even though he had to go on crutches.[27] Indeed, he was one of the most conscientious of commission members and was present forty-four times during the next two years.

Disestablishment became the subject of public debate in 1868 and 1869 when the Irish church was disestablished. Venn believed deeply in the establishment and wanted to see it maintained. Venn's policy for government of the churches overseas was based on maintenance of the supremacy of the crown. But when interest in disestablishment grew, he knew that he had to study the matter more seriously. He asked his son John to help him find books on disestablished churches, particularly the Protestant Episcopal Church in the United States. Was the church in America genuinely disestablished or were all churches equally established? What would disestablishment mean for the church in England and Ireland? He wanted to work out his own position on the question.[28]

Venn did not attend the CMS anniversary meeting in May 1868. This was already the second year since he gave up responsibility for the annual report. During that month he was again ill and could not work.[29] In the summer he resumed his work on Ritual Commission concerns. His outlook on the church in general was relaxed. He wrote to the bishop of Waiapu that "if God overturns the Establishment, I hope I shall cheerfully accommodate myself to a new state of things."[30]

The Ritual Commission dragged on but Venn's interest in it never flagged. Toward the end he had to be carried in a chair from the Dean's Yard of Westminster Abbey into the Jerusalem Chamber where the commission met. He had formed some alliances within the commission that he enjoyed. He and the bishop of St. David's became firm allies. "In nearly every division we have been on the same side—and he said to me the other day, 'we regard you as our Patriarch!' " Venn wrote to his son.[31]

Venn took the work of the Ritual Commission seriously. From the beginning he was dubious about its practical value. But he felt an honest effort should be made to clarify the issues. The commission presented four reports, which recommended that all variations on traditional vestments should be restrained, lights and incense were to be prohibited, the rubrics and Lectionary should be revised. Venn held out for the exclusion of the Apocryphal books from the Lectionary, but failed to win his point. The new Lectionary was the only concrete result of the commission's work.

Another responsibility fell on Venn's shoulders when the editor of the *Christian Observer* died in 1869. Venn assumed temporary responsibility, writing quite a few of the articles himself. Through the *Christian Observer* he attempted to create Evangelical interest in the Ritual Commission by interpreting its work and educating his readers in the history of ritual law and practice. An article titled "Alleged Evangelical Ritualistic Irregularities," was a statesmanlike review of charges brought against Evangelicals by the Ritualists that demonstrated prevalent attitudes of different periods of history, the ambiguity of laws, and the Evangelical attitude on each issue.

Venn's November 1870 review of the work of the Ritual Commission influenced some Members of Parliament to support legislative action on the commission recommendations.[32] Archbishop Tait sent a copy to Gladstone, who admitted that it placed the issues in clear perspective. At the archbishop's suggestion, Venn published the article as a separate pamphlet. The pamphlet was distributed to nearly three hundred members of both houses of Parliament and received favorable notice.

What had begun as a temporary responsibility turned into a permanent one. Month after month Venn edited the *Christian Observer*. Its future prospects seemed to pale. It was in financial trouble. Yet Venn felt it was important to maintain the journal as an Evangelical voice. His goal was to train several younger men to assume the editorship. The *Christian Observer* intended to continue in the founders' tradition of exposing false doctrine and superstition.

Meanwhile, Venn continued to carry CMS responsibilities. He was pleased with John Mee's work in the secretariat for the first several years. But Mee wanted to be Venn's successor and tried to secure the position for himself by resigning his salary and claiming legal precedence over the paid secretaries. This annoyed Venn, and the committee refused to accept the arrangement. Mee resigned. Once again plans for the future of the secretariat had suffered a setback. Venn, however, was feeling somewhat improved in health after two years of reduced activity, and he began handling more correspondence.[33]

In January 1870 Venn announced that he would retire from all active work in the CMS at midyear. The committee announced a call to prayer with a special service at the Church Missionary House to seek divine guidance in finding the successor to Venn.[34] By summer no successor had been found and Venn was still working, although he could now write only a few letters a day and some days none at all.[35]

Travel was becoming more burdensome and he went to Salisbury Square only twice a week. "Each visit brings upon me work at home so that with CMS and *Christian Observer* and Ritual Commission I am as much worked as my strength can sustain," he told his children.[36] Occasionally he remarked in his letters to missionaries about the infirmities of age.[37] And yet no successor was found.

Most of what he wrote for the *Christian Observer* during this period was either reviews or articles based on the work of the Ritual Commission.[38] He was also concerned about the apparent cleavage between the generations. He wrote "On separation between the younger and elder evangelicals,"[39] showing that differences of opinion had always existed and been respected among Evangelicals.

To foster an understanding attitude he published correspondence between his grandfather and the young Charles Simeon as an illustration of what the relationship between the generations might be.[40] He also took an interest in the question of church and state and published substantial articles on the subject.

In spite of these efforts, the existence of the periodical was threatened. The appearance of a new publication, *Evening News*, begun in April 1871, cut into the *Christian Observer*'s circulation. In the first month alone the *Christian Observer*'s circulation dropped by a hundred. Venn was determined to continue through the end of the year and then either let it die or turn it into a quarterly.[41]

Venn fell and injured himself in October 1871, but he kept at his work.[42] He could not really bear to close the *Christian Observer*, and he resisted the pleadings of Elliott, Garratt, and others who wanted to convert it into a quarterly. He saw that move as only a stopgap. "If such a voice can find no listeners in these busy days, let it cease. To have maintained a hearing for 70 years is a great fact."[43] So he carried on.

In January 1872 the Reverend Henry Wright was appointed by the CMS as honorary clerical secretary. Wright impressed Venn well. Venn was hopeful that he would soon be released from all responsibility. He still had the *Christian Observer* editorship on his mind. He told his son that as soon as an editor was found "I shall be ready to shut myself up and nurse my bad leg."[44]

Late in April, Venn suffered a serious fall and was unable to walk for some weeks. He recovered enough to continue going to Salisbury Square. He refused the committee's offer of a carriage and drove all the way. In June he made his last visit to Church Missionary House. His mind was as clear as ever, but his slowness of movement became an increasing burden.[45]

He now seemed to be removed from the secretariat. All his papers had been brought to his home, and Wright occupied Venn's room at Church Missionary House. He felt optimistic about the future of missions so that he could "see the possibility of the conversion of the whole world to the faith of Christ."[46] His appointment now was to await his dismissal.

Meanwhile, Venn still had the *Christian Observer* to edit.[47] During August he worked on an account of the Niger Mission and looked forward eagerly to the expected visit of Bishop Crowther early in the new year.[48] He also kept threatening to begin sorting and organizing his papers and letters. The current work of the CMS and the *Christian Observer* caused him to put it off.[49] His sister Emelia spent much time with him and offered to help him put his things in order, "but I will not let her set to work without me." In October he finally began to work on sorting his papers and was unhappy to find them in a confused state. He was tempted to destroy the whole collection rather than attempt to sort it, but he discovered some documents that belonged to the CMS and decided that it was the better part of wisdom to do the necessary if unpleasant task.[50]

Venn now felt cut off from the work of the Society and many of his old associates. In November he submitted his third and final resignation as honorary clerical secretary. On November 19 the Committee of Patronage nominated Venn to be a vice president of the Society. The committee voted the following resolution on November 26:

> That in confirming the Resolution of the Patronage Committee, and thus conferring on the Rev. H. Venn the highest distinction that is in their power to bestow, the Committee desire to express their sense of the utter inadequacy of such honour to represent the indebtedness of this Society to their beloved and honoured friend, and, at the same time, to record their devout thankfulness to Almighty God for the token of His favour towards them and their work in raising up one so specially qualified for the work he had to do.[51]

Venn accepted his election as a vice president with a letter in which he once again stated his concept of the secretariat. The secretaries were the executives of the committee, not mere clerks. At the same time he affirmed the high value he placed on the committee as the source of authority for the total work of the Society.

The elder Venn son, John, had married in 1867 and the younger, Henry, in 1869. The first grandchild was born the end of 1869 and two more were born before Venn died. His daughter Henrietta continued to make her home with her father. He was concerned that she be provided for after he was gone.

In December he wrote to his sons that he was gradually losing the use of his hands as well as his limbs. He had no premonition of an early death but he looked forward to their approaching visit. He wanted the family to speak freely and positively about the possibility that he would soon leave them in order to prepare Henrietta for his death.[52]

On December 30, 1872, Venn wrote to the senior Sierra Leone pastor, James Quaker.[53] His handwriting was now almost illegible. The following day he wrote his final letter. Again it was to Africa. This was to Henry Johnson, who had recently done outstanding work at Islington in languages and was now working on linguistics in Sierra Leone. He encouraged Johnson to return to England for further study in preparation for his witness among the Muslims.[54]

On January 9, 1873, Venn put in several hours' work with C. J. Elliott on a paper on the sacraments, which was to be published in the *Christian Observer*. In the evening he received his old friend CMS president Lord Chichester. The following day he suffered a stroke and was confined to bed. His mind remained clear, but he could hardly speak. The family came to his bedside and his elder son administered Holy Communion to his father. On January 13 he quietly died. The following Thursday, January 17, his funeral was held at Mortlake Church and, as he had instructed, he was buried in a simple grave in Mortlake Cemetery. The archbishop of Canterbury was unable to officiate at the funeral. In his place Bishop Russell, newly consecrated bishop of China, and the vicar of Mortlake led the service.

Tributes to Venn's life and work poured in from many parts of the world.[55] One of the most generous tributes came from Bishop Wilberforce with whom Venn had often differed. Wilberforce wrote to the family, "I honour especially in him the dedication of a life to a noble cause with an uncompromising entireness of devotion which had in it all the elements of true Christian heroism. You must look on his life as a grand epic poem which has ended in a *euthanasia* of victory and rest."[56]

His nephew James Fitzjames Stephen, who did not share Venn's religious views, nevertheless was moved by his character. "Henry Venn was the most triumphant man I ever knew," said Stephen. "I never knew a sturdier man." And when he learned of Venn's death, Stephen responded, "Somehow his life was so bold, so complete, and so successful that I did not feel the least as if his death was a thing to be sad about."[57]

The CMS immediately established the Henry Venn Native Church Fund to provide grants for native church development. In 1878 a steamer named the *Henry Venn* was built and sent to the Niger for Bishop Crowther's use.

NOTES

1. VB 130:194.
2. Knight, 1882, p. 328.
3. Ibid., p. 327.

4. CA1/L7, Aug. 22, 1862, to J. Quaker.

5. C/CE/L4, Dec. 27, 1862, to C. C. Fenn.

6. Venn MSS C34, July 31, 1863, to son John.

7. John Venn, Autobiographical Sketches (Venn MSS F27), pp. 102-5.

8. Venn MSS C34, Oct. 22, 1862, to son John.

9. Ibid., Oct. 27, 1866.

10. CCH/L2, Jan. 11, 1864, to Bishop of Victoria.

11. CN/L7, Nov. 26, 1864, to Bishop of Waiapu.

12. CI1/L6, Feb. 7, 1865, to J. Welland.

13. VB 147.

14. CN/L7, March 27, 1865, to Archdeacon H. Williams.

15. Knight, 1882, p. 342.

16. Venn MSS C34, Oct. 28, 1865.

17. CI2/L7, Jan. 26, 1866, to J. Thomas.

18. Venn MSS C34, Nov. 14, 1866.

19. LSA Minutes, Jan. 9, Feb. 3, March 13, and April 10, 1867.

20. CI3/L4, March 26, 1867, to T. K. Weatherhead; CA1/L8, Aug. 23, 1867, to J. Sass.

21. Knight, 1880, p. 424.

22. Quoted by Stock, II:654.

23. Venn MSS C34, Aug. 8, 1867.

24. Knight, 1880, p. 396.

25. Knight, 1882, Oct. 14, 1867.

26. Ibid.

27. Venn MSS C34, Dec. 9, 1867.

28. Ibid., March 27, 1868, to son John.

29. CI3/L4, May 20, 1868.

30. CN/L7, Sept. 1, 1868, to Bishop of Waiapu.

31. Venn MSS C34, May 17, 1869, to son John.

32. VB 189.

33. CA1/L8, Aug. 23, 1869, to H. Alcock.

34. *CM Record*, April 1870, pp. 97f.

35. CA1/L8, July 13, 1870, to J. Hamilton.

36. Venn MSS C34, Nov. 9, 1870, to John and Susie Venn.

37. VB 189.

38. CCH/L2, May 4, 1871, to T. McClatchie.

39. VB 186.

40. *Christian Observer*, 70:405, Jan. 1871, pp. 43-52.

41. Venn MSS C34, April 29 and Aug. 3, 1871, to son John.

42. Ibid., Oct. 9, 1871, to son John.

43. Ibid., Nov. 6, 1871, to son John.

44. Ibid., April 16, 1871, to son John.

45. Ibid., April 22, 1872, to son John.

46. Ibid., Aug. 4, 1872, to son John.

47. Ibid., Aug. 18, 1872, to Henrietta.

48. Ibid., Aug. 17, 1872, to Henrietta. No trace of his manuscript on the Niger Mission is to be found. Apparently it was never published.

49. Ibid., Aug. 20 and 21, 1872, to Henrietta.

50. Ibid., Oct. 11, 1872, to son John.

51. *CM Record*, Jan. 1873, p. 30.

52. Venn MSS C34, Dec. 22, 1872, to sons John and Henry.

53. CA1/L8.

54. CA1/L8, Dec. 31, 1872.

55. Obituaries of Venn appearing in the newspapers and periodicals of the day are listed in the bibliography.

56. Knight, 1882, p. 384.

57. L. Stephen, *Life of James Fitzjames Stephen*, pp. 87 and 300.

9

The Achievement of Henry Venn

Anyone who has filled an influential role as long as Henry Venn served the Church Missionary Society as honorary clerical secretary is bound to have accumulated both debits and credits to his account. Venn is no exception. In his lifetime he had his critics who objected to what they considered his autocratic administrative style or to specific decisions. They were less inclined to contest his basic insights and policies.

With the benefit of more than a century of history since Venn's death, how well does his work measure up to its promise? Peter Beyerhaus is representative of those who appreciate Venn's attempts at clarifying the goal of mission. In his judgment, "It was Venn's contribution that, after a long period of patriarchal, individualistic missionary work, he pointed the way to a 'church-centric' mission."[1]

Outstanding African historians who have taken stock of Venn's contribution from the angle of political development hold his name in high regard. According to E. A. Ayandele, Venn's indigenous church policy was attractive to the educated African for political rather than religious reasons. "It contained the principle of national independence in Church government" but was equally applicable to national political independence.[2]

Venn is not without his critics today. Those who have criticized him most sternly have been white Westerners. Stephen Neill has not hesitated to render a negative judgment. He charges Venn with theological wrongheadedness with his "sharp separation betweeen Church and mission," and, Neill says, when Venn's policies were actually put into practice, they produced "almost wholly disastrous" results.[3] He praises Bishop A. R. Tucker of Uganda as having advocated a much more correct ideal for the church–mission relationship. Neill's weighty criticisms call for careful examination of the record.

Venn began his tenure as CMS secretary during the period of British history that has been called the Age of Humanitarianism.[4] The humanitarian ideal directly shaped social attitudes. Humanitarians viewed the process of social transformation as conversion. They emphasized the importance of tapping the potential within an individual or a people. Such transformation had to be based on a voluntary, willed response from those being assisted. The classical liberal emphasis on respect for the individual was a key ingredient. This attitude of respect for the autonomy and integrity of the other extended to such questions as the control of the territory of another people.

The humanitarians could justify Britain's growing collection of colonies as only a temporary expedient.

Venn expressed his commitment to this philosophy of self-determination at many points. In Instructions to Missionaries in 1861, he exhorted them to "avoid putting yourself before them as a leader; rather stand behind them as a prompter and counselor." He insisted that "prompting to self-action is more important than inducing men to follow a leader."[5] The usual tendency is to feel that leadership means taking charge. Venn insisted that if one kept one's eye on the desired outcome, namely self-reliance, then a different approach must be taken. Rather than losing all influence with the young church, local adherents will gladly seek the counsel of a leader who respects their selfhood.

Along with an emphasis on inward and voluntary change, the humanitarians strongly opposed racism at a time when racialist concepts were on the rise.[6] By the 1850s theories of culture and race were being linked with evolution. Some of this theorizing was based on pseudo-scientific data, but it soon gained a wide following and rapidly altered the general public's attitude toward race. Christian missionaries during the 1850s and 1860s were among those who protested and argued against this powerful new idea, but to no avail. Eventually the missionaries would be swept up by this powerful stream. Even those who consciously opposed racism could never dissociate themselves from its taint.

Humanitarianism reached its crest about 1850. The next twenty-five years were a time of transition, which finally erupted into the Age of Imperialism for which the Berlin Congress of 1885 provides a convenient starting point and symbol. It was at this congress that the European powers partitioned West Africa as each vied for a share of that region.

Instead of the earlier "conversionist" ideal of the humanitarians, the imperialists advocated "trusteeship"—which translated into colonialism. They divided the world into two groups: the superior races and the lesser peoples. The lesser races were judged to be inherently incapable of developing to the same level as the superior races. But the superior races were duty-bound to come to the aid of the inferior peoples, helping them to manage their affairs. This they did by taking control of the territory of the weaker peoples to assure proper management of their affairs. "Trusteeship" rested on blatantly racist assumptions. Missionary societies and the people they commissioned as missionaries never successfully separated themselves from this new doctrine.

Venn's most creative period was the years 1846–61. His world-view was that of the humanitarian. During his final decade of service he struggled against the rising new tide. His most dramatic action was to secure the ordination of the first African Anglican bishop in 1864.

In the early 1850s Venn had begun to think about the possibility of consecrating an African and an Indian as bishops of their respective churches. He introduced the idea formally in 1857 in a letter to Mr. Labouchere, secretary for the colonies, suggesting that the time was ripe in West Africa.[7] In that letter he mentioned possible African candidates but concluded that Samuel Adjai Crowther was the only one who met all qualifications.

From the moment Venn first mooted his proposal, he began to meet missionary opposition. Henry Townsend, who with Crowther formed the leadership for the pioneer missionary party which went from Sierra Leone to Yorubaland to found the new mssion in 1846, appeared to want the bishop's mantle for himself and steadfastly opposed Venn's idea.[8] Other missionaries suggested that an African could not have jurisdiction over Europeans without a loss in prestige to the Europeans. Such opposition only steeled Venn's resolve to see an African consecrated bishop.

The man Venn had his eye on, Samuel Adjai Crowther, was a Yoruba who had been captured while a teenager by slavers. His ship was one of the fortunate few to be intercepted by a British patrol and forced to go to Freetown where the captives were freed. Young Adjai soon came into the care of missionaries, who gave him an education and brought him to Christian faith. In 1842–43 he attended the CMS Islington Institution and was ordained deacon and priest before returning to Sierra Leone. During this time in London, Venn met him for the first time. They forged a lifelong bond of friendship and mutual respect.

Crowther was not at all keen on Venn's proposal to make him a bishop. He knew his European missionary colleagues did not want him as their bishop and he understood the kinds of problems he would face if they were forced to accept him. He was also a man of great humility, deep piety, and commitment to his special vocation as Bible translator and evangelist. But he had a strong sense of duty and loyalty to Venn. In the end, Venn prevailed.[9] On June 19, 1864, Crowther was consecrated in Westminster Abbey as bishop of West Africa Beyond the British Territories. This meant that Venn had accepted a compromise with his missionaries in order to obtain the ordination at all. Crowther was assigned to head up the mission on the Niger rather than having charge of the Yoruba churches.

Venn could not justify Crowther's consecration on grounds that this represented the flowering of indigenous leadership, since Crowther was designated bishop of a territory whose language and culture were foreign to him. Venn also seemed to be contradicting his long-standing argument with high-church advocates of a mission being led only by a bishop, since Crowther was placed in charge of the Niger Mission—a mission he had headed since its founding in 1857. Initially no Europeans had been assigned to this mission. But Venn began clearing the way for Europeans to serve on the Niger under Crowther's supervision. He repudiated his earlier dictum of "native agency under European superintendence." He now advocated collegiality and mutuality.[10] Unfortunately all efforts to deploy European missionaries to the Niger during the first stage of that mission were aborted by death and various mishaps. It later proved to be extremely difficult to integrate Europeans into that mission in which only Africans had served the first thirty years.

For Venn there was almost a desperate urgency to break down the racist barriers that were beginning to rise against the non-Western peoples. He had always insisted that every people had the potential to achieve the same level of competence as Europeans—if given the opportunity. But he met an increasingly strong opposition in his own missionaries to such a conviction, and this attitude of superiority was now being reinforced by new theories of race. Venn wanted to make the point that every church had the right—indeed the capacity—to be headed by one native to its soil rather than a foreigner. In the end, Venn's vision of the indigenous church could not be sustained if racism or distinctions based on cultural differences gained the upper hand.

From the early days of his secretariat, the question that preoccupied Venn's mind was the new church: how to bring it into being through missionary agency; how to develop and protect its integrity; how to help it become rooted in the soil and economy of its native land; how to inspire this new church to become missionary in its self-understanding and practice. Another set of questions centered on the role of the missionary and mission agency: how to keep priorities clear and firm—not allowing the nature of the missionary task to be subverted by worthy, but distinctly different, purposes; how to eradicate missionary paternalism, which produces stultifying dependency in the new church; how to save the young church from the overpowering weight of the mission machine; how to encourage greater mobility on the part of the missionary agency; how to maintain missionaries in their vocation as pioneers instead of settling down as pastors of new churches, often at the expense of indigenous leadership.

Venn was not given the luxury of being able to develop his theories isolated from life. When in the 1840s he became convinced of how crucial it was that the new church become financially free of the mission, he set about implementing steps that would foster economic independence. He devolved responsibility for certain mission-sponsored programs on the local church in Sierra Leone as early as 1846 so they would gain experience in preparation for full self-government later. When the archbishop of Canterbury and the government approved creation of a bishopric of West Africa in 1852, Venn drafted the Constitution for a Native Pastorate. Contrary to the impression Neill gives that Venn precipitously inaugurated the Native Pastorate in 1860, he worked patiently—but deliberately—for many years to prepare both missionaries and church for what finally became the Native Pastorate Organisation.

Without a doubt, Venn would have agreed with Neill's contention that we dare not draw a "sharp separation between Church and mission" if we wish to remain faithful to Scripture. In a sermon he preached at the consecration of two missionary bishops on May 29, 1849, Venn emphasized the missionary responsibility of the whole church, a conclusion based on the primitive church at Antioch (cf. Acts 11:21ff.).[11] But Venn introduced further refinements. Like his contemporary Rufus Anderson, Venn differentiated between the work of a pastor and that of a missionary. For this he drew exegetical support from the Acts account of the early church.[12] Although Venn did not develop this point further, his instincts were sound. Not only did the apostle Paul emphasize the differences in ministry between himself and other leaders (cf. 1 Cor. 1:10–18) in practice, he adduced theological grounds for such specialization in the life on the church (cf. 1 Cor. 12, 14; Eph. 4:1–16) based on the Holy Spirit's grace-gifts.

In addition, Venn made a functional distinction between mission and missions. In the sermon already mentioned, he identified "the preaching of the Gospel to all nations, and to every creature," as the "paramount duty of the Church of Christ." The church is missionary by nature. But functionally the church sends missions of various kinds to many parts of the world. A mission is sent from one place to another. It is, by definition, foreign in sponsorship, leadership, support, and structure. Venn called this the "scaffolding," a temporary device to enable the building up of a new church in a place where there had been none.

Two further points need to be added. The work of the mission agency could be said to be completed only when the new church had itself caught the vision of mission and become part of the witnessing presence. Not only was this normative for every church everywhere; it was totally unrealistic to believe that the responsibility for world evangelization could be carried by a few Western missionary agencies. The Great Commission would be fulfilled only by enlisting the whole church worldwide in the great task of evangelization. One means of keeping this vision growing was for missionary agencies to set an example of continuous advance into the "regions beyond" rather than settling down. Venn specifically warned in his 1861 policy statement of the ways the "mission station" mentality endangers *mission*.[13]

Always concerned about deformations that long-term dependency spawns, Venn counseled patience and wisdom in implementing his suggestions for indigenizing a church. "In older missions," he said, "the change of system must be very gradual; for when a mission has grown up in dependence upon European missionaries and upon native agency salaried by European funds, the attempt to curtail summarily its pecuniary aid, before the introduction of a proper organization, will be like casting a person overboard before he has been taught to swim: it will be a great injustice to the native converts, and may seriously damage the work already accomplished."[14] Prudent leadership introduces innovations sensitively and responsibly.

As the oldest of the CMS's fields of labor, Neill rightly holds up Sierra Leone as furnishing the best test of Venn's ideas for bringing an indigenous church into its own after two generations of mission tutelage. The Native Pastorate Organisation, inaugurated in 1860, marked an important transition from mission to church. How abrupt and how sharp was the change?

In November 1860 ten Sierra Leonean pastors resigned their appointments by the Church Missionary Society and submitted their nine parishes and grammar school to the jurisdiction of the newly created Native Pastorate Organisation. This marked the transformation of these mission stations into regular parishes of the Sierra Leone church. The Native Pastorate assumed full responsibility for the support of the parishes and their ministry. The school had been financially independent already for some years and the churches had been contributing to the support of the pastors. Now the full burden of this support fell to them.

It is important to note the extent to which the CMS withdrew from Sierra Leone at this time. First, not all the parishes came under the new church structure. The Native Pastorate was not prepared to assume full responsibility and so four churches remained a CMS responsibility. The last of these was finally transferred to the Native Pastorate in 1877. Second, the CMS also continued to operate Fourah Bay College and the Female Institution. In the third place, the bishop of the Sierra Leone diocese was an Englishman who continued to draw a part of his financial support from the government.

In evaluating this experiment a generation later, Eugene Stock observed that it could not be considered a full-blown test of Venn's theory because of the continued strong participation by a white bishop and the CMS in the life of the church. Stock considered the creation of the Native Pastorate "a good first step towards that desirable *euthanasia* of the Mission."[15] But it was only a first step. Stock rates the experiment a qualified success during the first decade, but the climate began to change around 1870 and in the 1870s new problems emerged. By then Venn was no longer on the scene. His successors possessed neither his strong vision nor his administrative skill as they struggled to cope with changing circumstances.

In his book *The Story of a Mission*, T. S. Johnson, the first Sierra Leonean to reach the rank of bishop when he was consecrated assistant bishop in 1937, expressed pent-up anger and frustration over the fact that the foreign missionary continued as late as 1953 to exercise control over the church.[16] Johnson argued, "To-day the spirit of nationalism and racial self-respect is spreading, with the result that the younger Churches are growing rather restive under what they consider to be foreign domination—a kind of spiritual imperialism which is contrary to the due respect for humanity which is inherent in the Christian faith."[17] Venn had warned in Instructions to Missionaries in 1868 that precisely this was sure to be the outcome if the missionary failed to respect and trust the new church.[18] What happened during the intervening years? Do Johnson's angry words point to a failure of Venn's policies or, rather, a failure to apply Venn's policies by succeeding generations? What was the nature of the "paralysis" Neill says afflicted the Sierra Leone church "from which a whole century has not availed to deliver it"?[19] Bishop Johnson points in one direction; Bishop Neill in another.

Between 1850 and 1875 British public opinion underwent a far-reaching change. We do not yet have a satisfactory study of the complex drives and forces that came to flower as full-blown imperialism. Nor have we faced up to what that development has meant for the Christian movement worldwide. But that general shift in social attitudes toward other peoples of the world was matched by a new mood among Evangelicals from whose circles the fresh missionary recruits came. A new Christian ideology underlay the conflicts between Europeans and Africans.

This ideology, which came increasingly into play after 1870, "sprang from in the main a new vision of the ordering of the truly Christian life in this world."[20] This vision was the product of ferment within the Christian church in Great Britain and Europe rather than the result of missionary experience. Nevertheless missionaries avidly carried the results of these developments at home with them to their fields of labor, often attempting zealously to apply these new concepts and standards in Africa or Asia. They were ill-prepared to understand the problems and needs of fledgling churches in a strange culture.

The major source of influence on the new generation of CMS missionaries was revivalism as it came to be institutionalized in Keswick from 1874 onward. Keswick teaching stressed the possibility of "deliverance from the power of besetting sin, the attainment of victory in the little conflicts of everyday life."[21] This quest for holiness of life produced a puritanical concern for achieving and maintaining proper moral standards. The concern for spiritual vitality was fully justified, but the spirit in which these missionary novices presented their concerns often alienated their African associates.

The new generation of missionaries from the 1880s onward, many of whom were Cambridge graduates, soon made their impact wherever they went. One especially tragic episode involved the takeover of the Niger Mission by this new generation, sending Bishop Crowther to his grave discredited and broken. It is beyond our purposes here to recount this story in detail. It was not simply a case of European versus African. The CMS was attempting to protect itself against criticisms from several sides; for all his excellent qualities, Crowther proved to be a weak administrative leader and disciplinarian; the younger generation was critical of policies of the older generation of leaders; new missionaries like G. W. Brooke wanted to scrap the traditional theology in favor of Keswick theology as well as the whole mission method that the older theology entailed.[22] In the purge that Brooke and his colleagues carried out in 1891–92, the CMS disconnected nearly all African agents, and the young missionaries placed themselves firmly in control of the entire mission operation. Although the aged Bishop Crowther had graciously accepted the inevitable shortly before his death, other Africans were profoundly embittered and a deep crisis enveloped the entire church.

In London the CMS Committee recommended to the archbishop of Canterbury that an English bishop succeed Crowther and two Nigerians be consecrated assistant bishops. The Africans saw this move as a declaration of the failure of Crowther's episcopate and a vote of "no confidence" in Africans. A vocal minority within the committee sided with the Africans and argued that installing a European bishop at this date was a step backward.

On June 29, 1893, an Englishman, J. S. Hill, became bishop, and two Nigerians, Isaac Oluwole and Charles Phillips, were consecrated assistant bishops of the Niger diocese. In the words of J. B. Webster:

The date was carefully chosen. It was the twenty-ninth anniversary of Crowther's consecration. What tragic irony for Africans. The new settlement—a blatant reversal of the past—paraded as a forward step in the Venn tradition. It was the ultimate humiliation. In December the three bishops, accompanied by the largest party of English missionaries ever sent forth at one time, arrived on the West Coast.[23]

These steps produced two results. On the one hand, Anglican church–mission relations on the Niger remained strained for many years. On the other, many Nigerians withdrew and joined the African Church Movement and other independent churches.

Stephen Neill has held up Bishop A. R. Tucker of Uganda as offering a far sounder concept of mission-church relations than did Henry Venn. Across the African continent, Tucker was struggling with exactly the same problems as those the Niger church was facing at the same time. The first CMS party of missionaries entered Uganda in 1877. The missionaries baptized their first converts in 1882 and two years later three young Christians suffered martyrdom at the hands of anti-Christian elements. The following year Bishop Hannington was murdered as he was approaching the Ugandan border on his way to take charge of his new diocese. For the next several years repeated waves of persecution swept over the small flock of believers in Uganda. In 1888 the kabaka (king) ordered all missionaries to leave the country. Meanwhile the church had become an underground movement with both spiritual and political objectives. The church emerged from this period led by its own people and with a strong sense of selfhood. In early 1893 Bishop Tucker called special attention to "the deepened sense of responsibility evidently entertained by the members of the Church Council with regard to their office and work."[24] Apparently the importance of this fact escaped Tucker's missionary colleagues, who saw only weaknesses and problems in the church.

Tucker had arrived in 1890 with a group of young missionaries to work with the Ugandan church. They soon began talking of the need for a revival of the church. They were anxious about signs of nominalism and laxity in moral conduct. These missionaries were products of the Keswick movement and used Keswick categories in evaluating the state of the church. It is important to note that racial tension was not a problem at this stage. Missionary George Baskerville gathered round him a group of African colleagues and helpers who shared his home and work in a rare display of comradeship for a period of years.

In 1904 a member of the CMS Home Committee, Victor Buxton, visited Uganda and reported on missionary discussions: "A good deal was said on the one hand on their [i.e., the Ugandans'] unfitness on the whole for bearing responsibility; they were 'still mere children,' as one leading missionary remarked."[25] The emerging missionary consensus was "So long as it is necessary to send *missionaries* to Uganda, so long must they be the teachers, counselors, directors and leaders of the people."[26] And the growing strength of the mission made it increasingly possible to enforce the missionary will. During the first fourteen years of the mission in Uganda, only a handful of missionaries served. Their position was tenuous in every way. They were incapable of making the church submit to their wishes. Leadership of the church was in Ugandan hands. In 1904 the situation was quite different. The CMS now had seventy-nine missionaries, and the British colonial government was firmly in control. The power relationship stood in stark contrast to what it had been during the first years. This was the problem Bishop Tucker confronted repeatedly during his service in Uganda.

Both Venn and Tucker used architectural metaphors to describe their concept of a mission. Venn spoke of a mission as the "scaffolding." Proof that the scaffolding has served its purpose and can be removed comes when an indigenous ministry is installed as the "crown" or keystone of the spiritual building, the indigenous church.[27] Tucker described the mission as the timber core or pillar on which the arch of a building is erected. That core should be removed once the keystone was in place.[28]

What had become disturbing to Tucker was to discover through actual experience that the mission station—not indigenous leadership—had become the keystone of the arch. On crucial issues affecting church-mission relations the missionaries outmaneuvered the bishop. It was against the background of this missionary domination that he wrote the lines Neill has cited:

> In training native Christians in the art of self-government, it is a tremendous mistake to hold aloof from their organization, and this for the simple reason that if the work of the European Missionaries is carried on outside the limits of the native Church, there must be an outside organisation. In that case, the native Christian will not be slow to realize that the outside organization is the one which really settles whatever questions may be under discussion in the Church and that their own organisation is more or less a sham. . . . To my mind, the true attitude and spirit of the missionary towards those to whom he goes is included in the words: "Forget also thine own people and thy father's house." Let him therefore throw in his lot absolutely with the natives, identifying himself as far as possible with their life, work, and organization. Let him submit himself to the laws and canons of their Church.[29]

Tucker had discovered at firsthand what Venn had observed from greater distance: the entry of a mission usually leads to a power encounter, which frequently veers off into missionary domination and paternalism, stifling and threatening the vitality of the young church. They agreed that the mission as a foreign agency had to be temporary. Venn as a mission administrator saw this transition taking place through reassignment of the missionary to fresh territory once the new church achieved selfhood. Tucker as a bishop wanted to get rid of the mission apparatus, which he experienced as the means of missionary domination by integrating the missionaries into the life of the church and making them fully subservient to the church and its bishop.

Tucker proved completely incapable of winning his point with the missionaries assigned to his church. The missionaries in Uganda, as in Sierra Leone, reserved to themselves the right to determine when the church had achieved sufficient maturity to have a bishop chosen from within its own ranks. Rarely has the missionary timetable coincided with that of the church. The complaint of Bishop Johnson of Sierra Leone that the Europeans dragged their feet beyond all reasonable limits is not an isolated instance.

It is not difficult to see why the Venn ideal commends itself to members of the churches that are the result of missionary labors, while the Tucker ideal leaves them feeling anxious. Both Venn and Tucker saw the problem of missionary paternalism with penetrating clarity and had the courage to grapple with it. But neither of their approaches guarantees a certain outcome. In the end a system is no better than the people who administer and participate in it.

It was Henry Venn's achievement to perceive the importance of the mission–church relationship and propose a conceptual framework for dealing with it by seeking to place limits on the exercise of power by the missionary. He sought to do this both by limiting the length of time of missionary leadership and rechanneling missionary energies into fresh fields of service. Undoubtedly the climate of the age in which he lived made it easier to come to the conclusions he reached. He failed, however, to convince fully most of his own missionaries of his insights and policies. Consequently the next generation took their cues from other voices and led the missionary movement in a reversal of Venn doctrine—a course that proved to be a cul-de-sac from which our generation is still struggling to extricate itself. In this postcolonial time when most peoples and churches have gained their independence, Venn's vision seems to have been uncannily prescient.

We can recognize Venn's great contribution without ignoring weaknesses in his work. It is hardly fair to the man or his record, however, to hold him accountable for the failures of succeeding generations who frequently repudiated in practice—while affirming in theory—Venn's ideal for the indigenous church.

Indeed, Venn would be distressed at the sight of future generations slavishly applying policies created to meet the needs of a particular time. We cannot know how Venn would respond to the "great new fact of our time"— the presence of a worldwide body of Christ. The vision of churches indigenous to the cultures of the world, which know the meaning of having their integrity as well as being interdependent with other parts of the body, remains as valid today as ever. But the great challenge of continuing to release the rich resources and energies of that worldwide body of Christ for missionary witness without paternalism and the creation of new dependencies calls for action attuned to today's reality.

It was Henry Venn's gift to be able to grasp clearly the central issue while being unusually resourceful and flexible in working out a program response. It is the bane of lesser men and women to be inflexible in methods of work while having no clear perception of the larger issues at stake.

NOTES

1. Peter Beyerhaus and Henry Lefever, *The Responsible Church and the Foreign Mission*, p. 30.

2. E. A. Ayandele, *The Missionary Impact on Modern Nigeria 1842–1914*, p. 181. In addition, see the studies by J. B. Webster, J. F. A. Ajayi.

3. Stephen Neill, *A History of Christian Missions*, p. 260. Cf. Neill's comments in *Creative Tension* (Edinburgh House Press, 1959), pp. 87f., and *The Unfinished Task* (Edinburgh House Press/Lutterworth Press, 1957), pp. 166f.

4. Philip D. Curtin, *The Image of Africa*, p. 3, pp. 289–478.

5. VB 114:90.

6. Curtin, *Image of Africa*; " 'Scientific' Racism and the British Theory of Empire."

7. G/AC1/13, June 12, 1857.

8. CA2/085a, July 21, 1857, Townsend to Venn.

9. See Jesse Page, *The Black Bishop*.

10. VB 37:6–11; CA3/L1, May 23, 1860, Venn to Crowther. Neill's tendentious remark (*History of Missions*, p. 377) needs to be set alongside Stock's much more measured judgment (II:464).

11. Michael Green, *Evangelism in the Early Church* (Eerdmans, 1970), chap. 7. Cf. T. E. Yates, *Venn and Victorian Bishops Abroad*, pp. 197–201.

12. VB 125. He makes the same point in Instructions to Missionaries, March 12, 1860 (VB 114:90).

13. Ibid., pp. 308f.

14. Ibid., pp. 314f.

15. Stock, II:445ff.

16. T. S. Johnson, *The Story of a Mission*, pp. 117–27.

17. Ibid., p. 120.

18. VB 170.

19. Neill, *History of Missions*, p. 260.

20. Andrew Porter, "Cambridge, Keswick, and late-nineteenth-century Attitudes to Africa," p. 27.

21. Quotation by C. F. Harford, cited by Andrew Porter, "Cambridge," p. 15.

22. Andrew Porter, "Evangelical Enthusiasm, Missionary Motivation and West Africa in the Late Nineteenth Century: The Career of G. W. Brooke." G. O. M. Tasie, "The Story of Samuel Ajayi Crowther and the C.M.S. Niger Mission Crisis of the 1880s: A Reassessment," points up, as does Porter, that the causes of the crisis were complex. It cannot be explained in terms of interracial conflict alone.

23. J. B. Webster, *The African Churches Among the Yoruba*, p. 39.

24. John V. Taylor, *The Growth of the Church in Buganda*, p. 61.

25. Ibid.
26. Ibid., p. 87.
27. Stock, II:418.
28. Taylor, *Church in Buganda*, p. 86.
29. Ibid.

Appendix I
The Native Pastorate and
Organisation of Native Churches

First Paper, Issued 1851
Minute upon the Employment and Ordination of Native Teachers

General Principles

The advanced state of missions having rendered it desirable to record the views of the Society upon the employment and ordination of native teachers, the following particulars are given for the information of its missionaries:

1. In all questions relating to settlement of a native Church in any mission field, it is important to keep in view the distinction between the office of a *Missionary,* who preaches to the heathen, and instructs inquirers or recent converts—and the office of a *Pastor,* who ministers in holy things to a congregation of native Christians.

2. Whilst the work of a missionary may involve for a time the pastoral care of newly-baptized converts, it is important that, as soon as settled congregations are formed, such pastoral care should be devolved upon native teachers, under the missionary's superintendence.

3. The native teacher who approves himself "apt to teach" is appointed to the office of a *Catechist.* The office of a catechist has been always recognised in the Church of Christ for evangelistic work, his function being to preach to the heathen, and to minister in congregations of converts until they are provided with a native pastor.

4. As a general rule, a catechist should be presented to the Bishop for ordination only with a view to his becoming pastor of some specified native congregation or district. The case in which a native may be ordained for direct evangelistic work, or while engaged in missionary education, must be regarded as exceptional.

5. Ordination is the link between the native teachers and the native Church. Native teachers are to be regarded, after their ordination, as pastors of the native Church, rather than as the agents of a foreign Society, or of other independent parties. Their social position should be such as is suitable

Published as pamphlet in 1866. VB 157.

to the circumstances of the native Church; and their emoluments must be regulated by the ability of the native Church to furnish the maintenance of their pastors. Care must therefore be taken to guard native teachers from contracting habits of life too far removed from those of their countrymen.

6. The attempts which have been made by this Society to train up native missionaries and pastors by an European education, and in collegiate establishments, have convinced the Committee that, under the present circumstances of missions, native missionaries and pastors may be best obtained by selecting from among the native catechists those who have approved themselves faithful and established Christians, as well as "apt to teach," and by giving to such persons a special training in Scriptural studies, in the vernacular language.

7. While any district continues a missionary district, the native pastors located in it are, as a general rule, to be under the superintendence of a missionary or of some other minister, appointed by the Society; until, by the Christian progress of the population, the missionary district may be placed upon a settled ecclesiastical system: it being also understood that the Society is at liberty to transfer a native pastor to the office of a native missionary, and to place him in the independent charge of a missionary district if his qualifications have entitled him to that position.

8. It is desirable that all native congregations should contribute to a fund for the payment of the salaries of native pastors; but that no payment should be made direct from the congregation to the pastor.

9. To encourage native ordination, the Society will continue to pay to a catechist, who may be presented by them for ordination, the same salary which he received as catechist, as long as the infancy of the native Church may seem to require it; whatever addition may be requisite for his maintenance as an ordained pastor must be supplied from local resources, and, if possible, from native endowments, or the contributions of the native Church to a general fund for native pastors.

[NOTE: Paragraphs 2, 3, and 9 would imply that the infant congregations should be placed under the pastoral care of a native teacher (catechist), *who would be one of the Society's agents, receiving pay from the Society's funds.* This was subsequently modified. (See Second Paper, paragraphs 8 and 9.) Moreover, paragraph 9 in this first paper arranges that the native pastor should receive part of his salary direct from the Society, but the present regulation is that the whole of his salary should be drawn from the Native Church Fund; the Society's contribution, where necessary, being given in the form of a grant-in-aid to that fund.]

10. Regarding the ultimate object of a mission, viewed under its ecclesiastical aspect, to be the settlement of a native Church, under native pastors, upon a self-supporting system, it should be borne in mind that the progress of a mission mainly depends upon the training up and the location of native

pastors; and that, as it has been happily expressed, "the euthanasia of a mission" takes place when a missionary, surrounded by well-trained native congregations, under native pastors, is able to resign all pastoral work into their hands, and gradually to relax his superintendence over the pastors themselves, till it insensibly ceases; and so the mission passes into a settled Christian community. Then the missionary and all missionary agency should be transferred to "the regions beyond."

Second Paper, Issued July 1861

The work of modern missionaries is of a twofold character: the heathen are to be brought to the knowledge of Christ; and the converts who embrace the truth are to be trained up in Christian habits, and to be formed into a Native Christian Church. These two branches are essentially distinct; yet it is only of late years that the distinction has been recognized by appointing missionaries to the purely evangelistic branch under the designation of Itinerating Missionaries, in contradistinction from "Station" Missionaries.

Present System of "Station" Missionary Work and its Dangers

2. The missionary, whose labours are blest to the gathering in of converts, naturally desires to keep his converts under his own charge, to minister to them as a pastor, and to rule them as a native congregation. So, the two branches have become blended together; hence also the principles necessary for the evangelistic work, one of which is "taking nothing of the Gentiles," have insensibly influenced the formation of the native Christian Church—as if the word had been "taking nothing of the Christians." Whereas the Scriptural basis of the pastoral relation, within the Church of Christ, is "they that preach the Gospel should live of the Gospel"—"the ox that treadeth out the corn should eat of the same"; so that while the Missionary properly receives his support from a foreign source, the native Pastor should receive his from the Native Church.

3. Under this system, the Missionary takes charge of classes of Candidates for Baptism, Classes of Candidates for the Lord's Supper, and Communicants-classes. The Missionary advances the converts from one class to another at his discretion. When the converts become too numerous or too scattered for the individual ministry of the Missionary, he appoints a Catechist or other Teacher, and the Society pays him. The Society establishes Schools and pays for the Teachers. As the Mission advances, the number of Readers, Catechists, and Ordained Pastors, of Schools and Schoolmasters, is increased. But all is dependent upon the Missionary: and all the agency is provided for at the cost of the Society.

4. The evil incident to this system is threefold:

(1) In respect of the Missionary: his hands soon become so full that his

time and energy are wholly occupied by the converts, and he extends his personal labours to the heathen in a continually decreasing ratio. His work also involves more or less of secularity and account-keeping. The character of a simple Missionary is complicated with that of the director and paymaster of the Mission.

(2) In respect of the converts: they naturally imbibe the notion that all is to be done for them—they are dependents upon a foreign Mission, rather than members of a native Church. There may be the individual spiritual life, but there is no corporate life; though the converts may amount to thousands in number, they are powerless as a body. The principles of self-support, self-government, and self-extension are wanting; on which depend the breath of life in a native Church.

(3) In respect of the Missionary Society: the system entails a vast and increasing expense in its oldest missions; so that, instead of advancing to "the regions beyond," it is detained upon old ground; it is involved in disputes about native salaries, pensions, repairs of buildings, etc.: and as the generation baptised in infancy rise up under this system, the Society has found itself in the false position of ministering to a population of nominal Christians, who in many instances give no assistance to the progress of the Gospel.

5. This system of Church Missions often contrasts unfavourably with the missions of other denominations, in respect of the liberality of native converts in supporting their own teachers, and of their self-exertion for the extension of the Gospel: as in the case of the American Baptist Mission among the Karens of Burmah, of the Independents among the Armenians of Asia Minor, and the wonderful preservation and increase of Christianity in Madagascar after the expulsion of European missionaries. The unfavourable contrast may be explained by the fact, that other denominations are accustomed to take part in the elementary organisation of their churches at home, and therefore more readily carry out that organisation in the missions. Whereas in our Church the clergy find everything relating to elementary organisation settled by the law of the land; as in the provision of tithes, of church-rates, of other customary payments, in the constitution of parishes, and in parish officers. Our clergy are not prepared for the question of Church organisation; and, therefore in the missions they exercise the ministry of the Word without reference to the non-existence of the organisation by which it is supported at home.

Improved System and Its Principles

6. The dangers and imperfections of Church Missions must be remedied by introducing into the native Church that elementary organisation which may give it "corporate life," and prepare it for its full development under a native ministry and an indigenous episcopate.

7. For the introduction of such elementary organisation into the native Church, the following principles may be laid down:

I. It is expedient that native converts should be trained, at as early a stage as possible, upon a system of self-government, and of contributing to the support of their own native teachers.

II. It is expedient that contributions should be made by the converts themselves, for their own Christian instruction, and for schools for their children; and that for this purpose a Native Church Fund for an assigned missionary district should be established, into which the contributions should be paid. The fund must, at first, be mainly sustained by grants from the Missonary Society, these grants to be diminished as the native contributions spring up. Whilst the fund receives grants from the Society, the Parent Committee must direct the mode of its management.

III. It is expedient that the native teachers should be divided into two classes, namely—

(1) Those who are employed as assistants to the Missionary in his evangelistic work, and who are paid by the Society.

(2) Those who are employed in pastoral work amongst the native Christians, who are to be paid out of the Native Church Fund, whether Schoolmasters, Readers, Catechists, or ordained Pastors, as the case may be; so that they may be regarded as the ministerial agents of the native Church, and not as the salaried agents of a Missionary Society.

IV. It is expedient that the arrangements which may be made in the missions should from the first have reference to the ultimate settlement of the native Church, upon the ecclesiastical basis of an *indigenous* episcopate, independent of foreign aid or superintendence.

Practical Suggestions for Carrying Out the Improved System

To carry out the foregoing principles, it is suggested:

8. That, in conformity with Principle I., the converts should be encouraged to form themselves for mutual support and encouragement into *"Christian Companies."* (Act. iv. 23. The literal translation would have been "their own friends or relatives." The translators of the Bible adopted the term "company" to denote the new and close brotherhood into which Christians are brought. In Africa the term has already been adopted for their native associations.) The members of such companies should not be too numerous, or too scattered, to prevent their meeting together in familiar religious conference. Local circumstances will decide the convenient number of a company: upon its enlargement beyond that number it should be divided into two or more companies.

One of each company should be selected, or approved of, by the Missionary, as an elder, or *"Christian Headman,"* to call together and preside over the companies, and to report to the Missionary upon the moral and religious condition of his company, and upon the efforts made by the members for extending the knowledge of Christ's truth. Each Christian company should be encouraged to hold *weekly meetings* under its headman, with the occasional presence of the Missionary, for united counsel and action, for reading the Scriptures and prayer, and for making contributions to the Church fund—if it be only a handful of rice, or more, as God shall prosper them. (Principle II.)

Monthly Meetings of the Christian Headmen should be held under the Missionary, or some one whom he may appoint, at which meetings the headmen should report upon their respective companies, hand over the contributions, receive from the Missionary spiritual counsel and encouragement, and commend their common work, in united prayer, to the great Shepherd and Bishop of Souls.

As long as converts are thus dependent for their Christian instruction upon their headmen, with only occasional ministrations of the agents of the Society, the work must be regarded as the evangelistic work of the Society.

9. *The First Step* in the organisation of the native Church will be taken when any company, or one or more neighbouring companies unitedly, shall be formed into a *congregation having a schoolmaster or native teacher located amongst them, whose salary is paid out of the Native Church Fund* (Principle III.). This step may be taken as soon as the company or companies so formed into a congregation contribute a fair amount, in the judgment of the Missionary, to the Church Fund.

10. *A Second Step* in the organisation of the native Church will be taken when one or more congregations are formed into a *Native Pastorate, under an ordained native, paid by the Native Church Fund* (Principle III.). This step may be taken as soon as the congregations are sufficiently advanced, and the payments to the Native Church Fund shall be sufficient to authorise the same, in the judgment of the Missionary and of the Corresponding Committee.

The Christian headmen of the companies comprised within a native pastorate should cease to attend the monthly meetings of headmen under the Missionary, and should meet under their native pastor.

As long as the Native Church Fund is under the management of the Missionary Society, the native pastors, paid out of that fund, must remain under the general superintendence of some missionary of the Society, who shall be at liberty to minister occasionally in their churches, and to preside jointly with the native pastors at the meetings of headmen and other congregational meetings; the relation between the native pastor and the missionary being somewhat analogous to that of curates with a non-resident incumbent.

11. A third step in the organisation of the native Church will be taken when, a sufficient number of native pastorates having been formed, *a District Conference* shall be established, consisting of pastors and lay delegates from each of their congregations, and the European missionaries of such

district. District conferences should meet periodically for consulting upon the native Church affairs, as distinguished from the action of the Society (Principle IV.).

12. When any considerable district has been thus provided for by an organised native Church, foreign agency will have no further place in the work, and that district will have been fully prepared for a native episcopate.

Concluding Remarks

13. There must be a variety of details in carrying into effect these suggestions. A mere outline is given above; but it will be seen that the proposed scheme of organisation will prepare the native Church for ultimately exhibiting in its congregational and district conferences the counterpart of the parish and the archdeaconry, under the diocesan episcopacy of our own Church system.

14. The proposed organisation of the mission Church is adapted to the case as it is, where the native Church is in a course of formation out of a heathen population by the agency of a Missionary Society with limited resources. Under such circumstances, a Society must commence its work by accustoming the converts to support their own institutions in the simplest forms, so that the resources of the mission may be gradually released, and be moved forward to new ground. In other words, the organisation must work upwards. When a sufficient *substratum* of self-support is laid in the native Church, its fuller development will unfold itself, as in the healthy growth of things natural. Had the problem been to organise a mission where ample funds exist in the hands of a Bishop and his clergy, for the evangelisation of a whole district, as well as for the future endowment of its native Church, the organisation might work downwards, beginning with a diocesan council, forming the converts into districts and parishes, building churches and colleges, etc. These have been too much the leading ideas in modern missions; and European ideas easily take root in native minds. But past experience seems to show that such a system, even if the means were provided, would be too apt to create a feeble and dependent native Christian community.

15. The foregoing suggestions must be modified according to the previous system which may have prevailed in a mission. In older missions the change of system must be very gradual; for when a mission has grown up in dependence upon European missionaries and upon native agency salaried by European funds, the attempt to curtail summarily its pecuniary aid, before the introduction of a proper organisation, will be like casting a person overboard before he has been taught to swim: it will be a great injustice to the native converts, and may seriously damage the work already accomplished.

16. On the other hand, in new missions the missionary may from the first encourage the inquirers to form themselves into companies, for mutual instruction and reading the Scriptures and prayer, and for making their weekly

collections. It should be enjoined upon each company to enlarge its numbers by prevailing upon others to join in their meetings. The enlargement of a Christian company, so as to require subdivision, should be regarded as a triumph of Christianity, as a festive occasion of congratulation and joy, as men rejoice "when they divide the spoil."

17. If the elementary principles of self-support and self-government and self-extension be thus sown with the seed of the Gospel, we may hope to see the healthy growth and expansion of the native Church, when the Spirit is poured down from on high, as the flowers of the fertile field multiply under the showers and warmth of summer.

Third Paper, Issued 8 January 1866

1. The first Minute of the Committee of the Church Missionary Society upon the subject of the native Church was issued in 1851; but at the end of ten years so little progress had been made towards the formation of native Churches, that in July 1861 the Committee issued a second minute on the organisation of native Churches in missions, in which various practical directions were given for the establishment of a Native Church Fund and of Native Church District Conferences. The object of the present paper is to record, for the encouragement of their missionaries, the progress which has been since made in native Church organisation, and to point out some practical measures for the more speedy establishment of self-supporting, self-governing, and self-extending native Churches.

Review of the Progress Made Towards Native Church Organisation

2. The Committee trust that throughout their missions *the distinction is now understood and recognised between a Mission and a Native Church—* that is, between the agency employed by a Foreign Missionary Society to evangelise any people, and the agency to be employed in pastoral ministrations to Christian congregations.

3. The greatest advance in native Church organisation has been made in Sierra Leone, the earliest mission of the Society. There nine out of twelve missionary districts have been formed into self-supporting native pastorates. The nine native ministers and the village schools are all supported by the contributions of the native Church, assisted, to some extent, by a grant-in-aid from the Society. These native ministers are no longer under the direction of the Society, but of the European Bishop of Sierra Leone and a church council. In this mission a circumstance occurred which holds out an important example to other missions. Two native ministers, who had been educated and ordained in England, and had for twelve years been acting as missionaries of the Society, had to choose between continuing in that position or resigning their connection with the Society, and casting in their lot with the native

Church. They wisely chose the latter, as most for the advantage of their country. The result has fully justified their choice. Their superior qualifications have acted beneficially upon the whole body of native pastors. Had they, in consequence of these superior qualifications, retained their position as missionaries of the Society, the native church would have suffered loss, and the rest of the native pastors might easily have become discontented.

4. Throughout India and Ceylon the native Christians have been of late years in a measure aroused to the duty of supporting their native pastors. In some districts sums have been raised as endowments for this purpose. In South India these endowments amount to the sum of 3,300L.; but hitherto these endowments have been accumulating, and have therefore afforded no relief to the current expenses of the mission. In many congregations contributions are raised for building and repairing of churches and for church expenses; but in very few cases have any contributions been made for relieving the Society from the charge of native ministrations. In the province of Tinnevelly 1,500L. a year is raised by the native Churches for various religious and benevolent objects, while the Society wholly supports the native pastors, catechists, and village schools, at a cost of 4,000L. a year beyond the expense of European agency.

5. It is obvious from the foregoing statements that, even in the most advanced missions of India, measures are required to make the support of native ministers by native congregations more effective. In other missions, in India and elsewhere, measures have yet to be taken for raising native contributions for the native Church.

Need of the Formation of a Separate Native Church Fund

6. The development of the resources of the native Church will be greatly promoted, in the judgment of the Committee, by a separation between the Native Church Funds and the Funds of the Society. For as long as the contributions for the support of the native Church are paid into the treasury of the Society, the Society is regarded as the paymaster, and not the native Church. Besides which, as long as the native Church agency and the missionary agency are paid out of one treasury, the distinction between the native Church and the mission is liable to be lost sight of, and the two agencies are, by the native Christians, blended into one and the same.

7. The separation of the two funds can only be satisfactorily effected by placing the Native Church Fund under the management of a local committee, or Church council, comprising, as in Sierra Leone, Europeans and natives. To such a separate fund the Society may contribute grants-in-aid, gradually diminished as the native Church contributions increase, until the native Church is able to sustain the whole charge of the native pastorate. In a former minute the managing body of such a Native Church Fund was called a "District Conference"; but as the term "conference" is generally employed for the meetings of missionaries, the designation of "Council," as in Sierra

Leone, more exactly represents the executive body of a native Church, and points also to the relative position of that body in respect of the missionary of the district, and ultimately of the native Bishop.

8. The Church Council, or managers of the fund, will naturally be entitled to exercise some superintendence over the agents supported by the fund. Regulations must therefore be adopted for securing a proper selection of the members of the Church Council, and for the right exercise of the powers of the council, under the united action of Europeans and natives.

9. The principles on which the Native Church Fund and Church Councils should be regulated have been already partly explained in the former minutes on "Native Church Organisation," but they may be now stated in a more distinct and practical form.

I. That native contributions for the support of native teachers should be commenced from the first formation of a Christian congregation, even though there be but a single congregation; but they should never be paid direct from any congregation to its pastor or resident catechist, but to *a native church fund*, which must be available for the support of all the native teachers of an assigned district, according to regulated scales of salaries.

II. That whilst the native contributions are inadequate to the whole support of the native teachers of such a district, the Society shall supplement the native Church fund by grants-in-aid; and as long as the Society thus contributes or carries on a mission within the district, *the treasurership* and ultimate control of the native Church fund must rest with the Society.

III. That as soon as a district contains three or more separate congregations under native pastors, *a Native Church Council* should be formed for the distribution of the fund, for consulting upon the interests of the native Church, and for the general superintendence of its affairs.

IV. That in every church council, as long as the district remains a missionary district, a missionary or other person appointed by the Society shall be the chairman, whose concurrence shall be necessary to the validity of the council, and who shall submit the proceedings of the council to the Committee of the Society.

V. The members of the council should be appointed periodically, and should consist of two members appointed by the chairman, three native pastors appointed by the pastors, and three native laymen appointed by the congregations.

VI. That the foregoing arrangements be subject to revision by the Parent Committee from time to time, until the native Church fund ceases to receive aid from the Society, or the district is placed under a permanent ecclesiastical system.

10. The Committee feel assured that the establishment of a separate native Church fund will not only afford great relief to the resources of the Society, but will have far more important benefits, by training up the native

Church to manage its own affairs independently of European superintendence, and by affording to the heathen a visible and convincing proof of the reality and stability of native Christianity.

Suggestion of a Native Episcopal Commissary, Preparatory for a Native Suffragan Bishop

11. With a view further to promote the independence of the native Church at as early a period as possible, it may be suggested *that the Bishop of the diocese should appoint from time to time a Native Minister as his Commissary,* to visit and make himself acquainted with the native teachers and their pastoral work, and that the commissary should attend the church councils as an assessor, with the chairman, and that he should report his visitations to the Bishop. This arrangement is proposed as a preparation for the appointment of a native suffragan bishop, when the native Church is sufficiently organised, and the Bishop of the Diocese shall be prepared to make such an appointment.

Reasons for a Missionary Society Not Placing Native Ministers in the Position of European Missionaries

12. The Committee may refer, in connection with this subject, to applications they have lately received from more than one quarter to place some of the native pastors in the position of European missionaries, as in the earlier stages of missionary operations. The first Minute seems indeed to hold out the prospect to native pastors of such a missionary position, as an advancement and reward of faithful service. But the case is now altered. Experience has proved that the employment by a foreign Missionary Society of native ministers on the footing of English missionaries impedes, in many ways, the organisation of the native Church. The native Church needs the most able native pastors for its fuller development. The right position of a native minister, and his true independence, must now be sought in the independence of the native Church, and in its more complete organisation under a native Bishop. At the same time the Committee reserve to themselves the power, in exceptional cases, of transferring a native pastor to the list of missionaries or assistant missionaries; but this must only be done when the general interests of the Society require it, and not as a reward or advancement of an individual. The example of the African missionaries, who transferred themselves to the position of native pastors, points out a more excellent way.

The Native Church Fund May for a Time Be Relieved of the Charge of Elementary Schools

13. In the foregoing remarks the Committee have confined their view to the support and superintendence of the pastoral agency of the native

church, as exercised by native pastors or resident catechists or readers. They have not touched upon the support of schools, because they regard Anglo-vernacular schools and boarding schools as missionary agency; and they think that it will greatly facilitate the arrangements for supporting native pastors if the vernacular schools are provided for, as a temporary arrangement, by the Society, or by other local resources, as, in South India, all female education is supported by the South India local fund, until the native Church organisation is sufficiently established to support the vernacular schools. The native pastors and the church council should, nevertheless, regard it as an essential part of their duty to watch over these schools, and to promote their efficiency.

[NOTE: The original pamphlet included an appendix, "Proposal of a native bishop in Tinnevelly," which is here omitted. The proposal was first issued in 1865. W.R.S.]

Appendix II
Politics and Missions

We are met together to take leave of a large body of missionaries going to distant and widely differing fields of labour—to West Africa, India, Ceylon, China, and the Mediterranean.

The Committee have so frequently addressed their missionaries upon the main principles and chief motives of missionary work, that they feel justified in omitting these upon the present occasion; in order to touch upon a topic of great practical importance, which the present aspect of the missionary field brings into prominent notice—namely, the proper conduct of a missionary in respect to social and political questions which may seem to be connected with the progress of his spiritual work.

The one object of the Church Missionary Society is to provide for the preaching of the Gospel of Christ to those who have not yet received it; and to train up the Christian converts in the doctrine and discipline of the Church of England.

But the blessings of the Gospel when received tend to elevate the social position of the converts, and to instruct them in the true principles of justice and humanity: and so to quicken in their minds the sense of the wrongs they may suffer through oppression and misgovernment. A knowledge also of Christian duty, while it secures obedience to the sovereign powers, limits that obedience to things lawful in the sight of God as defined in His Word; and so far often interferes with the institutions of heathen and Mohammedan Governments.

The relation, also, in which the missionary stands to his converts, necessarily connects him with their temporal welfare. Going among the people with a message of love upon his lips, and with the spirit of love in his heart, he soon wins the confidence beyond all other persons of his race. He becomes their best friend—their faithful adviser. His message embraces their temporal as well as their spiritual interests, for "godliness" hath the "promise of the life that now is, and of that which is to come." They have, therefore, a claim upon him for advice, and assistance against injustice and wrong.

The missionary has, moreover, a message to declare, on proper occasions, to those in authority, on their responsibility to God, by whose ordinance they exercise the right of government.

Instruction to Missionaries, delivered September 28, 1860. VB 118.

However earnestly, therefore, the faithful missionary may strive to confine himself to his one great work, the ministry of the Gospel of salvation, he is liable to be involved in many questions of a social and political kind. And he cannot always escape the reproach cast upon his Divine Master and upon His Apostle, of being the enemy of Caesar, or of turning the world upside down.

The difficulty which a Christian missionary always finds in shaping his course in such matters, with "the wisdom of the serpent, and the harmlessness of the dove," is much increased in seasons of national, political, or social excitement. And the fields of labour to which you are designated are so circumstanced. In India, society yet heaves under the recent terrible catastrophe, and questions have been lately raised, in respect of the civil rights of Christian converts, of the system of ryotry in the cultivation of indigo, of the Christian action of Government, and of its officers—in which the missionary may be more or less necessarily involved. In the sphere of our missions in Africa and in China, civil wars rage, and in the former country, our missionaries are severally living under governments at open war with each other. In Asia Minor, and throughout the Turkish Empire, social and political affairs are in a state of terrible effervescence.

Into such fields of labour, you are going forth as the messengers of the Prince of Peace—to preach "glory to God in the highest, and on earth peace, good-will towards men." How blessed the commission! yet how arduous and perilous its right execution!

The Committee would therefore desire to furnish you, by the Divine blessing, with advice for the guidance of your conduct, and, with an affectionate assurance of their sympathy, to encourage and cheer you in your future difficulties.

I. The general rule in such cases has been laid down in the printed "Regulations explanatory of the relation between the Church Missionary Society and the missionaries connected with it," in these words: "Every missionary is strictly charged to abstain from interfering in the political affairs of the country or place in which he may be situated."

The terms of this rule are necessarily broad and somewhat indefinite—political affairs is a wide term. There are worldly politicans who would desire to include in their exclusive province national education, the State support of idolatry, the social institution, as it is called, of slavery, the treatment of the aborigines, the private religious action of Government officers. As soon as a minister of religion touches these questions an outcry is apt to be raised, as if he were meddling with politics.

But such subjects as these are not simply "political affairs." They are of a mixed character.

The great principles of justice, humanity, and Christian duty lie at the root of these questions. Those principles are, as matters of investigation and of public exposition, the special province of the minister of religion. It is for the minister of religion to propound these principles, and to suggest their proper application. Such mixed questions, therefore, cannot by any just interpretation be included in those "political affairs" from interfering with which the missionary is to abstain. A missionary is bound to remonstrate if he believes the great principles of justice, humanity, and Christian duty to be violated; and the politician is bound, on his part, to vindicate his adherence to those principles, in the course which he thinks it right to pursue. In all such questions, therefore, it was the wisdom of the governing powers to listen to the suggestions of the missionary body, and to secure their co-operation; if the authorities, on the other hand, decline or oppose their suggestions, the missionary is driven to an appeal to public opinion as a last resource, and the Government may be, sooner or later, compelled to yield that which Christian principle demands: and too often, after loss of time and opportunity, and after controversial dissension, equally disadvantageous to all the parties concerned.

A few specific cases which have occurred in the history of this Society will serve to illustrate the foregoing statement.

1. The earliest political question in which the Society was involved was that of slavery: first, the abolition of the slave trade; afterwards, the abolition of slavery. This Society nobly and prominently denounced the sin and evil of slavery, while it was yet maintained as a social institution, and protected by numerous acts of the legislature. Other missionary societies having labourers before ourselves in slave colonies, bore the brunt of the contest upon the spot. Their missionaries were denounced as political agitators, till at last the missionary, Smith, was cast into a jail, and tried as a rebel. This act called forth the indignation of the British Parliament, and the authority of the Imperial Government was interposed to vindicate the rights of justice and humanity in the person of the injured missionary. Through such conflicts the good cause at length triumphed, and slavery was abolished.

2. Another great political question, in which the missionaries were involved, was the liberty of preaching the Gospel to the natives of India. Here again, the first brunt of actual conflict was borne by the missionaries of another society—the illustrious Carey, Ward, and Marshman. Their memoirs, lately published, exhibit an instructive example of the delicacy and difficulty of such questions as we are handling, and how gradually the right and liberty were conceded, for which the missionary and his friends contended.

3. So also, by the missionary and his friends, the question of Government connection with idolatry, in India, was first raised, and was mainly supported by the evidence of the missionary. Here, also, the advocates of a Christian policy were frequently denounced as disturbers of government. Even the eminent Christian bishop, Dr. Corrie, received an official rebuke for pressing this question upon the attention of Government. The cause of Christian duty was, however, supported by the voice of the nation, and at length the very principles which had been at first opposed as the theory of fanatics, were embodied in a formal despatch of His Majesty's Government.

4. So, also, in Travancore the missionaries have thought themselves compelled, on several occasions, to stand up for the civil rights of the converts,

and their efforts have been blessed with success. Even when the Government of Madras censured the missionaries for appearing in courts of justice as the friend of the oppressed Christian, the Home Government reversed the censure, and vindicated the conduct of the missionary, as being the natural and proper guardian of the just civil rights of the convert.

5. On a late occasion, a missionary of this Society furnished this Committee with a statement of the effects which he had witnessed of an order of the supreme Government of India, in respect of the private action of Christian officers towards Christian enquirers of the 24th Punjab Native Infantry. The Committee thought it right publicly to remonstrate against this proceeding. The Government, in consequence of this remonstrance issued a despatch explanatory of that order, which has happily removed the difficulties which a misunderstanding of the order had created; and the Committee rejoice now to add that the good work in the regiment, arrested for fifteen months by that misunderstanding, has been renewed, and the baptism of several soldiers of the regiment has since taken place.

6. At this present time a social question is agitated between the indigo planter of Bengal and the ryot cultivator. When, a few years ago, the cause of the ryot was advocated by the missionary, the missionary was denounced as a meddler in matters beyond his province. At length, however, the supreme Government has instituted a Court of Inquiry, and has placed a missionary, as a fair representative of the ryot, among the Commissioners, and has subpoenaed other missionaries to give evidence on oath of the cases of alleged oppression which have come under their notice; thus vindicating the right of the missionary to assist in the adjustment of this question. The result of the enquiry is not yet known, and therefore the Committee abstain from further remark upon this particular case.

These six instances will sufficiently illustrate our position that there are many questions of a mixed character, which, though partly political, fall within the province of the missionary, and in the adjustment of which the authorities may advantageously avail themselves of the co-operation of the missionary body. These questions, it is impossible to deny, are becoming daily more and more prominent and important. For it is a characteristic of the age that the religious element enters into every great question—even in the congress of European nations.

II. The Committee now proceed to offer you a few practical directions in respect of such questions as have been described.

1. The Committee affectionately, but earnestly, warn each missionary, especially every young missionary, not to take up supposed grievances too hastily; but to wait and consult with other Christian men till they have ascertained the reality and importance of any alleged social or civil wrong. Remember that these "mixed" questions form the exceptions to the general rule of strict abstinence from interfering in political affairs. This rule must be applied to all such matters as do not palpably involve the great principles of justice, humanity, or Christian duty. The Committee say *palpably*, because the inge-

nuity of some minds will see a connection which is not generally recognised. All political measures might be thus excepted from the prohibition, and the rule become a nullity. But common sense has established a distinction, and it will be well for the missionary to err on the side of abstinence from doubtful questions, rather than to interfere in matters which will not be allowed by sober judges to belong to his province.

2. When, however, the missionary is unavoidably involved, in the line of his duty, in questions having a political aspect, let him guard against a political spirit—that is, against the spirit in which the politicians of this world strive together. He must stand clear of all party strife. The apostolic injunction is—"The servant of the Lord must not strive; but be gentle unto all men, apt to teach, patient, in meekness instructing them that oppose themselves; if God peradventure will give them repentance to the acknowledging of the truth." In conformity with this rule, the missionary should never assume a position of hostility to the ruling powers, or have recourse to public censure, or the lash of newspaper invectives. Let him rather address the authorities in respectful and confiding terms, as those upon whom God has laid the responsibility of upholding the great principles of Christian duty. If such addresses be unheeded, let a temperate statement of the case be transmitted to the Missionary Directors at home, with such particulars as will bear the closest sifting, and as the missionary is prepared to avow before the public.

3. Avoid, even in the most pressing cases, being drawn into the vortex of mere political discussions; for it will prove a painful interruption to your happier duties. Much precious time is necessarily lost in those discussions which might have been spent in winning to Christ souls, who should have been your crown of rejoicing in the day of the Lord. Even your conferences with your brethren on such topics will be far less profitable to the soul, than if the time had been wholly devoted to spiritual things. And you will be liable to be drawn into still less profitable connection with the men of the world, who will court the aid of a spiritual man for the sake of a secular object, though they sneer at his religion. All these, and many other considerations, make the true missionary shrink from political discussions, make him walk warily while engaged in them, and make him most thankful to escape from their entanglements.

4. When compelled by a sense of duty to take an active part in exceptional cases, be the more careful to observe the standing rule of the Society, in its legitimate scope and intention, in all other political relations. These will embrace the ordinary course of Government, in respect of which you must exhibit in your own conduct, as well as inculcate upon all others, the spirit of the apostolic injunction, "Tribute to whom tribute is due; custom to whom custom; fear to whom fear; honour to whom honour." You must especially strive to stand aloof from all questions of political leadership—of political partisanship; whether officers of Government be favourable or unfavourable to missionary work, whether they patronise or oppose, let the missionary avoid all appearance of political intrigue. The cordial and courteous recognition of

the official position of an opponent will be the best means of disarming his opposition. A candid construction of his measures will conciliate, while a severe criticism will raise needless animosity.

III. The missionaries who labour under Christian rulers, in the dependencies of Great Britain, will be enabled, under ordinary circumstances, to carry on their work without concerning themselves with the course of the Government. But the case is more difficult with those who labour amidst uncivilised nations and governments. The injunction to abstain from all interference with political affairs is obviously not applicable when the native government is mixed up with national superstitions and social institutions, which violate all justice and humanity; when the magistrate's sword is in the hands of every petty chief, or self-constituted oppressor; when human sacrifices form a part of the political constitution.

In such a situation the first missionaries found themselves in the Susu Mission of Africa and in New Zealand. Yet while the rule stood, some conscientious men hesitated to instruct the natives in political maxims, or to protest against their existing atrocities. For the relief of their conscience, the following note was added to the rule by the Committee, and was printed for many years in the "Explanatory Regulations."

"It is not intended, however, by this regulation to preclude missionaries who may be stationed in New Zealand, or in other regions which are uncivilised, and which do not enjoy the protection of a fixed Government, from bringing the natives acquainted with such Christian and civil institutions, as in process of time their situations may require; or from using their influence in such countries to preserve or restore peace, in conformity with the spirit of a minister of the Gospel."

In the spirit of this explanation, the Society at home and the missionaries in New Zealand took a leading part in the discussion of the great national question of the colonisation of those islands. When the first Governor, Captain Hobson, was sent out to negotiate with the chiefs for the transfer of the sovereignty to the Queen of Great Britain, he obtained the assistance of the missionaries of this and of the Wesleyan Society to bring about that event. No one took a more prominent part than the senior missionary of the Church Missionary Society. The services of the missionaries were publicly acknowledged by the Governor and the Home Government; and, on a special occasion, the Governor thus addressed the Legislative Council on its being opened December 14, 1841:

"Whatever difference of opinion may be entertained as to the value and extent of the labours of the missionary body, there can be no doubt that they have rendered important services to this country; or that, but for them, a British colony would not at this moment be established in New Zealand."

The voice of the missionary, which was thus mainly instrumental in bringing the New Zealand chiefs to accept the Treaty of Waitangi, is now rightly lifted up on behalf of the chiefs against, as they believe, an attempted violation of its letter and spirit.

On a late review of the printed form of the "Explanatory Regulations," the note was omitted, because New Zealand had become a British colony, and the missions of the Society in Western Africa were then under British Government, and it was thought that the good sense of Christian missionaries would sufficiently qualify the rule in exceptional cases. But the state of the Yoruba Mission recalls one part of the appended note to our attention. In the present day a civil war has broken out between three of the towns in which missionaries reside. Ijaye and Ibadan have made war against each other, and Abeokuta has unhappily joined in the conflict. The several missionaries in these towns have been thus placed in most difficult positions. The Commitee are not prepared to judge of the conduct of each missionary, or of his conduct in all respects. But the Committee have seen quite enough to induce them to urge upon you, who are going to the Yoruba Mission, with affectionate importunity, the old injunction of "using your influence to preserve or restore peace in conformity with the spirit of a minister of the Gospel."

IV. The Committee will conclude with a few words of general encouragement and advice suggested by the circumstances which have called forth these instructions.

1. Remember that seasons of special political conflict, or social excitement, have always been seasons of special promise and hope to the Church of Christ. The King of Zion has an iron sceptre to break down all opposition to an advancing gospel. Political convulsions are the execution of His judgment. At the very time when He thus wields that iron sceptre, He enjoins upon His Church to proclaim the message—"Kiss the Son, lest He be angry." "When the judgments of the Lord are in the earth, the inhabitants of the world will learn righteousness." We have seen this most manifestly in the improved prospect of our Indian Missions since the Mutiny. And every observer of God's dealings with the world will supply abundant illustrations. It is refreshing to think how often the work of mercy and grace is silently advancing amid the crash of human affairs. Let the man of faith repose upon this thought. In the darkest hours the eye and ear of flesh may discern nothing but the flash of lightning, and hear only the roll of thunder; but let the ear of faith catch the sound of the still small voice, and let the man of faith then ply in patience, prayer and faith his special mission.

2. Let the Committee remind you also that such critical times as they allude to are also to the Christian times of special trial and temptation, and he needs then to place a double guard upon his temper and spirit, lest he be carried away by the stream into an exhibition of worldly tempers, lest his good should be evil spoken of, through his hasty language or exaggerated statements. There will be perils on all sides. The missionary may be often in personal danger; such a time is an occasion for showing his faith in a special providence—that he does not fear with the fear of men of the world—that he can stay himself upon his God. There may be dangers to his reputation; especially when the missionary stands up as the friend of the aborigines, in opposition to the oppression of unprincipled European settlers. Those of us who

are old enough to remember the agitation of the slavery question, can remember the torrents of calumny and of coarse abuse with which the white man attempted to overwhelm Wilberforce, Macaulay, Stephen, and all other champions of the negro race. We can remember also the calm and loving composure with which it was borne, as a part of the costs which had been counted.

3. The Committee do not attempt to give you more than very brief hints on these topics. They have confidence in the reflections which will arise in your own minds; but above all, they commend you to the grace and guidance of an ever present Saviour, who has promised to send you the almighty aid of the Holy Comforter; who will manifest Himself to His servants who suffer for His name's sake at the present day, as He did to His Apostle Paul. When, "the night following" the tumult in the Council at Jerusalem, "the chief captain feared lest Paul should have been pulled in pieces,"—"the Lord stood by him, and said, 'Be of good cheer, Paul: for as thou hast testified of me in Jerusalem, so must thou bear witness also at Rome.' "

[NOTE: The rest of this Instruction is addressed to each missionary individually, discussing assignment details. W. R. S.]

Bibliography

(For abbreviations used, see listing on p. xvi)

Part 1   Writings by and about Henry Venn

A. Venn's Correspondence

Henry Venn's letters are preserved in the Church Missionary Society Archives, London. An index to all Venn letters, including a résumé of the contents of each letter, has been prepared. The following CMS Letterbooks contain the Venn Correspondence:

Ceylon C/CE/L2 (1835–50) to C/CE/L4 (1859–75)
China C.CH/L1 (1834–63) to C.CH/L2 (1863–76)
East Africa C.A5/L1(1842–77)
Mauritius C/MA/L1 (1857–85)
Mediterranean CM/L3 (1838–54) to CM/L5 (1854–64)
Missions—Miscellaneous G/AC1/3 (1838–42) to G/AC1/18 (1871–73)
New Zealand CN/L4 (1840–45) to CN/L7 (1862–78)
Niger C.A3/L1 (Jan. 1858 to Oct. 1872)
North India C.I1/L2 (Feb. 1842) to C.I1/L7 (1866–73)
North West America C/C1/L1 (1821–46) to C/C1/L3 (1860–75)
Sierra Leone C.A1/L3 (Nov. 1841) to C.A1/L8 (Dec. 1872)
South India C.I2/L3 (1836–42) to C.I2/L7 (1867–73)
West India C.I3/L2 (1835–55) to C.13/L4 (1865–73)
West Indies CW/L3 (1839–58)
Yoruba C.A1/L4 (Feb. 1850) to C.A2/L4 (Aug. 1872)

Venn family correspondence and manuscripts are also deposited at CMS and catalogued: Venn MSS, F1, etc.

B. Venn's Printed Writings

Bibliography of Henry Venn's Printed Writings with Index, compiled by Wilbert R. Shenk (Herald Press, 1975), gives complete information on each item and where it may be located. The following bibliography gives basic information on each of them. All references in the book to items from this bibliography are abbreviated VB, followed by the number assigned that item and the page(s) cited. For example, VB 170:317 refers to item number 170 in the *Bibliography,* page 317.

1825

(1)   *Remarks on the propriety of applying the funds of the British and Foreign Bible Society, to the circulation of such foreign versions as contain the Apocrypha, in places where no other versions will be generally received.* London: Knight and Bagster. Second edition with Preface. Pp. 31.

1828

(2)   *Academical studies subservient to the edification of the church.* A sermon preached in the Chapel of Queens' College, Cambridge, March 2. Cambridge: Harwood and Hall. Pp. 28.

1831

(3)   *The single talent well employed; or, the history of Ruth Clarke, for thirty years, servant of the late Henry Venn, M.A.* London: John Hatchard and Son. (1834, 8th edition; 1839, 12th edition.) Subsequently published as: *The history of Ruth Clark; or, the single talent well employed.* [London: J. Groom, [1855?]. Pp. 36.

1834

(4)   *The life and a selection from the letters of Henry Venn.* London: John Hatchard and Son, 1834 (1835, 1836, 1837, 1839). Pp. xvi–585.

1838

(5)   Memoir of Henry Venn, M.A., prefixed to new edition of *The Complete Duty of Man.* London: Tegg and Son, 1838, v-xxiii.

(6)   Letter on ecclesiastical relations of the Church Missionary Society. December 18.

1838 or 1839

(7)   *Islington Hymn Book.* HV a chief compiler.

1839

(8)   Remarks on the constitution and practice of the Church Missionary Society, with reference to its ecclesiastical relations. Appendix II, 39th Report.

1840

(9)   "The Rev. H. Venn on certain strictures on the life of his grandfather." To the editor of the *Christian Observer.* CO, 40(29), May 1840, pp. 261-6.

1841

(10)   Address of the Committee of the Church Missionary Society, on its present financial situation. Dec. 13. Pp. 4. Signed by Venn, Davies, Coates.

(11)   Circular letter from the Committee of the Church Missionary Society to the missionaries (re finance). [Dec.]. Pp. 3. Signed by Venn, Davies, Coates.

1842

(12)   Address to King of Prussia. Feb. Signed by Chichester, Venn, Davies, Coates. CMR, XIII (2), Feb. 1842, p. 46.

(13)   Fourah Bay Institution Buildings' Fund. (A full description of the Society's policy re higher education.) September 29. Signed by Venn, Davies, Coates.

1843

(14)   Letter to local association secretaries on plans for removing financial difficulties of the Society. Jan. 10. Pp. 2. Signed by Venn, Davies, Coates.

(15)   Regulations for the Church Missionary Society's Institution at Islington. As revised Jan. 27. Pp. 7. Signed by Venn, Davies, Coates.

(16)   *The hope and joy of re-union in the heavenly state* [John 14:1-3]; a sermon together with a sermon by John Venn, *The power which quickens, preserves, comforts, and finally perfects the believer* [Ephes. 1:19-23]. Preached on the occasion of the death of Mrs. Eling Elliott, April 23, 1843. London: Hatchard and Son, pp. 1–18.

(17)   Statement of the proceedings of the Committee of the Church Missionary Society in the case of the Rev. W. T. Humphrey. April 25, 1843. Signed by Venn, Coates, Davies. Proceedings 1842–43. Vol. 17, Appendix, pp. 113-43.

(17a)   Instructions to missionaries. October 16.

1844

(18)   Correspondence between Bishop Terrot and the CMS. Jan. 20; March 1 and 6. Pp. 10. *The Record,* No. 1725, May 9, 1844, p. 3.

(18a)   Instructions to missionaries. May 27.

(19)   *A sermon on the occasion of the death of Josiah Pratt.* October 20. [I Peter 4:10–11.] London: Seeleys, Hatchards, Nisbet. Pp. 24.

(20)   Correspondence between the Rev. Henry Venn, Hon. Sec. of the CMS and the Ven. Samuel Wilberforce, Archdeacon of Surrey, in reference to a speech delivered at York by the Archdeacon, on the 26th of October last. (This circular contains the Archdeacon's apology and the withdrawal of certain insinuations, Nov. 14.) Pp. 4.

1845

(21)   Appeal of the members of the Church Missionary Society for a memorial of the late Rev. Josiah Pratt, B.D., late secretary of the Society. March 28. Pp. 3. Signed by Venn, Davies, Coates.

(22)   Statement of the Committee of the Church Missionary Society, in reference to land purchased by the Missionaries in New Zealand. July 8. London: Church Missionary House. Pp. 16. Signed by Venn, Davies, Coates.

(23)   Bishopric of Prince Rupert's Land. September 5. (Appeal for subscriptions towards endowment.) Pp. 3. Signed by Chichester, Dandon M.P., Ashley M.P., Alexander Beattie, Benjamin Harrison, Henry Kingscote, John Labouchere, William Niven, William Short, Henry Venn.

(24)   Madras and South India Mission—Papers relative to the education of the natives of India, through the medium of the English language. September. London: Church Missionary Society. Pp. 16. Signed by Venn, Davies, Coates.

1846

(25)   *The present position and future prospects of the Church Missionary Society.* Presented to Islington Clerical Meeting, Jan. 7. London: Church Missionary House. Pp. 22.

(26)   "On the employment of native labourers in missionary stations: an exchange by letters to the editor." CO, Jan. & Feb. 1846, pp. 17–19; 81–3.

(27)   To the Association Secretaries of the Church Missionary Society. Feb. 9. Pp. 3. Signed by Venn, Davies, Coates.

1847

(28)   Suggestions for the improvement of the social and intellectual condition of the native Africans at Sierra Leone. Pp. 3.

1848

(29)   (Address to Archbishop of Canterbury re acceptance of Vice-patronage of CMS.) March 13. CMR, XIX(5), May 1848, pp. 99–100.

(30)   Address of the Committee to the members and friends of the Society (relative to the Jubilee), June. Signed by Venn, Tucker, Straith. *Jubilee Volume 1848-49,* pp. v–xiv.

(31)   Circular letter to Secretaries of Associations, containing hints and suggestions in reference to the Jubilee Year and Jubilee Day. [Sept. 1848]. Pp. 3. signed by Venn, Tucker, Straith.

(32)   *The founders of the Church Missionary Society and the first five years.* CMS Jubilee Pamphlet No. 5, Sept. London: Church Missionary House, 1848. Pp. 31.

(33)   Instructions to missionaries. Oct. 31. Signed by Venn, Tucker, Straith. *Jubilee Volume 1848-49,* 3-16.

(34)   Rules for reducing unwritten languages to alphabetical writings in Roman character with reference especially to the languages spoken in Africa. Editor, Henry Venn. October. Pp. 7.

(35)   Letter read and adopted by the Jubilee Meeting of the Church Missionary Society, 2nd, Nov. (Addressed to native Christians in areas where the Society was at work conveying message from the meeting.) Pp. 4. Signed by Chichester, Venn, Tucker, Straith.

(36)   "The results of modern missions." CO, 48(132), Dec. 1848, pp. 805-7.

1849

(37)   *A sermon at the consecration of the Right Rev. G. Smith, Bishop of Victoria, and the Right Rev. D. Anderson, Bishop of Rupert's Land,* May 29. [Acts 21:21-22]. London: Hatchards and Seeleys. Pp. 31.

(38)   Report of a Sub-Committee to consider existing regulations respecting the marriage of students and missionaries, June 11; Report of the Sub-Committee upon the financial arrangements between the CMS and its missionaries, Dec. 11. Appendix contains HV's letter to the principal of the CMS Institution (Islington), October 8, 1861. Pp. 16.

(39)   *Preface to S. W. Koelle, Narrative of an expedition into the Vy Country of West Africa and the discovery of a system of syllabic writing recently invented by the natives of the Vy Tribe.* Sept. 6. London: Seeleys and Hatchards. Pp. ii–vi.

(40)   Instructions to missionaries. October 5. CMI, I(7), Nov. 1849, pp. 162-68.

(41)   The Missionaries' Children's Home. (A statement of intention.) October 30. Pp. 2. Signed by Venn, Tucker, Straith.

(42) Jubilee Statement read (in part) at Jubilee meeting, Exeter Hall, Nov. 2. *Jubilee Volume 1848–49,* pp. 179–257.

(43) Memoranda for the use of a deputation of the Church Missionary Society appointed to wait upon Viscount Palmerston, to solicit protection for the liberated Africans, being British subjects, who have emigrated from Sierra Leone to Badagri and Abeokuta, and for the European missionaries who reside at these places. [1849]. (Meeting with Palmerston took place Dec. 4.)

1850

(44) Minutes upon the position of native ministers in a mission, and upon the distinction between a mission and the pastoral charge of native converts, n.d. [Collation of minutes of April 12, 1848, and Jan. 8, 1850.] Pp. 3.

(45) Statement respecting the comparative economy of the Church Missionary and Wesleyan–Methodist Missionary Societies, in reply to certain statement in the "Watchman" Newspaper, etc. January. Pp. 4. Signed by Venn, Tucker, Straith.

(46) The African Squadron, Petition of the Committee of the Church Missionary Society, deprecating the diminishing or removal of the Squadron. March 19. Pp. 3. Signed by Chichester, Venn, Straith.

(47) Rupert's Land Diocesan Fund. April 22. Pp. 4.

(48) *Colonial church legislation—a letter to Sir Robert Harry Inglis, Bart, M.P.* May 8. Pp. 20. London: John Hatchard.

(49) Instructions to missionaries. Aug. 20. CMI, I(8). Oct. 1850, pp. 425–31.

(50) Minutes of the Committee of the Church Missionary Society, in reply to a statement, contained in the Report of the Derby Association of the Society for the Propagation of the Gospel in Foreign Parts, and referring to the operations of the Church Missionary Society. Nov. 11. Pp. 4. Signed by Venn, Tucker, Straith.

(50a) Report of the Sub-Committee to consider the eligibility of removing the students of the Institution to the country. Dec. 9. Pp. 8. *Laws, Regulations and Policies of the CMS.* No. VII.

1851

(51) Instructions to missionaries. Jan. 2. CMI, II(2). Feb. 1851, pp. 39–45.

(52)   Address of the Committee of the Church Missionary Society on the present crisis. Jan. 13. (On the subject of papal aggression.) Signed by Venn, Tucker, Straith, CMR, XXII(3), March 1851, pp. 65–8.

(53)   Correspondence between the secretary of the Church Missionary Society and secretary of the Hibernian District of the Church Missionary Society in Dublin in reference to deputational arrangements in Ireland, Jan. 18; Feb. 20. Pp. 3.

(54)   Instructions to missionaries. June 20. CMI, II(8) Aug. 1851, pp. 185–91.

(55)   The case of Archdeacon Henry Williams, in reply to a statement by the Rev. E. G. Marsh. Oct. 13. Pp. 24. Signed by Venn & Straith.

(56)   A letter to the Lord Bishop of London in ref. to the operations of the C.M.S. in Syria, Palestine, etc., for the benefit of the Greek and Oriental Church. Nov. 20. Proceedings of the CMS, 1851–1852, Vol. 21, Appendix II, pp. 208–13.

(57)   Instructions to missionaries. Dec. 5. CMI, III(1), Jan. 1852, pp. 18–21.

(58)   Minute upon the employment and ordination of native teachers. (First paper.) N.B. Subsequently included in the pamphlet *The Native Pastorate and Organisation of Native Churches,* 1866. See (157).

(59)   Character of Edward Bickersteth. Appendix to T. R. Birks, *Memoir of Edward Bickersteth.* London: Seeleys, [1851]. 2nd edn., 1852.

1852
(60)   (Letter to the Bishop of Hong Kong re the claim of the American Episcopalian Bishop to exercise episcopal authority over CMS missionaries.) Aug. 24. Pp. 4.

(61)   (Official statement re Home for Missionaries' Children.) Sept. Pp. 2. Signed by Venn, Straith.

(62)   Instructions to missionaries. Nov. 1. CMI, III(12), Dec. 1852, pp. 285–7.

1853
(63)   Statement respecting the clergymen in connexion with the Church Missionary Society, who have been compelled to relinquish missionary work through Providential circumstances, and have returned home under the sanction of the Committee, able to under-

take ministerial work, and in many cases equal to full discharge of laborious duties, but who are yet without preferment, and very inadequately provided with a maintenance for their families. Jan. Pp. 2. Signed by Venn, Knight, Straith.

(63a) Sierra Leone Native Church. Articles of a proposed arrangement between the Bishop of Sierra Leone (Dr. Vidal) and the Church Missionary Society, in respect of the regulation of the Native Church in the Colony of Sierra Leone (March 1853), pp. 7.

(64) *The responsibilities of the seniors of the university as respects the salvation of souls.* A sermon at Cambridge, I Cor. 3:10-15, preached before the University of Cambridge April 17, 1853, on the occasion of the death of J. Scholefield. London: Seeleys; Cambridge: Macmillans, pp. 18.

(65) The memorial of the Church Missionary Society, for Africa and the East, presented to the Right Hon. the Earl of Aberdeen, First Lord of the Treasury, etc., etc., etc., in reference to the renewal of powers to the Hon. East India Company. May 27. Pp. 23. Signed by Chichester, Venn, Knight, Straith.

(66) "Lord Langdale and the Gorham Judgment" CO, 53 (186), June 1853, pp. 413–25.

(67) Minutes of the Committee of the Church Missionary Society on the present state and future prospects of China. Oct. 10. Pp. 15.

1854
(68) Some account of the efforts made by the African Native Agency Committee, to promote the growth of cotton in Africa and of other exportable produce by means of native African agency itself. Jan. 1. Pp. 25.

(69) Native Church Organisation—extract from letter to Lord Bishop of Madras, Jan. 3.

(69a) Address, annual meeting, London Society for Promoting Christianity Amongst the Jews, May 5. *Jewish Intelligence,* 20, June 1854, pp. 178–80.

(70) Special appeal for the enlargement of the Society's means: the need of men, and the men needed. May 8. Pp. 3. Signed by Venn, Chapman, Straith, Graham.

(71) Instructions to missionaries. June 16.

(72) Circular to the Society's missionaries in India, June 27. Pp. 2. Signed by Venn, Chapman, Straith, Graham. (re government plans for education.)

(73)   Circular to missionaries re the finances of the Society, urging more local self-support. June. Pp. 2. Signed by Venn, Chapman, Straith.

(74)   Documents connected with the proposal of the Bishop of New Zealand Church. July. Pp. 16.

(75)   Instructions to missionaries. Sept. 5.

(76)   Instructions to missionaries. Oct. 13.

(77)   Preface to *Memoir of the Rev. John James Weitbrecht,* compiled by his widow, Mary Weitbrecht. London: James Nisbet and Co., 2nd edn., 1854. Pp. v–vi.

1855
(78)   Instructions to missionaries. [Jan. 16].

(78a)   Regulations explanatory of the relation between the CMS and the students, missionaries, and catechists, connected with it. Feb. Pp. 8. *Laws, Regulations and Policies of the CMS,* No. II.

(79)   Report of a meeting for establishment of a "Stranger's Home," for Asiatics, Africans, South-Sea Islanders, and others, occasionally residing in the metropolis. March 28. Pp. 26. Speech by HV. Pp. 5–7.

(80)   Instructions to missionaries. June 1.

(81)   Circular to the Society's Missionaries. Nov. 20. Pp. 3. Signed by Venn, Chapman, Straith, Holl. (Generally re the finances of the Society, urging more local self-support.)

(82)   Minute adopted by the Committee of Correspondence. Dec. 4. Pp. 4. Signed by Venn, Chapman, Straith, Holl. (Re scruples of certain missionaries in Bengal in respect of government grants-in-aid.)

1856
(83)   Letter of the Rev. Henry Venn to the Bishop of Melbourne, on the employment of unpaid lay preachers. Jan 1. Pp. 4.

(84)   Memorial of the committee of the Church Missionary Society upon the extension of the Episcopate in India, April 14, 1856; and Statement of the Committee of the Church Missionary Society, to accompany a memorial, upon the extension of the Episcopate in India, April 13.

(85)   Circular minute on missionary unions. April 14. Pp. 3. Signed by Venn, Chapman, Straith. (Earlier arguments restated and earlier decisions confirmed.)

(86)   Minute of Committee of the Church Missionary Society upon the state of its finances at the close of the year ending 31st March, 1856, adopted April 14. P. 1. Signed by Venn, Chapman, Straith, Holl.

(87)   Instructions to missionaries. June 5. CMR, 27(7), July 1856, pp. 153–54.

(88)   Extension of West-African commerce, more especially with reference to the Niger and Tshadda—Deputation to Lord Palmerston, etc. July 18. CMR, XXVII(8), Aug. 1856, 181–84.

(89)   Minute on the different departments of business connected with the secretariat of the Church Missionary Society. July 22. Pp. 7.

(90)   Instructions to missionaries. Oct. 10. CMI, XIII(1), Jan. 1857, pp. 19–22.

(91)   *Colonial church legislation. An inquiry into the ecclesiastical law of the colonies and dependencies of Great Britain; and into the best means of remedying its defects; with observations by the Lord Bishop of Melbourne.* London: Seeley, Jackson, and Halliday. Pp. 23.

1857
(92)   Minute on polygamy. Jan. 12.

(93   Instructions to missionaries. June 5. CMI, VIII(7), July 1857, pp. 154-60.

(94)   *The treasure in earthen vessels. II Cor. 4:7. A sermon preached in the Parish Church of St. Marylebone, June 11, at the consecration of the Hon. & Right Rev. John Thomas Pelham, D.D., Lord Bishop of Norwich.* To which is appended an historical sketch of the revival of evangelical preaching in the Church of England. London: Seeley & Co. Pp. 16.

(95)   "The crisis in India—Remarks on the supposed connexion between missions and the outbreak in India." [August]. CMI, VIII, 1857, special attachment, pp. 8. (See p. 7 for Venn statement.)

(96)   Minute of the C.M.S. on the Indian Mutiny in its connexion with Christian missions and the future government of India upon Christian principles. Sept. 29, 1857. Signed by Venn, Knight, Chapman, Straith.

(97)   Special appeal for India. Dec. 1. Signed by Venn, Knight, Chapman, Straith.

(98)   A memorial to the Queen on the Indian crisis, Dec.; to which is attached: the policy of the Indian government in respect of

religion—an explanatory statement to accompany the memorial to Her Majesty the Queen from the vice-patron, president, vice-presidents, friends, and supporters of the Church Missionary Society, on the Indian Crisis. Pp. 40.

1858

(99)   Statement of the Committee of the Church Missionary Society upon the Indian Crisis. Jan. 12.

(100)   A sermon on the occasion of the death of the Rt. Rev. Daniel Wilson, Bishop of Calcutta and Metropolitan of India, Acts 20:24, February 14, in *Three Sermons preached on the occasion of the death of D. Wilson, Bishop of Calcutta,* by the Bishop of Winchester, H. Venn, etc. London: Seeley, Jackson, and Halliday. Pp. 12.

(101)   Minute of the Committee of the Church Missionary Society on the question of "The extension of the episcopate" in India. A compilation of the memorial, April 14, 1856, and statement, April 13, 1857, with introduction and closing paragraphs added. March 30. Pp. 4. Signed by Chichester, Venn, Knight, Chapman, Straith.

(102)   Letter to a friend on the views of the Committee of the Church Missionary Society on the extension of the episcopate in India. April 12. Pp. 4.

(102a)   Report of public meeting. May 20, of Christian Vernacular Education Society for India. *Occasional Paper,* No. 2, July. See p. 8ff for Venn's address.

(103)   Ecclesiastical relations of the Church Missionary Society in India. July. Pp. 16. Signed by Venn, Knight, Chapman, Straith. (N.B. This document includes Appendix II to the *39th Annual Report.*)

(104)   Deputation to Lord Stanley. Aug. 7. Pp. 19. See pp. 16–18 for remarks by Venn (an extract from *The Record,* Aug. 9, 1858.)

(104a)   Candidates and students. Laws and regulations relating to candidates for missionary employment and students of the Institution at Islington. Nov. 8. Signed by Venn, Knight, Chapman, and Straith. *Laws, Regulations and Policies of the CMS,* No. VI.

1859

(105)   *Memorial to the Rev. Thomas Gajetan Ragland.* Cambridge University Church Missionary Association. *Occasional Papers,* No. 2. Jan. London: Seeley, Jackson and Halliday. Pp. 23.

(106)   "Special fund for India" (an explanation). CMR, n.s., IV(1), Jan. 1859, p. 1.

(107)   Special appeal for labourers. Feb. 23. Pp. 4. Signed by Venn, Knight, Chapman, Straith.

(108)   Terms of acceptance of candidates (Minute), May 31.

(109)   Bible education committee for India—deputation to Lord Palmerston and Sir Charles Wood. Aug. 5, 1859.

(110)   Instructions to missionaries. Oct. 14.

(111)   Letter to the *Times*: "West African Cotton." Nov. 10. Pp. 5.

(112)   Regulations for corresponding committees, missionary conferences, etc. (India). December. Pp. 16.

(113)   *A plea for an open and unfettered Bible in the Government schools of India.* Pp. 12.

1860

(114)   Instructions to missionaries. March 12. CMI, XI(4), April 1860, pp. 89–92.

(115)   Memorial to the Right Honourable Viscount Palmerston, on the national importance of steam navigation upon the River Niger, for the encouragement and protection of lawful commerce, and the more effectual suppression of slave trade. March 15. Pp. 3. Venn is one of many signatories.

(116)   *Recent policy of Indian government in respect of progress of Christianity among the natives of India.* Occasional Papers on India, No. 8. March. Pp. 12. Unsigned.

(116a)   "The educational wants of India." Review of (1) *Christian Education for India in the mother tongue,* by W. Arthur; (2) *Educational destitution in Bengal and Behar,* Calcutta, 1858; (3) *The policy as established by law, of the Indian Government, opposed to the neutral policy in respect of Christianity,* the Church Missionary Society, 1860. CO, 59(271), July 1860, pp. 494–501, Part 1; 59(272), Aug. 1860, pp. 574–79, Part 2.

(117)   "The Bible in Indian Schools." Petition presented to the House of Lords. July 2. CMR, N.S.V.(8), Aug. 1860, pp. 233–35.

(118)   Instructions to missionaries. Sept. 28. Pp. 24. London: Church Missionary House. Signed by Venn, Knight, Chapman, Straith, Dawes.

(119)   Letter to Mr. Royston of the Madras Corresponding Committee about new plans for the organisation of the mission in relation to the local church. Sept. & Oct. 2. Pp. 7. Signed by Venn, Knight, Chapman, Straith, Dawes.

(120)   *The policy, as established by law, of the Indian government, opposed to the neutral policy, in respect of Christianity.* London: Church Missionary Society. Pp. 12. Unsigned.

1861

(121)   Memorial of the Church Missionary Society to His Grace the Secretary of State for the Colonies on the present circumstances of New Zealand Jan. 4. Pp. 7. Signed by Chichester.

(122)   Further remarks on New Zealand affairs. April 23. London: Church Missionary House. Pp. 18.

(123)   Speech at the Anniversary of the British and Foreign Bible Society. April 30.

(123a)   "West Africa; viewed in connection with slavery, Christianity, and the supply of cotton." Review of (1) *A pilgrimage to my motherland,* by Robert Campbell, 1861; (2) *Ten years' wandering among the Ethiopians,* by T. J. Hutchinson, 1861; (3) *Reports of the Church Missionary Society,* 1858–1860; (4) *Papers of the Cotton Supply Association,* Manchester, 1860, 1861; (5) *Papers of the African Aid Society,* 1860, 1861; (6) Report of Debates in the House of Commons, *The Times,* Feb. 27, 1861. CO, 60(281), May 1861, pp. 289–403.

(124)   Instructions to missionaries. June 21. CMI, XII(8), Aug. 1861, pp. 183–88.

(125)   Minute on the organisation of native churches. July 9. (Second paper.) N.B. Original title: Present system of "station" missionary work and its dangers. Subsequently included in *The Native pastorate and organisation of native churches,* 1866.

(126)   Minute on the conviction and imprisonment of the Rev. James Long for libel. Sept. 24. Pp. 6.

(127)   The position and Prospects of the Church Missionary Society. Nov. 19. Pp. 3.

1862

(128)   An address to Colonel Sir Herbert B. Edwardes, K.C.B., Commissioner of the Cis-Sutlej States, Punjab, on occasion of his return to India, with some notice of his reply. Jan. 3. London: Church Missionary House. Pp. 10.

(129)   Instructions to missionaries. Jan. 24. CMI, XIII(3), March 1862, 49–53.

(130)   Address to the Committee on taking possession of the Committee room in the new mission house. March 7.

(131) *The missionary life and labours of Francis Xavier taken from his own correspondence: with a sketch of the general results of Roman Catholic missions amoung the heathen.* London: Longman, Green, Longman, Roberts & Green. Pp. 324.

1863
(132) *Sermon preached on the occasion of the death of Mrs. Wilson.* Rom. 16:1–2. Feb. 1. London: B. Seeley. Pp. 7–20.

(133) Memorial of the Church Missionary Society to his Grace the Duke of Newcastle, Her Majesty's Secretary of State for the Colonies, etc. March 17, 1863. Pp. 4. Signed by Chichester, Venn, Knight, Dawes. (Re the policies of Governor Freeman at Lagos— a protest against.)

(134) Instructions to missionaries. March 26. CMI, XIV(5), May 1863, pp. 109–13.

(135) To the Right Honourable Sir Charles Wood, Bart., M.P., Secretary of State for India. Oct. 12. (First draft.) Pp. 3. Signed by Chichester, Venn, Long, Dawes.

(136) To the Right Hon. Sir C. Wood, Bart., M.P., etc., etc. (Final submission.) (Representation re education in India.) Pp. 4.

(137) Letter to the *Times* concerning the Bishop of Oxford's Speech. Nov. 11. P. 10.

(138) Memorandum of several points brought under notice of Sir Charles Wood, H.M. Secretary of State for India, by a deputation of the Church Missionary Society, on presenting the Society's memorial upon government grants-in-aid to schools in India. Nov. 26. Pp. 2.

(138a) "The Bishop of Oxford on missions." CO, 62(312), December 1863, pp. 899–907.

(139) I. Venn letter re. missionaries at Abeokuta, with attachments:
    1. Memorial of CMS to Duke of Newcastle
    2. Despatch, Duke of Newcastle to Governor Freeman
    3. Gov. Freeman to Duke of Newcastle
    4. Duke of Newcastle to Freeman
    5. Gov. Freeman to Duke of Newcastle
    6. Newcastle Despatch
    7. Acting Governor's Despatch
    8. Idem.
    9. Duke of Newcastle to Acting Governor
  II. Venn's letter re conduct of missionaries:
    1. Venn to Earl Russell, Dec. 1, 1862
    2. Enclosure: H. Townsend to Venn, July 2, 1862

Parliamentary Papers, Irish University Press edn. Colonies: Africa: Nigeria, No. 63, Sessions 1840–87 (July 25, 1863).

1864

(140)   Remarks upon a leading article in the "Buckingham Advertiser and Free Press" of Saturday, Feb. 20th, 1864. Mar. 3. Pp. 2.

(140a)   Bishop Daniel Wilson's journal letters. Review of *Bishop Daniel Wilson's Journal Letters.* Edited by Daniel Wilson, 1863. CO, 63(314), Feb. 1864, pp. 138–43.

(141)   Proposed minute on the re-marriage of native converts' bill. n.d., pp. 6. [March–April, 1864].

(142)   (Statement to Archbishop of Canterbury respecting the West African Native Church.) April 11. Pp.4.

(143)   Royal Commission on clerical subscription—subscription to articles the safeguard of a church's liberties. Speech in Jerusalem Chamber, April 25. Knight, 1882, pp. 491–7.

(144)   "Church politics: the royal commission." CO, 64(317), May 1864, pp. 347–61. Unsigned.

(145)   Appeal from the Committee of the Church Missionary Society to their friends throughout the country. July 11. Postscript dated July 22. Signed by Chichester, Maude, Venn, Long, Fenn, Dawes.

(146)   West African Native Bishopric Fund. [1864]. Revised in 1870. Pp. 2.

1865

(147)   *Retrospect and prospect of the operation of the Church Missionary Society* (being the substance of an address delivered to the Islington Clerical Meeting). Jan. 10. London: Church Missionary House. 2nd edn., 1865. Pp. 25.

(148)   Obituary of the Rev. Henry Venn Elliot. (Reprinted from the CO, 65[328], April 1865, pp. 303–8.)

(149)   Report based on HV tract concerning present missionary situation. CO, 65(328), April 1865, pp. 317–8.

(150)   Basle Missionary Society's Jubilee, 1865. May 8. Pp. 3. Signed by Chichester, Maude, Venn, Long, Dawes. (Greetings to the Society.)

(151)   Instructions to missionaries. June 16.

(152)   Draft of letter to the secretary of the corresponding committee, Calcutta, on the re-marriage of converts' bill. June. Pp. 7. Signed by Venn, Long, Fenn, Dawes.

(153)   Proposal of a native bishop in Tinnevelly, issued July 1865. July 10. Pp. 4.

(154)   Instructions to missionaries. Dec. 11. CMI, ns. II(1), Jan. 1866, pp. 17–19.

(155)   *West African Colonies. Notices of the British Colonies on the West Coast of Africa.* London: Dalton and Lucy, Pp. 39.

(156)   Minute on the native church endowments in the missions of the CMS. Jan. 8. Pp. 2.

(157)   Third paper on native Church organisation. Jan. 8. (N.B. This paper, along with the first two of 1851 and 1861, are issued together with the present one as a pamphlet: *The native pastorate and organisation of native churches* with appendix: "Proposal of a native bishop in Tinnevelly," issued July 1865.)

(158)   To the Right Honourable Edward Cardwell, M.P., Her Majesty's Secretary of State for the Colonies. Jan. 18. Pp. 4. Signed by Chichester and Venn.

(158a)   "Dr. Livingstone's second expedition to Africa." Review of *The Zambesi and its tributaries, and the discovery of Lakes Shirwa and Nyassa; being a narrative of an expedition during the years 1858–1864 in South-Eastern Africa,* by David Livingstone, 1866. CO, 65(343), July 1866, pp. 520–35.

(159)   Instructions to missionaries. June 29. CMI, N.S.II(9), Sept. 1866, pp. 264–67.

(160)   *Sermon after the funeral of Baron Northbrook,* preached Sept. 16. I Timothy 4:12. London: Dalton and Lucy. Pp. 3–16.

(161)   The address of the president, treasurer, committee, and secretaries of the Church Missionary Society for Africa and the East, to the Sierra Leone Missionary Association. Oct. 8. Pp. 10. Signed by Chichester, Maude, Venn, Fenn, Mee, Dawes.

(162)   Minute of the New Zealand Mission. Nov. 20. Pp. 7. Signed by Maude, Venn, Fenn, Mee.

1867

(163)   Letter of the Rev. Henry Venn, Honorary Secretary of the Church Missionary Society, to the Lord Bishop of Kingston (Jamaica), on the state of the Negroes of Jamaica. Jan. 7. Pp. 11.

(164)   Letter from the Committee of Correspondence of the Church Missionary Society to the Corresponding Committee at Madras. January. Pp. 8. Signed by Venn, Fenn, Mee, Hutchinson.

(165)   Palestine Mission: erection of a church at Nazareth. Correspondence also relating to that Mission. (HV letter dated Feb. 2, pp. 1–3.) Pp. 16.

(165a)   "Our churchmanship, and that of the ritualists." CO, 66(350), Feb. 1867, pp. 123–33.

(166)   Instructions to missionaries. July 23. CMI, N.S.III(9), Sept. 1867, pp. 277–80.

(167)   Church Missionary Society: statement, explanation, and appeal. Aug. 12. Pp. 3. Signed by Chichester, Maude, Venn, Fenn, Mee, Hutchinson.

(168)   Proposal for erecting a Protestant church at Nazareth. [1867]. Pp. 4.

1868
(169)   Royal commission in ritual—resolutions proposed for adoption by the Rev. H. Venn, Jerusalem Chamber, July 18, 22, Aug. 8, Dec. 8, 11, 1867, and Jan. 30, 1868.

(170)   Instructions to missionaries. June 30. CMI, N.S.IV(10), Oct. 1868, pp. 316–20.

(171)   "Growth of missionary spirit and effort in the University of Cambridge during the past fifty years": a paper read at Cambridge. December. CMI, N.S.VI(11), Nov. 1870, pp. 349–52.

(172)   The slave-trade of East Africa: is it to continue or be suppressed. (Unsigned but prepared by CMS secretariat. Incorporates Venn's concepts but appears to have been drafted by another secretary.)

1869
(172a)   "The committee room of the Church Missionary Society: a scene." CO, 68(374), Feb. 1869, pp. 142–48.

(173)   Instructions to missionaries. Jan. 5. CMI, N.S.V(3), March 1869, pp. 71–75.

(174)   "The ritual commission." Parts I and II. CO, 69(373 & 374), Jan. & Feb. 1869, pp. 1–17; pp. 81–97.

(175)   East African slave trade—draft of a proposed memorial to government. [Jan. 1869]. Pp. 7.

(175a)   "Alleged Evangelical ritualistic irregularities." CO, 68(375), March 1869, pp. 161–70.

(175b)   "Lunar Scenery." CO, 68(375), March 1869, pp. 170–78.

(176) To His Grace the Duke of Argyll, K.T. etc., Her Majesty's Secretary of State for India, etc., etc. The memorial of the president and committee of the society called the Church Missionary Society for Africa and the East. Feb. 16. Pp. 4. Signed by Chichester, Venn, Fenn, Mee, Hutchinson. CMI, N.S.V.(4), April 1869, pp. 121–22.

(176a) "Auricular confession and absolution in the Church of England." CO, 68(376), April 1869, pp. 241–52.

(177) "Change of the editorship of the *Christian Observer.*" CO, 69(377), May 1869, pp. 321–24.

(177a) "Former days not better than these." Review of *A sermon preached in Peterborough Cathedral,* at the first General Ordination of the Lord Bishop, by A. S. Farrar. CO, 68(377), May 1869, pp. 391–96.

(178) Instructions to missionaries. July 6. CMI, N.S.V.(8), Aug. 1869, pp. 242–46.

(178a) "The penitent thief." CO, 68(379), July 1869, pp. 481–86.

(179) "The Negro Bishop." CO, 69(381), Sept. 1869, pp. 641–50.

(179a) "Dean Goode's sermons." Review of *Sermons by the late William Goode,* Edited by James Metcalfe, 1869. CO, 68(381), Sept. 1869, pp. 666–77.

(180) Memorandum on the best means of providing episcopal superintendence for a native Christian church beyond Her Majesty's dominions. Nov. 10. Pp. 4.

(181) "Foreign Missions." Review of Dr. Rufus Anderson's *Foreign Missions, Their Relations and Claims* (1869). CMI, N.S.V(11), Nov. 1869, pp. 327–35.

(182) *Franz Xavier, Ein weltgeschichtliches missionsbild.* Translation into the German of *Francis Xavier* with substantial additions by Wilhelm Hoffmann. Wiesbaden/Darmstadt: Niedner.

1870
(183) "Bishop Hamilton's secession from the evangelical clergy." CO, 70(385), Jan. 1870, pp. 1–11.

(183a) "Christianity among the New Zealanders." Review of (1) *Christianity among the New Zealanders,* by the Right Rev. W. Williams, 1867; (2) *The past, present, and the future of New Zealand,* by R. Taylor, 1868; and (3) *Te Ika a Maui, or, New Zealand and the inhabitants,* by R. Taylor, 1870. CO, 69(389), May 1870, pp. 374–84.

(184)   Church Missionary Society. Special appeal. June. Pp. 3. Signed by Chichester, Maude, Venn, Fenn, Hutchinson.

(184a) "The Ritual Commission—the Lectionary." CO, 69(391), July 1870, pp. 481–91.

(185)   "The old key to the true interpretation of the baptismal service of the Church of England." (First drafted in 1850.) CO, 70(393), Sept. 1870, pp. 641–53.

(186)   "On separation between the younger and the elder evangelicals." CO, 70(393), Sept. 1870, pp. 688–91.

(187)   Instructions to missionaries. Oct. 21. CMI, N.S.VI(12), Dec. 1870, pp. 370–75.

(188)   Obituary: Rev. J. W. Knott, M.A. CO, 70(394), Oct. 1870, pp. 790–96.

(189)   "The ritual commission and its results." CO, 70(395), Nov. 1870, pp. 801–19. Also published separately, by one of the commissioners, *The Ritual Commission; the value and importance of its recommendations.* London: Hatchards, 1871.

(190)   Minute of the Society on the projected appointment of a missionary bishop to Madagascar. Signed by Chichester, Maude, Venn, Fenn, Barton, Hutchinson, and Lake. Dec. 12.

1871

(191)   Correspondence respecting the Madagascar bishopric. Dec. 21, Jan. 7, 1871. Pp. 3.

(192)   Instructions to missionaries. Jan. 20. CMR, N.S.I.(3), March 1871, pp. 91–97.

(193)   Memorandum to the Bishop of London re Madagascar bishopric. Feb. 10. Pp. 4.

(194)   The Church Missionary Society and the Madagascar bishopric. Mar. 21. Pp. 8.

(194a) "Bishop Cotton." Review of (1) *Memoir of G.E.L. Cotton, Bishop of Calcutta and Metropolitan,* Edited by Mrs. Cotton, 1871; (2) *Life of Right Rev. T. F. Middleton, Bishop of Calcutta,* by C. W. Le Bas, 1831. CO, 70(400), April 1871, pp. 241–64.

(194b) "The Gown or the Surplice." CO, 70(400), April 1871, pp. 291–301.

(195)   The Church Missionary Society and the Madagascar bishopric. March 21. Pp. 4. Signed by Venn, Fenn, Barton, Hutchinson, Lake.

(196)   Instructions to missionaries. July 25. CMI. N.S.VII(11), Nov. 1871, pp. 347–50.

(196a)   "The horrors of the West African slave trade reviving in East Africa." CO, 70:(405), September 1871, pp. 710–16.

(197)   Letter to Archbishop of York re proposal to establish a central board of missions. Oct. Pp. 4. Signed by Chichester, Venn, Fenn, Hutchinson, Lake.

(198)   "May parents be sponsors for their children at baptism?" CO, 71(406), Oct. 1871, pp. 739–44.

(199)   The Protestant church at Nazareth. Nov. Pp. 4.

1872

(200)   Consecration of churches in India. (Letters to the Bishop of Calcutta, Jan. 10, p. 7, and July 19, p. 10. G/AZ/1/2.)

(201)   Proposal of diocesan boards, or church unions, for the management of the home operations of church societies. Jan. 1872.

(201a)   "The Episcopal Church in America: Baptismal regeneration and ritualism." CO, 71(413), May 1872, pp. 326–340.

(202)   Proposal to set apart the 20th Dec. 1872, as a day of special prayer for an increase of missionary labourers in the Church of England. July 8. Pp. 4. Signed by Venn, Fenn, Wright, Hutchinson, Lake.

(203)   Instructions to missionaries. July 16, 1872. CMI, N.S.VIII(8), Aug. 1872, pp. 240–46.

(203a)   "The Bennett judgment: what are the Evangelical clergy to do?" CO, 71(416), Aug. 1872, pp. 561–68.

(204)   Memorandum on the need of some modification of an order in council, May 1, 1848, respecting jurisdiction of the Bishop of Victoria (China). Aug. Pp. 4.

(205)   Memorandum on the subject of a missionary bishop for China. August. Pp. 7.

(205a)   "Day of united intercession amoung members of the Church of England for labourers in the missions." CO, 71(417), Sept. 1872, pp. 641–49.

(206)   "Providential antecedents of the Sierra Leone Mission." CO, 72(419), Nov. 1872, pp. 801–9.

(207)   Preface to Joseph Salter, *The Asiatic in England*. London: Seeley, Jackson and Halliday, 1873.

C. Books about Venn

Knight, William. *Memoir of the Rev. H. Venn—the missionary secretariat of Henry Venn, B.D., Prebendary of St. Paul's and Honorary Secretary of the Church Missionary Society,* with an introductory biographical chapter and a notice of West African commerce by his sons, the Rev. John Venn, M.A., and the Rev. Henry Venn, M.A. London: Longmans, Green, and Co., 1880.

————. *Memoir of Henry Venn, B.D.—Prebendary of St. Paul's and Honorary Secretary of the Church Missionary Society.* London: Seeley, Jackson, and Halliday, 1882. This is a substantially reorganized and modified edition.

Venn, John. *Annals of a clerical family: being some account of the family of William Venn, Vicar of Otterton, Devon, 1600-1621.* London: Macmillan and Co., 1904. For Henry Venn, see pp. 148-74.

Warren, Max. *To Apply the Gospel—Selections from the Writings of Henry Venn.* Grand Rapids, Mich.: W. B. Eerdmans Co., 1971. Introduction: "Henry Venn, the Man, His Thought and His Practice—An Interpretation," pp. 15-34.

D. Articles and Obituaries Relating to Venn

"The Decease of the Rev. Henry Venn," *The Record,* no. 5695, Jan. 15, 1873, p. 2.

Notice of death and obituary, *The Times,* Jan. 16, 1873, p. 1, col. 1; p. 9, col. 6.

"The Late Rev. Henry Venn," *The Record,* no. 5647, Jan. 20, 1873, p. 2.

In Memoriam, CMI, 9(1), Jan. 1873, p. 33.

In Memoriam, CMR, 18(2), Feb. 1873, pp. 57-61.

In Memoriam, CO, 72(422), Feb. 1873, pp. 81-2.

Elliott, Charles J. "Notice of the late Rev. Henry Venn," CO, 73(422), Feb. 1873, pp. 147-54.

Minute of the death of the Rev. H. Venn, CMS *Monthly Reporter,* no. 3, March 1873, pp. 101-2.

Money, C. F. S.: "The late Rev. Henry Venn," *The Christian Advocate,* 7(3), March 1873, pp. 161-83.

"Memorial to the Rev. Henry Venn, B.D.," CMR, 18(4), April 1873, p. 139-41. Also: *Pamphlets* II(2).

"The Rev. Henry Venn," CMI, 9(5) May 1873, pp. 129-47.

Lee, Sidney (ed.). "Venn, Henry (1796-1873)," *Dictionary of National Biography.* London: Smith, Elder and Co., 1909; 58(208-9).

Venn, J. A. (ed.). "Venn, Henry," *Alumni Cantabrigienses.* Cambridge University Press, 1954; II:VI, p. 283.

Warren, Max. "Venn, Henry (1796–1873)," in Stephen Neill, Gerald H. Anderson, and John Goodwin (eds.), *Concise Dictionary of the Christian World Mission*. London: United Society for Christian Literature/ Lutterworth Press, 1970, p. 634.

E. Reviews of Venn's Writings

The Life and Selections from the Letters of the late Rev. Henry Venn, M.A., reviewed in CO, Feb. 1835, pp. 116–27.

Colonial church legislation, reviewed in CO, 50(148), July 1850, pp. 504–12.

The responsibilities of the seniors as respects the salvation of souls, reviewed in CO, 53(188), Aug. 1853, pp. 560–64.

Colonial church legislation: an enquiry into the ecclesiastical laws of the colonies and dependencies of Great Britain, reviewed in CO, 56(220), April 1856, pp. 243–50.

A review of the Rev. H. Venn on St. Francis Xavier and Christian missions. London: Burns and Lambert, 1862. (reprinted from the *Weekly Register,* Nov. 8 and 15, 1862.)

The missionary life and labours of Francis Xavier, CO, 62(301), Dec. 1862. pp. 899–913.

Francis Xavier, reviewed in *Christian Advocate and Review,* III, May 1863, pp. 225–29.

"Venn and Hoffmann's Life of Xavier," CMI, 7(9), Sept. 1871, pp. 264–71.

F. Studies in Venn's Missionary Principles

Ajayi, J. F. Ade. "Henry Venn and the Policy of Development," *Journal of the Historical Society of Nigeria,* 1, no. 4, (Dec. 1959): 331–42.

Beyerhaus, Peter. *Die Selbständigkeit der Jungen Kirchen als missionarisches Problem.* Wuppertal-Barmen: Verlag der Rheinischen Missions-Gesellschaft, 1956. Chap. 1:1: "Henry Venn—the euthanasia of the mission," pp. 31–44. Chap. 4: "The Foundation of the Anglican Church on the Niger," pp. 123–62.

Beyerhaus, Peter, and Lefever, Henry. *The Responsible Church and the Foreign Mission.* Grand Rapids, Mich.: W. B. Eerdmans Co., 1964. Chap. 1, pt. 1, pp. 25–30, and chap. 4, pp. 65–73.

Coggan, F. D. *These Were His Gifts.* Exeter: University of Exeter, 1974. Chap. 3: "Henry Venn (1796–1873)," pp. 321–31.

Shenk, Wilbert R. "Henry Venn's Instructions to Missionaries," *Missiology* 5, no.4 (Oct. 1977): 467–85.

———. "Henry Venn's Legacy," *Occasional Bulletin of Missionary Research* 1, no.2 (April 1977): 16–19.

———. "The Missionary and Politics: Henry Venn's Guidelines," *Journal of Church and State* 24, no. 3 (Autumn, 1982): 525–34.

————. "Rufus Anderson and Henry Venn: A Special Relationship?" *International Bulletin of Missionary Research* 5, no. 4 (Oct. 1981): 168–72.

————. "T'owd Trumpet: Venn of Huddersfield and Yelling," *Churchman* 93, no. 1 (1979): 39–54.

Yates, T. E.: *Venn and Victorian Bishops Abroad.* London: SPCK, 1978.

Part 2   General Bibliography

Ajayi, J. F. A. *Christian Missions in Nigeria, 1841–1891.* Evanston: Northwestern University Press, 1965.

————. "The Development of Secondary Grammar School Education in Nigeria." *Journal of the Historical Society of Nigeria* 2 (1963).

————. "Henry Venn and the Policy of Development." *Journal of the Historical Society of Nigeria* 1 (1959):331–42.

————. "Nineteenth Century Origins of Nigerian Nationalism." Journal of the Historical Society of Nigeria 2 (1961): 196–210.

Ajayi, William Olaseinde. "A History of the Niger and Northern Nigerian Missions 1857–1914." Ph.D. dissertation, Bristol University, 1963.

————. "A History of the Yoruba Mission 1843–1880." Master's thesis, Bristol University, 1959.

Anderson, Rufus. *Foreign Missions, Their Relations and Claims.* New York: Scribners, 1869.

Anstey, R. "A Reinterpretation of the Abolition of the British Slave Trade, 1806–07." *English Historical Review* 87 (1972):304–32.

Ashwell, A. R., and Wilberforce, R. G. *Life of the Right Reverend Samuel Wilberforce.* 3 vols. London, 1880–82.

Ayandele, E. A. "An Assessment of James Johnson and His Place in Nigerian History, 1874–1890." Pt. 1, *Journal of the Historical Society of Nigeria,* 2 (1963):486–516.

————. "Background to the 'Duel' between Crowther and Goldie on the Lower Niger, 1857–1885." *Journal of the Historical Society of Nigeria* 4 (1967):45–63.

————. *The Missionary Impact on Modern Nigeria, 1842–1914. A Political and Social Analysis.* London: Longmans, Green and Co., 1966.

Balleine, G. R. *A History of the Evangelical Party in the Church of England.* 1908. Reprint. London: Church Book Room, 1951.

Ballhatchet, K. A. "Asian Nationalism and Christian Missions." *International Review of Missions* 46 (1957):201–4.

————. "The Home Government and Bentinck's Educational Policy." *Cambridge Historical Journal* 10 (1951):224–29.

Bateman, Josiah. *The Life of Daniel Wilson, D.D.* Boston, 1860.

————. *The Life of the Reverend Henry Venn Elliott.* 2d ed. London, 1872.

Battiscombe, Georgina. *Shaftesbury: The Great Reformer, 1801-85*. Boston: Houghton Mifflin Co., 1975.

Baumgarten, Michael. *The Acts of the Apostles* (3 vols.), or *The History of the Church in the Apostolic Age*. Edinburgh: T. and T. Clark, 1854.

Beaglehole, J. C. "The Colonial Office, 1782-1854." *Historical Studies: Australia and New Zealand* 1 (1941):170-89.

Beaver, R. Pierce (ed.). *To Advance the Gospel—Selections from the Writings of Rufus Anderson*. Grand Rapids: Wm. B. Eerdmans, 1967.

———. "Rufus Anderson's Missionary Principles." *In Christus prediking in de wereld*. Kampen: J. H. Kok, 1965.

Bell, Kenneth N., and Morrell, W. P. (eds.). *Select Documents on British Colonial Policy, 1830-1860*. Oxford: Clarendon, 1928.

Best, G.F.A. "The Evangelicals and the Established Church." *Journal of Theological Studies,* N.S. 10 (1959):63-78.

Beyerhaus, Peter. "The Three Selves Formula: Is It Built on Biblical Foundations?" *International Review of Missions* 53 (1964):393-407.

Biber, G. E. *Bishop Blomfield and His Times*. London, 1854.

Birks, T. B. *Memoirs of Edward Bickersteth*. 3d ed., 2 vols. London, 1852.

Blomfield, Alfred (ed.). *Memoir of Charles James Blomfield*. London, 1863.

Bowen, Desmond. *The Idea of the Victorian Church*. Montreal: McGill University Press, 1968.

Bradley, Ian C. *The Call to Seriousness: The Evangelical Impact on the Victorians*. New York: Macmillan, 1976.

Bright, John. *Speech on Legislation and Policy for India, June 24, 1858*. London, 1858.

Brilioth, Y. *Three Lectures on Evangelicalism and the Oxford Movement*. London, 1934.

Brown, Ford K. *Fathers of the Victorians*. Cambridge: University Press, 1961.

Burn, W. L. *Emancipation and Apprenticeship in the British West Indies*. London: Jonathan Cape, 1937.

Buxton, Thomas Fowell. *The African Slave Trade and Its Remedy*. London: Pall Mall, 1968.

Carey, S. Pearce. *Carey*. London: Marshall, Morgan and Scott, 1936.

Carus, William. *Memoirs of the Life of the Reverend Charles Simeon . . . with Selections from His Writings and Correspondence*. 2d ed. London, 1847.

Chadwick, Owen. *MacKenzie's Grave*. London: Hodder and Stoughton, 1959.

Church Missionary Society. *Register of Missionaries and Native Clergy, 1804-1904*. London: CMS, 1904.

Clark, G. Kitson. *Churchmen and the Condition of England 1832-1885: A Study in the Development of Social Ideas and Practice from the Old Regime to the Modern State*. London: Methuen, 1973.

———. *The English Inheritance*. London: SCM, 1950.

——. *The Making of Victorian England*. London: Methuen, 1962.

Cnattingius, Hans. *Bishops and Societies: A Study of Anglican Colonial and Missionary Expansion, 1698–1850*. London: SPCK, 1952.

Coates, Dandeson. *The New Zealanders and Their Lands*. London: Hatchards, 1844.

Cockshut, A. O. J. *Anglican Attitudes. A Study of Victorian Religious Controversies*. London: Collins, 1959.

(Conybeare, W. J.) "Church Parties." *Edinburgh Review* 98 (1853):273–342.

Cotton, Sophia A. *Memoir of Bishop Cotton*. London: Longmans, Green and Co., 1871.

Coupland, Reginald. *Wilberforce*. London: Oxford, 1923. 2d ed., 1945.

Crowder, M. A. *Church Embattled: Religious Controversy in Mid–Victorian England*. London: David and Charles, 1970.

Curtin, Philip D. *The Image of Africa: British Ideas and Action 1780–1850*. London, 1965.

——. " 'Scientific' Racism and the British Theory of Empire." *Journal of the Historical Society of Nigeria* 2 (1960).

De Jong, J. A. *As the Water Covers the Sea—Millennial Expectations in the Rise of Anglo-American Missions 1640–1810*. Kampen: J. H. Kok, 1970.

Delavignette, Robert. *Christianity and Colonialism*. New York: Hawthorn Books, 1964.

De Silva, K. *Social Policy and Missionary Organizations in Ceylon 1840–1855*. London: Longmans, 1965.

Duff, Alexander. *India and India Missions*. Edinburgh, 1839.

——. *Missions the Chief End of the Christian Church*. Edinburgh, 1840.

——. *What Is Caste? How Is a Christian Government to Deal With It?* Calcutta, 1858.

Ekechi, Felix K. *Missionary Enterprise and Rivalry in Igboland 1857–1914*. London: Frank Cass, 1972.

Elliot-Binns, L. E. *The Early Evangelicals: A Religious and Social Study*. London: Lutterworth, 1953.

——. *English Thought 1860–1900—The Theological Aspect*. London: Longmans, Green and Co., 1956.

——. *The Evangelical Movement in the English Church*. London: Methuen and Co., 1928.

Embree, A. T. *Charles Grant and British Rule in India*. New York: Columbia University Press, 1962.

Fieldhouse, D. K. "Imperialism: An Historiographical Revision." *Economic History Review,* 2d series, 14 (1962–63):187–209.

Fletcher, Irene M. "The Fundamental Principle of the London Missionary Society." *Transactions of the Congregational Historical Society,* 19 (1962–63):138–46, 192–98, 222–29.

Forster, E. M. *Marianne Thornton: A Domestic Biography*. London: Edward Arnold, 1956.

Fyfe, Christopher. *Africanus Horton—West African Scientist and Patriot.* New York: Oxford University Press, 1972.

Gallagher, J. "Foxwell Buxton and the New African Policy, 1838–1842." *The Cambridge Historical Journal* 10 (1950):36–58.

———, and Robinson, R. E. "The Imperialism of Free Trade." *Economic History Review,* 2d series, 6 (1953):1–15.

Gibbs, M. E. *The Anglican Church in India, 1600–1970.* Delhi: ISPCK (India Society for Promoting Christian Knowledge), 1972.

Gollock, Georgina A. *Eugene Stock.* London: CMS, 1929.

Goodall, Norman. *The "Fundamental Principle" of the London Missionary Society.* Livingstone Press, 1945.

Grant, Anthony. *The Past and Prospective Extension of the Gospel by the Mission to the Heathen.* Bampton Lectures. London, 1844.

Greaves, R. W. "The Jerusalem Bishopric, 1841." *The English Historical Review* 64 (1949):328–52.

Grey, Earl (Henry George). *The Colonial Policy of Lord John Russell's Administration.* 2 vols. London: Richard Bentley, 1853.

Griffiths, Sir Percival. *The British Impact on India.* London: MacDonald, 1952.

Hair, P. "CMS 'Native' Clergy in West Africa to 1900." *The Sierra Leone Bulletin of Religion,* 4 (1962):71.

Hanna, William. *Memoirs of the Life and Writings of Thomas Chalmers, D.D.* 4 vols. Edinburgh, 1849–52.

Hennel, Michael. "A Little-Known Social Revolution." *Church Quarterly Review* 143 (1954):189–207.

———. "Henry Venn of Huddersfield." *The Churchman* 68 (1954): 92–99.

———. *John Venn and the Clapham Sect.* London: Lutterworth, 1958.

Hinchliff, Peter. "The Selection and Training of Missionaries in the Early Nineteenth Century." In *The Mission of the Church and the Propagation of the Faith,* ed. G. J. Cuming, pp. 131–36. Cambridge: University Press, 1970.

Hole, Charles. *The Early History of the Church Missionary Society for Africa and the East to the End of 1814.* London: CMS, 1896.

Hopkins, Hugh Evan. *Charles Simeon of Cambridge.* London: Hodder and Stoughton, 1977.

Howse, Ernest Marshall. *Saints in Politics—The "Clapham Sect" and the Growth of Freedom.* London: George Allen and Unwin, 1952, 1971.

Ifemesia, C. C. "The British Enterprise on the Niger 1830–1869." Ph.D. dissertation, University of London, 1959.

———. "The 'Civilizing' Mission of 1841: Aspects of an Episode in Anglo-Nigerian Relations." *Journal of the Historical Society of Nigeria* 2 (1962):291–310.

Ingham, Kenneth. "The English Evangelicals and the Pilgrim Tax in India, 1800–1862." *Journal of Ecclesiastical History* 3 (1952):191–200.

————. *Reformers in India 1793–1833. An Account of the Work of Christian Missionaries on Behalf of Social Reform.* Cambridge: University Press, 1956.

Johnson, T. S. *The Story of a Mission—The Sierra Leone Church: First Daughter of C.M.S.* London: SPCK, 1953.

Jones, M. G. *Hannah More.* Cambridge: University Press, 1952.

Kling, B. B. "The Bengal Indigo Disturbances, 1859-1862: A Study in the Origins of Political Activity in Modern Bengal." Ph.D. dissertation, University of Pennsylvania, Philadelphia, 1960.

Knaplund, Paul. *Gladstone and Britain's Imperial Policy.* London: George Allen and Unwin, 1927.

————. *James Stephen and the British Colonial System, 1813–1847.* Madison: University of Wisconsin Press, 1953.

————. "Mr. Oversecretary Stephen." *Journal of Modern History* 1 (1929):40–66.

————. "Sir James Stephen and British North American Problems, 1840–1847." *Canadian Historical Review* 5 (1924):22–41.

Knorr, Klaus. *British Colonial Theories, 1570–1850.* London: Frank Cass and Co., 1963.

Knutsford, Viscountess (Holland, Margaret Jean). *Life and Letters of Zachary Macaulay.* London: Edward Arnold, 1900.

Lepsius, Carl Richard. *Standard Alphabet.* London: Seeley's, 1855.

Liddon, Henry Parry. *Life of E. B. Pusey.* London: Longmans and Co., 1893–97.

(Liverpool) *Conference on Missions, 1860.* Edited by Secretaries to the Conference (G. D. Cullen, E. Steane, J. Mullens, and H. C. Tucker). London: James Nisbet and Co., 1860.

Long, G. E. "India and the Evangelicals." *London Quarterly and the Holburn Review,* 6th series, 32 (1963): 140–47.

Long, James (Rev.). *Vernacular Christian Literature for Bengal.* Calcutta, 1850.

Marshall, T. W. M. *Christian Missions, Their Agents, Their Method, and Their Result.* London, 1862.

Marshman, J. C. Evidence before Select Committee of the House of Commons, 1853. *Parliamentary Papers.* Vol. 29. London, 1852–53. Pp. 26–27.

Mayhew, Arthur. *Christianity and the Government of India.* London: Faber & Gwyer, 1929.

————. *The Education of India.* London: Faber & Gwyer, 1926.

McAdoo, H. R. *The Spirit of Anglicanism, a Survey of Anglican Theological Method in the Seventeenth Century.* London: A. and C. Black, 1965.

Meacham, Standish. "The Evangelical Inheritance." *Journal of British Studies* 3 (1963):88–104.

————. *Henry Thornton of Clapham 1760–1815.* Cambridge: Harvard University Press, 1964.

Morrell, W(illiam) P(arker). *British Colonial Policy in the Mid-Victorian Age: South Africa, New Zealand, the West Indies.* Oxford: Clarendon Press, 1969.

Myklebust, Olav Guttorm. *The Study of Missions in Theological Education.* 2 vols. Oslo: Egede Instituttet; Hovedkommisjon Forlaget Land og Kirke, 1955–57.

Neill, Stephen C. *Colonialism and Christian Missions.* London: Lutterworth and McGraw-Hill, 1964.

———. *A History of Christian Missions.* Baltimore: Penguin Books, 1964.

Newsome, David H. "The Churchmanship of Samuel Wilberforce." In *Studies in Church History,* vol. 3, ed. G. J. Cuming, pp. 23–47. Leiden: Brill, 1966.

———. *The Parting of Friends.* London: John Murray, 1966.

Oddie, G. A. "India and Missionary Motives, c. 1850–1900." *Journal of Ecclesiastical History* 25 (1974):61–72.

———. "The Reverend James Long and Protestant Missionary Policy in Bengal, 1840–1872." Ph.D. dissertation, University of London, 1963–64.

Orr, J. Edwin. *The Second Evangelical Awakening in Britain.* London: Marshall, Morgan and Scott, 1949.

Page, Jesse. *The Black Bishop: Samuel Crowther.* London: Hodder and Stoughton, 1908.

Paton, William. *Alexander Duff—Pioneer of Missionary Education.* London: SCM, 1923.

Pinnington, John. "Church Principles in the Early Years of the CMS: The Problem of the 'German' Missionaries." *Journal of Theological Studies,* 20 (1969):523–32.

Porter, Andrew. "Cambridge, Keswick, and late-nineteenth-century Attitudes to Africa." *The Journal of Imperial and Commonwealth History* 5, no. 1 (Oct. 1976):5–34.

———. "Evangelical Enthusiasm, Missionary Motivation and West Africa in the Late Nineteenth Century: The Career of G. W. Brooke." *The Journal of Imperial and Commonwealth History* 6, no. 1 (Oct. 1976):23–46.

Pratt, Josiah, and Pratt, J. *Memoir of the Reverend Josiah Pratt, B.D.* London: 1849.

Rack, H. D. "Domestic Visitation: A Chapter in Early Nineteenth Century Evangelism." *Journal of Ecclesiastical History* 24 (1973):357–76.

Robinson, Ronald, and Gallagher, John. *Africa and the Victorians.* London: Macmillan, 1961.

Rosselli, John. *Lord William Bentinck.* London: Chatto and Windus, 1974.

Sawyerr, Harry. "Christian Evangelistic Strategy in West Africa: Reflections on the Centenary of the Consecration of Bishop Samuel Adjayi Crowther on St. Peter's Day, 1864." *International Review of Misions* 54 (1965):343–52.

Smyth, Charles (H. E.). "The Evangelical Movement in Perspective." *Cambridge Historical Journal* 7 (1943):160–74.

––––––. *Simeon and Church Order. A Study of the Origins of the Evangelical Revival in Cambridge in the Eighteenth Century.* Cambridge: University Press, 1940.

Soloway, Richard A. *Prelates and People. Ecclesiastical Social Thought in England 1873–1952.* London: Routledge and Kegan Paul, 1969.

Spear, Percival. "Bentinck and Education." *Cambridge Historical Journal* 6 (1938):78–101.

Speer, Robert E. "The Science of Missions." *The Missionary Review of the World.* Jan. 1899, pp. 27–37.

Spring, David. "The Clapham Sect: Some Social and Political Aspects." *Victorian Studies* 5 (1961):35–48.

Stephen, Caroline Emelia (ed.). *The Right Honourable Sir James Stephen.* Gloucester, 1906.

Stephen, James (Sir), K.C.B. *Essays in Ecclesiastical Biography.* 2 vols. 3rd ed. London: Longman, Brown, Green, and Longmans, 1853.

Stephen, Leslie (Sir). *Life of Sir James Fitzjames Stephen, Bart.* London: Smith, Elder and Co., 1895.

Stephenson, A. M. G. *The First Lambeth Conference 1867.* London: SPCK, 1967.

Stock, Eugene. *History of the Church Missionary Society.* 4 vols. London: CMS, 1899, 1916.

––––––. *My Recollections.* London: James Nisbet and Co., 1909.

––––––. "Voices of Past Years." *Church Missionary Review* 63 (1912): 149–55, 289–96, 537–43, 606–13, 660–67.

Storr, Vernon F. *The Development of English Theology in the Nineteenth Century, 1800–1860.* London: Longmans, Green and Co., 1913.

Stunt, T.C.F. "John Henry Newman and the Evangelicals." *Journal of Ecclesiastical History* 21 (1970):65–74.

Swan, William. *Letters on Missions.* 2d ed. London, 1843.

Tasie, G.O.M. "Christianity in the Niger Delta, 1864–1918." Ph.D. dissertation, University of Aberdeen, 1969.

––––––. "The Story of Samuel Ajayi Crowther and the C.M.S. Niger Mission." *The Ghana Bulletin of Theology* 4:7 (Dec. 1974):47–60.

Taylor, John V. *The Growth of the Church in Buganda.* London: SCM Press, 1958.

Townsend, G. *Memoir of the Reverend Henry Townsend.* London, 1887.

Trevelyan, G(eorge) M(acaulay). *British History in the Nineteenth Century and After: 1782–1919.* London: Penguin Books, 1965.

Tucker, H. W. *Memoir of the Life and Episcopate of George A. Selwyn.* London, 1879.

Van Den Berg, Johannes. *Constrained by Jesus' Love—An Inquiry into the Motives of the Missionary Awakening in Great Britain in the Period between 1698 and 1815.* Kampen: J. H. Kok, 1956.

Venn, John. (Statement re) "Evangelical Kerygma." *Christian Observer* 6 (1807):742ff.

———. *Sermons.* 3 vols. London, 1814–17.

Venn, John (b. 1834). *Annals of a Clerical Family: Being Some Account of the Family of William Venn, Vicar of Otterton, Devon, 1600–1621.* London: Macmillan and Co., 1904.

Walker, F. Deaville. *The Romance of the Black River.* London: CMS, 1930.

Walls, A. F. "A Christian Experiment: The Early Sierra Leone Colony." In *The Mission of the Church and the Propagation of the Faith,* ed. J. G. Cuming, pp. 107–29. Cambridge: University Press, 1970.

———. "Missionary Vocation and the Ministry—The First Generation." In *New Testament Christianity for Africa and the World,* ed. Mark E. Glasswell and Edward W. Fashole-Luke, pp. 141–56. London: SPCK, 1974.

———. "The Nineteenth Century Missionary as Scholar." In *Misjonskall og forskerglede,* pp. 409–21. Oslo: Universitetsforlaget, 1975.

Walsh, J. D. "Joseph Milner's Evangelical Church History." *Journal of Ecclesiastical History* 10 (1959):174–87.

———. "Origins of the Evangelical Revival." In *Essays in Modern English Church History,* ed. G. V. Bennett and J. D. Walsh, pp. 132–62. London: A. and C. Black. 1966.

———. "Yorkshire Evangelicals in the Eighteenth Century." Ph.D. dissertation, Cambridge University, 1956.

Ward, William Reginald. *Religion and Society in England 1790–1850.* London: Bastford, 1972.

Warren, Max. *Christian Mission and Social Reform.* London: SCM, 1967.

———. *The CMS: A Study of Its Nature and Function.* London: CMS, 1943.

———. *The Functions of a National Church.* London: Epworth Press, 1964.

———. *The Idea of the Missionary Society.* 1943.

———. "The Missionary Expansion of *Ecclesia Anglicana.*" In *New Testament Christianity for Africa and the World,* ed. Mark E. Glasswell and Edward W. Fashole-Luke, pp. 124–40. London: SPCK, 1974.

———. *The Missionary Movement from Britain in Modern History.* London: SCM, 1965.

———. *Unfolding Purpose: An Interpretation of the Living Tradition Which Is CMS.* London: CMS, 1950.

———. "Why Missionary Societies and Not Missionary Churches?" *The Student World* 1–2 (1960). Reprinted in *History's Lessons for Tomorrow's Mission,* pp. 149–56.

Wesbster, James Bertin. *The African Churches Among the Yoruba 1882–1922.* Oxford: Clarendon Press, 1964.

———. "The Bible and the Plough." *Journal of the Historical Society of Nigeria* 2 (1963):418–34.

White, Gavin Donald. "The Idea of the Missionary Bishop in Mid-Nineteenth Century Anglicanism." S.T.M. dissertation, General Theological Seminary, New York, 1968.

Wilberforce, Robert I. and Samuel (eds.) *The Correspondence of William Wilberforce*. 2 vols. London, 1840.

——. *Life of William Wilberforce*. 5 vols. London, 1838.

Wilberforce, Samuel. *The Letter-Books of Samuel Wilberforce*. Transcribed and edited by R. K. Pugh. Aylesbury: Buckinghamshire Record Society and the Oxfordshire Record Society, 1970.

——. *Speeches on Missions*. London, 1874.

Willmer, Haddon. "Evangelicalism 1785–1835." Hulsean Prize Essay. Cambridge: University Library, 1962.

Wilson, D(aniel). *Journal Letters* (of Bishop D. Wilson). London, 1863.

Wilson, H. S. (ed.). *Origins of West African Nationalism*. London: Macmillan, 1969.

Wood, Charles (Sir). *Speech on Bill for the Government of India*. London, June 3, 1853.

Woodward, Llewellyn (Sir). *The Age of Reform, 1815–1870*. Oxford: Clarendon Press, 1962.

Young, G. M. (3d). *Speeches by Lord Macaulay with His Minute on Indian Education*. London: Oxford University Press, 1935.

INDEX

169